KARABAKH

The Road to Peace

Rustam Musevi

KARABAKH
The Road to Peace

A History of Conflict Between
Armenia and Azerbaijan

Hazar Global Press

Karabakh: The Road to Peace
A History of Conflict Between Armenia and Azerbaijan

Written and adapted by Rustam Musevi

Published by Hazar Global Press
St. Paul, Minnesota, USA

Library of Congress Control Number: 2026900268

ISBN: 979-8-9994622-5-1

Printed in the United States

First Edition: 2026

For the fallen and the displaced, may their memory be a light toward peace, and may neighbors one day find a way to stand beneath the same sky.

Content

Author's Note

This book was written by an independent researcher and writer whose engagement with the Karabakh conflict is shaped by both personal background and sustained research. I was born and raised in Baku and came of age during the final years of the Soviet Union and the early stages of the First Karabakh War. Although I did not live in an active combat zone, the conflict unfolded alongside the political and social transformations that defined everyday life in the capital. These experiences inform my interest in the subject, but they are not presented here as evidence or argument.

My familiarity with the region predates the outbreak of war. As a child, I spent time in Fuzuli and the Shaumyan district, and in 1988, I traveled to Armenia by bus with my father, when crossing borders was still possible. These experiences provide personal context, but the analysis in this book rests on documented sources rather than recollection.

The research for this book was conducted primarily after the 44-Day War of 2020 and the events of 2023. It draws on policy documents, legal texts, official statements, archival materials, and regional and international media reporting. I also engaged in qualitative conversations with members of Azerbaijani diaspora communities in the Upper Midwest of the United States, focusing on their perceptions of the conflict and its aftermath. These discussions informed my understanding but are not quoted directly, and no individuals are identified.

I do not write on behalf of any institution. My prior academic work, including graduate-level research on diaspora communities completed independently at Saint Mary's University of Minnesota, informs my approach but does not define the format of this book. While this is not an academic thesis, it follows similar principles: careful sourcing, attention to context, and an effort to avoid attributing collective responsibility.

Throughout this book, place names reflect the layered history of the South Caucasus rather than a single political convention. Many locations, particularly in and around Karabakh, have Azerbaijani, Armenian, Soviet-era, and locally used names that coexist in historical records and lived memory. I use names such as *Karabakh, Nagorno-Karabakh, Stepanakert, Khankendi, Yerevan, Erevan*, and many others, depending on the historical context, source, and readability. This approach is intended to support clarity and historical accuracy, not to assert ownership, legitimacy, or preference. The variation itself is part of the region's history and reflects the complexity the book seeks to explain. This book does not seek to judge, accuse, or reach legal conclusions. It does not advance claims regarding genocide, war crimes, or historical entitlement. Such determinations belong to legal and institutional processes. The purpose here is explanatory: to trace how the conflict developed, how competing narratives were formed and sustained, and how Armenians and Azerbaijanis now confront the challenge of moving from war toward an uncertain peace.

I have deliberately avoided activist language. The aim is not persuasion but clarity. Where suffering is described, it is done with specificity rather than symbolism. Where responsibility is examined, it is framed in political and historical terms rather than moral absolutes. The central concern throughout is how societies interpret conflict once the fighting has ended.

Writing about a conflict that has shaped one's own historical moment requires restraint. Complete distance is neither possible nor desirable, but uncritical alignment is equally limiting. This book proceeds from the belief that acknowledging complexity is essential, and that any durable peace depends not on erasing the past, but on understanding it with greater precision.

Preface

This book was written at a moment when the conflict over Karabakh had moved from active war to its aftermath, while much of the existing literature no longer reflected conditions on the ground. Many widely cited accounts were produced before the 44-Day War of 2020 or before the events of 2023. Others focus narrowly on episodes of fighting, often separated from the longer histories of Armenia, Azerbaijan, and the South Caucasus as a whole. This book revisits the subject in light of recent developments. It presents an updated chronology that situates the conflict within its broader regional and historical setting.

Rather than attempting to reproduce the historical record in exhaustive detail, this book deliberately chooses to be selective. The histories of Armenia, Azerbaijan, and Karabakh span centuries and encompass a vast range of events, documents, debates, and personal experiences. To include every episode or interpretation would require thousands of pages and risk obscuring the larger patterns that shaped and sustained the conflict over time.

Instead, the book provides a concise historical foundation, a clear account of the conflict's major phases, and an analysis of the political and regional dynamics that influenced its course. The aim is not to replace specialized scholarship or archival research, but to offer a coherent narrative explaining how the conflict emerged, evolved, and reached its current stage. Geography, imperial legacies, demographic change, and political transformation are treated as interconnected forces within the South Caucasus, a region whose histories cannot be understood in isolation from one another.

Many local experiences and individual perspectives necessarily fall outside the scope of this volume. Readers seeking deeper detail will find a substantial body of scholarship, archival material, and expert analysis available in libraries and online. This book is intended as an entry point: a framework for understanding the conflict as a whole, clarifying its complexity, and encouraging further independent inquiry.

For similar reasons, visual material is used sparingly. Photographs and historical maps are widely accessible through public archives and digital collections. Rather than reproducing readily available images, the book prioritizes narrative explanation and analytical clarity. Maps are included only when necessary to orient the reader and illustrate key structural changes.

The book is written for a broad readership: general readers seeking clarity, students and analysts looking for an accessible reference, policymakers interested in historical and regional context, and members of diaspora communities seeking to understand better how the region arrived at its present condition. Although the chapters follow a chronological structure, they may be read either sequentially or independently. Taken together, these choices reflect the book's central purpose: not to offer a definitive account, but to present a clear and balanced framework for understanding the Karabakh conflict and the conditions shaping the search for peace.

This approach also defines the book's ethical and analytical stance. It does not seek to judge, assign collective blame, or advance a legal verdict. It is not a memoir, a manifesto, or a political brief. Questions of legal responsibility and contested terminology are addressed in the main text when relevant to understanding specific events. The emphasis throughout is explanation rather than adjudication. The analysis draws on publicly available sources, including academic research, policy documents, media reporting, and open interviews in multiple languages. As with any examination of a prolonged and contested conflict, interpretations will differ, and disagreement is both expected and unavoidable.

My perspective has also been shaped by personal experience. I grew up in Baku during a period marked by rapid political change and social fracture. The city's neighborhoods, workplaces, and schools included people of different ethnic backgrounds, including Armenians. Some relationships endured the upheavals of the late Soviet period and the war years, continuing through displacement and migration, including friendships that remain active today in the United States. I have also known families who severed such ties entirely, holding entire communities responsible for violence and loss. These contrasting responses reflect the uneven ways conflict reshapes social bonds among people who once lived side by side.

These experiences reinforced a basic observation that civilians bear the primary consequences of war. Political decisions taken by governments and leaders disrupt everyday life through displacement, economic dislocation, institutional breakdown, and prolonged insecurity. In the Karabakh conflict,

Armenian and Azerbaijani families alike experienced the loss of relatives, the destruction of homes, and decades spent away from places that had defined their social and personal worlds. Some died in combat; others continue to live with the long-term effects of violence and uncertainty.

I did not experience frontline fighting or prolonged displacement, and I do not equate my experience with those who did. Nevertheless, I recognize the scale and persistence of loss on all sides and the ways it continues to shape memory, identity, and political attitudes. This recognition informs the book's approach. Its purpose is not to reconcile grief or prescribe forgiveness, but to present the conflict with sufficient care, proportion, and context to move beyond simplified blame. Any lasting peace will depend not on forgetting the past, but on understanding it without reducing entire societies to enemies.

Throughout the chapters that follow, loss and trauma are addressed directly. Over more than a century, the conflict has taken lives, displaced families, disrupted economies, and left enduring psychological scars among Armenians and Azerbaijanis. Acknowledging this human cost is essential. Equally important is resisting zero-sum thinking, the assumption that one side's security or dignity can exist only at the expense of the other. Such thinking has prolonged the conflict long after the battles ended.

This book seeks to clarify the past, explain the present, and help readers think more carefully about the future. It does not promise simple conclusions. Instead, it offers context, chronology, and analysis, believing that informed understanding can support more constructive discussion. The region's stability, economic development, and long-term peace depend not on the repetition of inherited narratives, but on understanding how those narratives were formed and how they might evolve.

This book aims to explain how the Karabakh conflict developed, why it endured for so long, and why the choices made after the wars matter as much as the wars themselves. The road to peace is shaped by societal interpretations of the past and visions for the future. By emphasizing context rather than judgment, this book seeks to contribute to a more informed discussion to support a stable future grounded in peace and mutual prosperity.

The South Caucasus and the location of the Karabakh

Map of the Caucasus. Source: United States Central Intelligence Agency, 2004. Public domain Source:

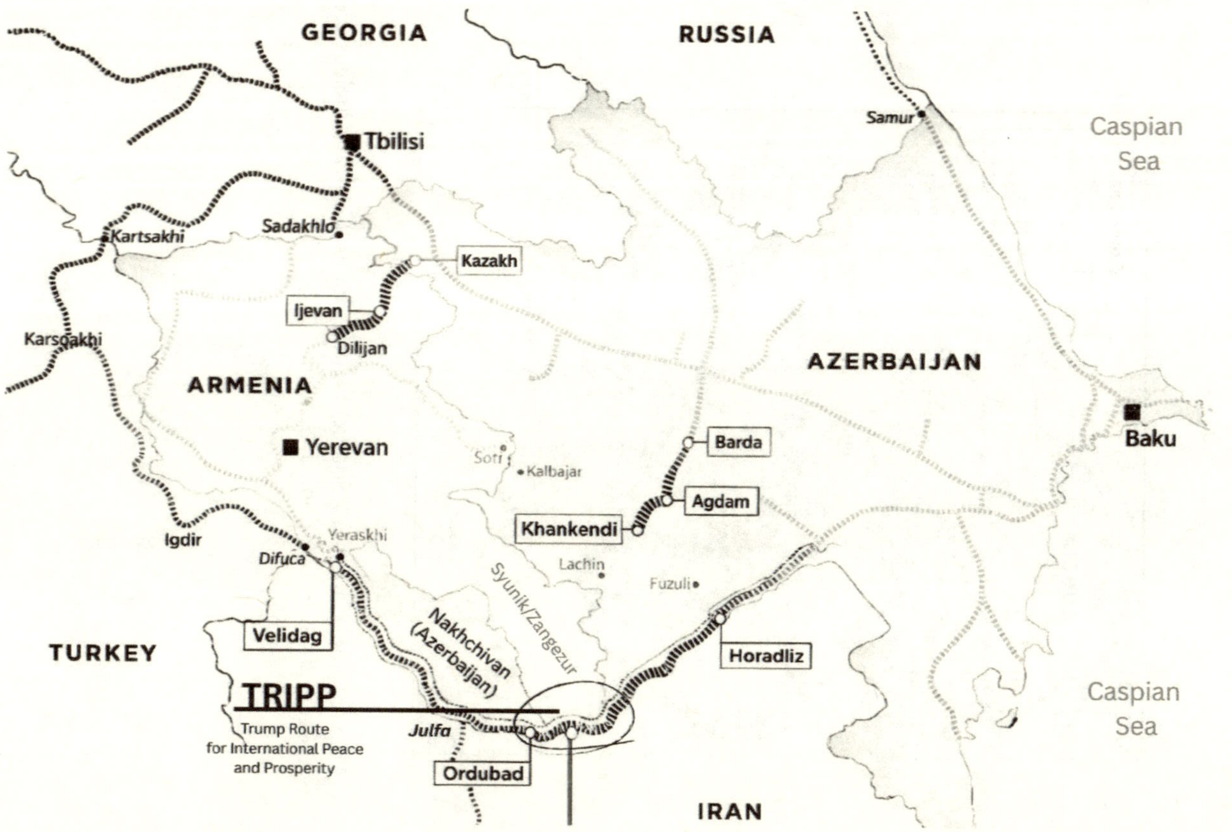

Regional Transportation Corridors and Proposed TRIPP Route

The Land Called Karabakh

On a warm August day in 2025, the White House became the setting for a moment widely presented as historic. Azerbaijani President Ilham Aliyev and Armenian Prime Minister Nikol Pashinyan, hosted by U.S. President Donald J. Trump, signed a joint declaration intended to mark the end of one of the most protracted and most violent conflicts of the post-Soviet era. For decades, the dispute over Nagorno-Karabakh had resisted diplomatic resolution, leaving tens of thousands of dead and nearly a million people displaced. The public gestures exchanged during the ceremony, including handshakes, smiles, and brief informal remarks, stood in stark contrast to the hostility that had defined relations between the two societies for over a generation.

The declaration, however, did not produce uniform reactions. Within segments of the Armenian diaspora, particularly in Western countries, skepticism emerged almost immediately. For years, diaspora organizations had urged successive governments in Yerevan to resist compromise, emphasizing historical loss and warning against concessions to Baku. These positions, articulated from outside the region, reflected deep emotional investment in the conflict but were often disconnected from the economic, political, and security constraints facing Armenia itself. Through lobbying efforts, advocacy campaigns, and cultural institutions abroad, reconciliation was frequently portrayed as a strategic weakness rather than a political recalibration.

Diaspora discourse also shaped interpretations of the departure of Karabakh's Armenian population. Many residents left after the 2020 war and the subsequent Azerbaijani advances for various reasons, including fear, uncertainty, and personal calculations, all under intense social pressure. As departure became the dominant response, conformity and fear of isolation narrowed perceived alternatives. Diaspora leaders subsequently framed the exodus as evidence of renewed ethnic cleansing, reinforcing a narrative of injustice that cast doubt on the durability and legitimacy of the Washington agreement. In this framing, the declaration signaled the erasure of Armenian presence and rights in Karabakh.

Beyond Armenian communities abroad, the peace initiative also unsettled regional powers. Russia and Iran have long viewed the South Caucasus as central to their strategic environments. Moscow maintained deep military and economic ties with Armenia, while Tehran regarded the region as both a buffer and a critical corridor for northward connectivity. Armenia's growing engagement with Washington, alongside the prospect of closer ties with Turkey and Azerbaijan, was interpreted in both capitals as a challenge to established influence. What U.S. officials described as a "new beginning" was viewed in Moscow and Tehran as a shift that weakened their political and economic leverage in the region.

Much of this unease converged around a transport initiative highlighted during the peace talks: the Trump Route for International Peace and Prosperity (TRIPP). Supporters presented the project as a mechanism to reconnect east–west trade routes, linking mainland Azerbaijan with its Nakhichevan exclave and onward to Turkey. Proposals included railways, highways, energy pipelines, and fiber-optic infrastructure running through southern Armenia. Although framed as a breakthrough, the concept itself was not new. Similar routes functioned during the Soviet period and reappeared as a contested provision of the 2020 ceasefire agreement, making transport connectivity one of the most sensitive and unresolved elements of postwar negotiations.

The proposal remained controversial. Critics in Armenia argued that the route, often depicted without Armenian checkpoints, risked undermining sovereignty, despite assurances that Armenia would retain jurisdiction and that any transit arrangement would operate under international management frameworks. For opponents, TRIPP appeared less as a neutral infrastructure project than as a geopolitical instrument advancing the strategic interests of Azerbaijan and Turkey while placing additional pressure on Armenia.

With all its complexity, the path toward peace emerged from decades of war, political deadlock, episodes of ethnic violence, and entrenched mistrust between Armenian and Azerbaijani societies. To understand how a conflict long considered insoluble reached this point, it is necessary to begin with Karabakh itself—the mountainous core of the South Caucasus and the focal point of one of the region's most enduring disputes. The significance of the 2025 declaration becomes clear only in contrast to what preceded it. From the late 1980s onward, fighting over Karabakh claimed more than thirty thousand lives in the first war alone, displaced nearly a million people, and devastated once-thriving towns. The 2020 war added thousands more casualties in just forty-four days, redrawing borders and deepening mistrust. For Armenians and Azerbaijanis alike, the conflict was experienced directly, shaping family histories, patterns of displacement, and social attitudes across generations.

What is Karabakh?

Karabakh is a landlocked, mountainous region of the South Caucasus, internationally recognized as part of Azerbaijan and located near Armenia. Framed by the Araz (also known historically as the Araxes) and Kura rivers, it spans about 1,700 square miles (roughly 4,400 square kilometers). The landscape of Karabakh, stretching across the southwest-ern flanks of the Lesser Caucasus, includes the districts of Jabrail, Fizuli, Khojavend (known in Armenian sources as Hadrut), Aghdam, Khojaly, Tartar (Terter), Shusha, and Khankendi. Much of the terrain rises above 3,120 feet (950 meters), the Murov mountains range to the north, crowned by Gamish mountains at 3,724 meters, and the Karabakh range to the west, where Boyuk Kirs (2,725 m) and Gizgala (2,843 m) overlook the valleys below.

The mountains dominate the Araz Valley to the south and southeast, overlooking the lowlands that stretch eastward toward Baku, the capital of Azerbaijan. Winters bring heavy fog and snow from November through April, while summers are mild, making the land productive with orchards, vineyards, mulberries, and grains. In the uplands, rainfall sustains dense oak, beech, hornbeam, and walnut forests. Rivers born of snowmelt and rain, including the Tartar, Khachin, Ghaggar, Kondalan, and Hakari rivers, carve through the mountains before joining the Kura and Araz. For centuries, they have served as vital arteries for farming, fishing, and settlement. Karabakh's natural wealth has long given it both economic and cultural significance.

Positioned between the Black Sea to the west and the Caspian to the east, these mountains have long served as both barrier and bridge, slowing the movement of people while channeling plants, animals, and cultures through narrow corridors. This funnel effect helped make the Caucasus one of the richest biodiversity zones in the temperate world, home to more than 6,300 plant species (1,600 found nowhere else) and a remarkable range of wildlife, from gray wolves and lynx to golden eagles and the increasingly rare Caucasus leopard.

Throughout history, Karabakh's highlands have been as formidable as they were fertile, their rugged terrain making them challenging to conquer. Strategically, the elevated ground favored defense, providing natural strongholds such as Shusha, whose medieval fortress once guarded the surrounding valleys and still stands today as a symbol of the region's enduring military and cultural importance. For centuries, the mountains also served as a place of refuge. During invasions and wars, people from the exposed lowlands often fled upward into Karabakh's valleys and fortresses, where the landscape offered protection. This movement of refugees over time helped shape the region's cultural mosaic, where Muslim and Christian communities lived side by side, each leaving its imprint on Karabakh's history and identity.

Karabakh's name, rooted in both Turkic and Persian, combines kara, meaning black or dark and often used to denote rich, fertile soil, with bagh, the Persian word for garden. For centuries, the name reflected the region's agricultural abundance in its valleys and orchards. During the Soviet era, the region was formally designated as the Nagorno-Karabakh Autonomous Oblast (NKAO), and this designation became the standard reference throughout the conflict. In Russian, *nagornyy* means mountainous, reflecting the highland core of the broader Karabakh region, which historically extended into the surrounding lowlands of Azerbaijan. Armenians, however, refer to the area by its ancient name Artsakh, which was revived in the late twentieth century as part of their claim to the territory. Beyond names, Karabakh has long carried an allure: a crossroads of empires, a place of poets and warriors, silk and wine, monasteries and mosques. For centuries, the region supported both Christian and Muslim communities, even as rival empires contended for control of its valleys and mountain passes.

The history of Karabakh cannot be understood without reference to the two societies most closely bound to it. Over long historical periods, Armenians and Azerbaijanis lived as neighbors under successive imperial systems, including Arab, Mongol, Persian, Ottoman, Russian, and later Soviet rule. This extended coexistence left discernible cultural traces. In music, dance, and cuisine, shared forms emerged through common musical structures, overlapping dance traditions, and foodways shaped by local agriculture, herbs, and viticulture. To outside observers, Armenians and Azerbaijanis often appeared culturally and physically similar, their societies shaped by the same mountains and valleys and by shared historical experiences. Even in language, where distinctions are clear, borrowed terms and familiar expressions reflect sustained contact and exchange.

I encountered this shared social world directly while growing up in Baku. My classmates, teachers, and neighbors included Armenians, Russians, and Jews. We celebrated birthdays and holidays, spent time in one another's homes, and shared humor that relied on ethnic stereotypes without hostility. Until 1988, I do not recall nationality or ethnicity functioning as a dividing line in everyday life. That social environment changed abruptly with the onset of the conflict, which fundamentally altered relationships that had previously been taken for granted.

However, these similarities should not be mistaken for sameness. Armenians and Azerbaijanis followed different historical paths and developed distinct identities. Religion has been one dividing line, with Islam predominating among Azerbaijanis and Christianity among Armenians, alongside differences in language and script. Their national narratives diverged under the pressures of empire and modern nation-building, producing rival memories and competing claims. Claims that these cultural and historical differences make coexistence impossible are ultimately unproductive. Acknowledging difference is not the same as denying common ground. Understanding both the deep ties that once connected Armenians and Azerbaijanis, and the differences later amplified by political agendas and diaspora-driven rhetoric is essential to grasp why Karabakh became such a contested space and why peace proved so elusive. To understand how these identities were shaped and why their paths collided in Karabakh, it is necessary to examine the histories of Azerbaijan and Armenia themselves.

To begin, this book examines the history of Azerbaijan, followed by a parallel examination of Armenia's history. This structure is not intended to privilege one narrative over another, but to establish the historical foundations necessary to understand a conflict that is often presented without adequate context. Much of what follows regarding Karabakh cannot be understood without awareness of Azerbaijan's historical trajectory, from its roots in Caucasian Albania and later Muslim khanates to its incorporation into the Russian Empire and the Soviet Union. The history of Armenia is equally essential and is examined in its own right, with attention to its distinct experiences of empire, religion, and nation-building. Considered together, these histories reveal how two peoples who shared empires, borders, and cultural space came to develop sharply different memories of the same land.

Brief History of Azerbaijan

The history of Azerbaijan stretches back to antiquity, spanning both sides of the Araz River. To the south lies what is today Iranian Azerbaijan, centered on Tabriz and the Lake Urmia basin. Despite being separated by international borders, these northern and southern lands served as cross-roads between the South Caucasus and the Iranian plateau, creating a continuous cultural world linked by trade routes and kinship ties. Over the centuries, Greeks, Romans, Persians, Arabs, Mongols, and Russians each left their imprint, blending nomadic and sedentary ways of life into a rich cultural mosaic. Understanding this complex history is crucial for grasping how Azerbaijani identity has developed and why the region of Karabakh holds such enduring significance in the nation's narrative

Long before the modern Republic of Azerbaijan emerged as a nation, and before the name Azerbaijan came into political use for the territory north of the Araz River, the lands between the Caucasus and the Zagros were inhabited by various nomadic highland tribes. Mesopotamian inscriptions from the fourteenth and thirteenth centuries BCE record the Kuti, Lullubi, and Turukkum as loose confederations of mountain peoples who moved seasonally between valleys and pastures. They eventually merged into stronger states and ceased to exist as distinct groups, but aspects of their culture remained among later peoples such as the Hurrians and the Medes, contributing to the cultural landscape of the South Caucasus.

By the first millennium BCE, the Kingdom of Manna emerged south of Lake Urmia, the first organized state clearly identifiable in the region. Positioned between Assyria and Urartu, Manna built fortified towns, developed irrigation, and played rivals against one another, even appearing in the Book of Jeremiah for its alliance with Assyria. Its independence, however, proved fragile. By the late seventh century BCE, the kingdom was absorbed into the rising Median Empire under Cyaxares. Its systems of governance and metalworking influenced the Medes and later the Achaemenid Persians. Under Darius I, Persian rule extended north of the Araz River, and Herodotus later recorded Caspian–Albanian contingents fighting in the Greco-Persian Wars, indicating that these northern lands were already integrated into the Achaemenid imperial administration and military system.

The fall of Persia to Alexander the Great in the fourth century BCE once again redrew the map. Nonetheless, the rugged landscape north of the Araz River, in the southern reaches of the Lesser Caucasus, limited effective imperial control. Out of this turbulence came the kingdom of Atropatene, founded by the Median satrap Atropates. Though modest in size, it endured by balancing between Seleucid and Parthian power. Atropatene preserved Zoroastrian traditions while absorbing Greek and Persian influences, and its name endured, evolving over centuries into Azerbaijan. This continuity linked the ancient tribes, Manna, and the Medes to later dynasties, giving Azerbaijan deep historical roots in resilience, adaptation, and cultural layering.

Caucasian Albania

By the fourth century BCE, diverse tribal groups in the eastern Caucasus had coalesced into a polity known as Caucasian Albania. Its territory extended from the Caspian littoral to the foothills of the Greater Caucasus, encompassing a fertile yet contested landscape that Greek and Roman writers portrayed as both prosperous and martial. Numismatic evidence from centers such as Qabala and Shamakhi points to active trade networks, while inscriptions at Gobustan record the presence of Roman legions advancing into the region. Situated between competing imperial spheres, Caucasian Albania emerged as a frontier state whose development was shaped by sustained external pressures. Like other small polities in the region, Caucasian Albania's fate was shaped by the ambitions of its neighbors. Roman forces passed through the territory in the first century BCE, Persia treated it as a strategic buffer, and nomadic incursions periodically tested its defenses. Despite these pressures, the kingdom endured for centuries under a branch of the Arshakid dynasty, whose rulers navigated shifting allegiances between eastern and western powers.

In the fourth century, King Urnayr I formally adopted Christianity, aligning the kingdom with the Christian traditions spreading across the Caucasus. Early ecclesiastical centers developed in the region, including sites traditionally associated with the area of present-day Shaki, reflecting the establishment of an indigenous Albanian Christian church. This religious orientation, however, remained vulnerable to external pressure. Under Sasanian dominance, rulers such as Vache II were compelled to renounce Christianity and restore Zoroastrian practices, only to reassert their Christian affiliation following a later rebellion. These reversals did not signal religious instability so much as the limits of political autonomy, as Caucasian Albania remained caught between rival imperial and spiritual spheres.

The last Albanian ruler to leave a lasting mark was Javanshir (also rendered Juansher) (642–680), who confronted Khazar incursions, negotiated with Byzantium, and engaged diplomatically with the Arab Caliphate in Damascus. Through this balancing strategy, he secured Caucasian Albania a final generation of relative autonomy. After his death, the Arab Caliphate gradually absorbed the kingdom in the early eighth century. Caucasian Albania disappeared as a political entity, but its legacy endured in chronicles, inscriptions, and architectural remains scattered across Karabakh and the surrounding highlands. In later centuries, both Armenian and Azerbaijani historical traditions invoked the Albanian past to assert continuity with the vanished kingdom, transforming it into a lasting subject of historiographical debate. With the end of Albanian statehood, Karabakh and the wider eastern Caucasus entered a new era marked by the gradual spread of Islam, reshaping the region's political structures and cultural life.

Arab Caliphate and Resistance

By the early seventh century, the South Caucasus was marked by sustained imperial competition. Repeated wars between the Byzantine and Sassanian empires, compounded by pressure from the Khazar Khaganate, weakened regional stability and local autonomy. Arab expansion into the region unfolded within this context, introducing new administrative authority alongside the gradual spread of Islam. Following the collapse of Sassanian rule in the mid-seventh century, Arab forces advanced into what is now Azerbaijan. Cities such as Ardabil, Mughan, Shirvan, Beylagan, and Barda entered into agreements that combined military submission with the payment of tribute. By the early eighth century, Arab authorities had consolidated control over Caucasian Albania. They reduced Khazar influence in the region, bringing an end to the Mihranid dynasty, the local Albanian ruling house of Iranian origin.

These changes reshaped the region's religious landscape. Zoroastrianism declined with the fall of Sassanian patronage, while Islam spread more rapidly in the southern lowlands and urban centers. Christian communities in the north initially retained their faith as protected peoples, subject to the jizya tax. Over time, however, ecclesiastical autonomy narrowed. The Albanian Church was subordinated to the Armenian Apostolic hierarchy, and the use of the Albanian script gradually disappeared, reflecting the broader political and religious integration of the region into the caliphate.

Arab administrators reorganized the region as Arran, a territorial unit extending from Derbent in present-day Dagestan to areas south of the Kura basin and introduced population transfers to consolidate control. This new order, however, encountered sustained resistance. Uprisings erupted in Shamkir, Ardabil, Shirvan, and across Arran, culminating in the Khurramite movement led by Babek Khorramdin (often rendered as Babak). During the early ninth century, Babek mobilized a broad coalition of rural communities, local elites, and dissident religious groups, achieving a series of military successes that for a time expelled caliphal forces from large parts of Azerbaijan. His capture and execution in 837 marked the suppression of the revolt and the reassertion of Abbasid authority. In later historical memory, Babek's resistance came to occupy a prominent place, particularly in Azerbaijani historiography, where it has been interpreted as an early expression of opposition to external domination rather than as a unified nationalist movement in the modern sense.

From Sajid to Atabeks: Azerbaijan Before the Mongols

The emergence of the Sajid dynasty marked an early phase in the political rise of Turkic military elites in Azerbaijan. Founded by Ab'l-Saj Divdad, a Turkic commander serving within the Abbasid military system, the dynasty took root when his son Muhammad was appointed governor of Azerbaijan in 898. From their base in Ardabil, the Sajids extended authority across Arran and parts of Armenia, compelling local rulers to acknowledge their rule through tribute. For a brief period, their domain stretched from Derbent in the north to Zanjan in the south, bringing much of the region under a single administration.

Under their most powerful ruler, Yusuf ibn Abu'l-Saj, the dynasty asserted its dominance forcefully, including military campaigns against Armenian rulers. The capture and execution of King Smbat I of Armenia in 914, carried out in Dvin, underscored the shifting balance of power in the South Caucasus. Although the Sajids remained formally subordinate to the Abbasid Caliphate, their relations with Baghdad alternated between cooperation and defiance. Following Yusuf ibn Abu'l-Saj's death in 928, the dynasty quickly declined. Even so, the Sajids left a lasting imprint by consolidating Azerbaijan and Arran under Turkic-led rule, foreshadowing the emergence of later dynasties that would shape the region's medieval political landscape.

In the decades that followed, Azerbaijan became the stage for a succession of dynasties, each leaving its imprint while struggling to hold together a diverse land. The Salarids, rising in the mid-10th century from the Kengerli tribes, briefly revived Azerbaijani power under Marzban ibn Muhammad. From Ardabil, he extended authority into Sheki, Barda, and Armenia, but his reign was scarred by tragedy. In 944, Barda, one of the great cities of the Caucasus, was sacked by Rus raiders, an event later immortalized by Nizami Ganjavi in *Tragedy of Barda*. Internal disputes after Marzban's death fractured the dynasty, and by the century's end, the Salarids had faded.

Their place was taken by the Ravvadids, originally an Arab family centered in Tabriz, who consolidated power in 981. Their rule coincided with renewed migrations of Oghuz Turkic groups into Azerbaijan, a development that contributed significantly to the region's evolving cultural and linguistic landscape. The Ravvadids resisted pressure from Georgian and Byzantine forces and later confronted the Seljuks' advance. By the mid-eleventh century, however, an earthquake severely damaged Tabriz, and Seljuk expansion soon absorbed their weakened domain.

At the same time, the Shaddadids, a Kurdish dynasty later incorporating Turkic elements, rose to prominence in Ganja. From there, they extended control over Arran, Shamkir, and Nakhichevan. Their construction projects, including bridges and fortifications such as the Khudaferin crossings over the Araz River, reflected both strategic ambition and administrative capacity. Like the Ravvadids, the Shaddadids ultimately yielded to Seljuk dominance, thereby consolidating Seljuk authority across much of the region.

By the late eleventh century, Azerbaijan was firmly under the influence of the Seljuk Empire, serving as a frontier province of an empire that stretched from Central Asia to the Mediterranean. From this political landscape emerged the Eldiguzids, also known as the Atabeks of Azerbaijan, one of the most powerful dynasties of the medieval period. Their founder, Shams al-Din Eldiguz, rose from Seljuk military service to become the effective ruler of Azerbaijan in the mid-twelfth century. Governing first from Nakhichevan and later from Tabriz, the Atabeks presided over a period of political consolidation and cultural vitality. Contemporary chroniclers referred to Eldiguz as the "Great Atabek," a title reflecting an authority that at times extended from the Caucasus into northern Iran. Under their rule, substantial armies were maintained, scholars and poets received patronage, and major cities developed into centers of administration, learning, and commerce.

This power, however, proved vulnerable to both external pressure and internal fragmentation. A resurgent Georgia, under King David IV and later Queen Tamar, launched repeated incursions into Arran and Karabakh, including the sackings of Ganja and Beylagan. By the early thirteenth century, internal rivalries had weakened Atabek authority, leaving the dynasty exposed. In 1225, their rule collapsed, first under the advance of Jalal al-Din

Khwarazm Shah and soon afterward before the far greater force of the Mongol invasions. The Mongol arrival marked a decisive rupture in Azerbaijan's political and social order, ending the era of regional dynasties and ushering in a new imperial phase.

Mongol Invasions and the Age of Timur

The Mongols first struck Azerbaijan in the 1220s, devastating cities like Nakhichevan and Beylagan, while Tabriz survived by paying ransom. A harsher invasion in 1231 left Ganja deserted and compelled local rulers to accept Mongol authority. By the mid-13th century, Hulegu Khan, a grandson of Genghis Khan, established the Ilkhanate. This Mongol successor state ruled much of Iran and the South Caucasus, with Tabriz as its capital and Karabakh as its summer residence. Although Ghazan Khan declared Islam the state religion, heavy taxes and internal strife weakened the state, and by the 1350s it collapsed under pressure from the Golden Horde.

Out of this turmoil rose Timur (Tamerlane), the Turco-Mongol conqueror of Central Asia, who clashed with Tokhtamysh, khan of the Golden Horde, and swept through the Caucasus. His campaigns left a mixed legacy. Cities were looted and damaged, yet later rebuilt, and his alliance with Shirvan Shah Ibrahim I helped elevate Shirvan's influence in the region. After Timur died in 1405, a power vacuum emerged, filled by rival Turkoman tribal confederations. The Kara Koyunlu, led by Gara Yusif, established Tabriz as their capital in 1410, while their rivals, the Aq Qoyunlu under Uzun Hasan, later built an even larger realm stretching from Azerbaijan into Iraq and Anatolia. By the end of the fifteenth century, both dynasties were weakened by internal rivalry and external pressure. Nonetheless, their rule left durable political and cultural centers, most notably Tabriz, which emerged as a significant seat of power. Monumental projects such as the Blue Mosque in Tabriz and the Shirvanshah Palace in Baku testify to the architectural and artistic legacy of this period. These foundations facilitated the rise of the Safavids. This dynasty originated in Azerbaijan and went on to establish a new Iranian empire grounded in Persian political institutions and cultural traditions.

The Safavid Empire

By the late sixteenth century, the Safavid Empire was showing signs of structural weakness. After the death of Shah Tahmasp I in 1576, succession disputes and court intrigues weakened the throne, and under Muhammad Khodabandeh, the Ottomans seized Tabriz while the Uzbeks pushed into Khorasan. Collapse seemed imminent until Tahmasp's grandson, Abbas I, seized power in 1587.

Shah Abbas restored stability through reforms, notably by building a modern standing army and centralizing finances. He shifted power away from unruly tribal elites. Though forced to cede much of Azerbaijan and Georgia to the Ottomans at first, Abbas regrouped and by 1603 launched campaigns that restored these lands to Safavid control. The Treaty of Zuhab (1639) fixed much of the frontier, securing Azerbaijan and Erivan for Persia while leaving Iraq and Van to the Ottomans.

Abbas also turned outward. He expelled the Portuguese from Hormuz with English support. He tied Iran to global trade, making silk from Shirvan and Karabakh central to the economy. Karabakh's mulberry groves fed the silk industry, linking the region directly to Safavid prosperity. Cultural life also flourished: poets like Fuzuli and new schools and madrasas made the early seventeenth century an artistic high point.

But Abba's achievements did not last. By the eighteenth century, weak rulers, famines, and corruption hollowed the state. In 1722, Afghan forces captured Isfahan, ending Safavid power. Russia under Peter I seized Baku and the Caspian coast, while the Ottomans advanced into Georgia and Armenia, dividing much of the South Caucasus between them. Safavid loyalists briefly rallied under Tahmasp II with the help of Nadir Khan, a brilliant commander who recovered large parts of Iran and the Caucasus that had been lost to Afghan, Ottoman, and Russian advances. By 1736, Nadir had taken the title of Nadir Shah and founded the Afsharid dynasty. His military campaigns extended from India to the Caucasus, but heavy taxation and continuous warfare provoked widespread unrest, culminating in an assassination in 1747 that shattered imperial authority, leaving a political vacuum across the South Caucasus that a new generation of local rulers would soon fill.

The Karabakh Khanate

In the mid-eighteenth century, the South Caucasus fragmented into a series of small khanates, semi-autonomous principalities ruled by local khans, including Ganja, Baku, Sheki, Shirvan, Nakhichevan, and Erivan. Each struggled to survive between Persia, the Ottoman Empire, and a rising Russia. Among them, Karabakh emerged as a formidable power under Panah Ali Khan Javanshir.

A leader of the Javanshir clan, Panah Ali Khan, took advantage of the vacuum left by Nadir Shah's death. He recalled deported Muslim families, rebuilt communities, and established fortresses to secure his rule. First at Bayat, then Shahbulag, and finally Shusha, he created defensible strongholds that anchored his khanate. Shusha, built high on an inaccessible plateau, became both fortress and symbol, a permanent seat of authority in a volatile age.

Karabakh's rise faced challenges. The region included five Armenian melikdoms: Varanda, Khachen, Dizak, Jraberd, and Gulistan. Their rulers controlled fortified strongholds, maintained local militias, and built ties with external powers. Panah Ali Khan skillfully blended diplomacy with coercion, securing a marriage alliance with Varanda while applying military pressure on the remaining melikdoms and gradually limiting their autonomy. By the time Ibrahim Khalil Khan, his son and successor, reigned, the meliks had been reduced to vassal status, with their political authority absorbed into the orbit of Shusha.

By the late eighteenth century, the khanate had become a regional power. Shusha's legendary 33-day defense against Agha Mohammad Qajar of Persia siege in 1795 cemented its reputation for resilience. Though briefly captured in 1797, the shah's sudden assassination spared Karabakh from destruction. Survival, however, remained precarious. As imperial powers closed in from every direction, the khanate stood at the threshold of a new age, in which the terms of its autonomy would be decided not on the battlefield but at the negotiating table.

Russian Expansion into the Caucasus

By the dawn of the nineteenth century, the Caucasus became the arena of a new contest. Persia, under the Qajar dynasty, sought to hold its northern territories, while Russia, emboldened by victories in Europe, pressed steadily southward. North of the Araz River, political authority was fragmented, leaving local rulers vulnerable to outside pressure. In 1801, Tsar Alexander I annexed Kartli-Kakheti, and within a year the rulers of Derbent, Guba, and Lankaran accepted Russian patronage. The conquest soon escalated, and in 1804, General Pavel Tsitsianov stormed Ganja, killing its ruler Javad Khan and much of the city's population before renaming it Elizavetpol.

This brutality set the stage for the first Russo-Persian War (1804–1813). Abbas Mirza, son of Fatali Shah Qajar, mustered large forces but could not stop the Russian advance. In 1805, the Karabakh khanate signed the Treaty of Kurekchay, placing itself under Russian protection, soon followed by Sheki and Shamakhi. In the course of Russia's advance, Shusha fortress became a Russian garrison, while Baku fell after a naval bombardment. By the Treaty of Gulistan in 1813, Persia ceded Karabakh, Ganja, Sheki, Shamakhi, Derbent, Guba, Baku, and Lankaran to Russia. The second war (1826–1828) concluded with the Treaty of Turkmenchay, which resulted in Russia annexing Erivan and Nakhichevan, and promoting large-scale Armenian resettlement into the South Caucasus, subsequently altering the region's demographics.

Russian policy deliberately encouraged Christian resettlement into Muslim-majority lands. Armenians moved in large numbers from Persia and the Ottoman Empire, Germans were settled around Ganja, and Russians entered Karabakh and Shirvan. By the 1830s, the Armenian share of Karabakh's population had quadrupled, while Muslims declined in Erivan. This approach consolidated imperial authority while introducing tensions that would resurface later. Resistance was frequent but fractured: rebellions in Lankaran, Guba, and Sheki through the 1830s were swiftly suppressed.

Despite unrest, the Russian Empire imposed a program of modernization. Railroads linked Baku to Tiflis and the Caspian coast, industry grew, and oil transformed Baku from a provincial town into a global hub, attracting investors from Europe. By the late nineteenth century, the city had become the world's leading oil center. Beneath this rapid modernization, imperial governance relied on strategies that deepened social and ethnic divisions. Imperial policies and administrative practices exacerbated communal tensions between Christian Armenians and Muslim Azerbaijanis, contributing to outbreaks of violence in 1905–1906 across Baku, Shusha, and other towns. The clashes resulted in widespread destruction, the burning of villages, and hundreds of deaths. In their aftermath, Azerbaijani political organizations such as Difai and Musavat emerged, initially focused on community defense and gradually articulating broader national and political aspirations.

World War I further destabilized the region. Baku's oil became a critical resource for the Allied war effort. At the same time, most Azerbaijani Muslims were excluded mainly from frontline service and instead subjected to special taxation and labor obligations. At the same time, a small number of Azerbaijani officers from elite families advanced within the imperial military hierarchy. Figures such as Aliagha Shikhlinski and Samed-bey Mehmandarov earned the tsar's confidence. They established reputations for professional competence and the army leadership.

In southern Azerbaijan, the collapse of imperial authority created space for political experimentation. In 1920, Sheikh Muhammad Khiabani led a brief uprising in Tabriz, proclaiming the autonomous entity of Azadistan. Although the movement was swiftly suppressed, it reflected persistent currents of political activism and demands for autonomy in the region, shaped by wartime disruption and the broader disintegration of imperial rule.

The collapse of the Russian Empire in 1917 opened space for a new political order in the South Caucasus. On May 28, 1918, the Azerbaijan Democratic Republic (ADR) was proclaimed in Tiflis. It became the first parliamentary, secular republic in the Muslim world. Under the leadership of figures such as Mammad Amin Rasulzadeh and Fatali Khan Khoyski, the new state adopted a tricolor flag of blue, red, and green, symbolizing Turkic heritage, democratic aspirations, and cultural identity shaped by Islam.

From its inception, the republic faced severe challenges. War and revolution had left widespread famine, epidemics, and large refugee populations, while unresolved territorial disputes with Armenia and Georgia strained the fragile state. Baku, whose oil fields were central to regional and international interests, remained outside the government's control until September 1918, when Ottoman and Azerbaijani forces entered the city following the collapse of the Bolshevik-led Baku Commune. After relocating its capital to Baku, the ADR struggled to govern amid competing pressures, including the presence of British occupation forces, armed confrontations involving Armenian forces in Karabakh and Zangezur, and growing Bolshevik influence across the region.

Despite its fragile circumstances, the ADR laid essential foundations of statehood. It established a parliamentary system that included representatives not only of the Muslim majority but also Armenians, Russians, Jews, and Germans, reflecting the country's social and ethnic diversity. The government expanded public education, founded higher educational institutions, and enacted legislation granting women equal political rights. It also formed a national army, which engaged in fighting in Karabakh and clashed with Armenian forces near Askeran in 1920. On the diplomatic front, the ADR dispatched a delegation to the Paris Peace Conference and secured de facto recognition from several major powers.

However, the republic's position remained deeply precarious. The defeat of the Ottoman Empire in World War I deprived Azerbaijan of its principal military supporter. At the same time, British backing proved limited and temporary. Armed confrontations with Armenian forces continued in Karabakh and Zangezur, while Bolshevik power consolidated to the north and revolutionary pressures mounted internally. In April 1920, advancing Red Army units entered Azerbaijan amid political fragmentation and unrest. After just twenty-three months, the Azerbaijan Democratic Republic ceased to exist. Its collapse marked the end of a brief experiment in independence, but its institutions, political ideas, and symbols endured as a lasting reference point for later Azerbaijani statehood.

Soviet Azerbaijan

On April 28, 1920, Bolshevik forces entered Baku and proclaimed Soviet rule. The Azerbaijan Democratic Republic was dissolved, and a new government was formed under the Council of People's Commissars, nominally headed by Nariman Narimanov but effectively subordinated to the Eleventh Red Army and Moscow's authority. The first phase of Soviet consolidation was marked by coercion and political repression. The national army was disbanded, senior military officers were arrested or executed, and large numbers of intellectuals, clergy, landowners, and former officials were imprisoned, exiled, or killed. Private property was confiscated, key industries, including oil, were nationalized, and land reforms dismantled the prewar elite while imposing new production quotas on rural communities.

Armed resistance emerged almost immediately. Uprisings broke out in Ganja, Karabakh, Zagatala, and Lankaran, often led by former officers of the ADR army or local leaders. These revolts briefly challenged Soviet authority but were suppressed by Red Army units with significant loss of life. Many participants fled south into Iran, while those who remained were subjected to surveillance, arrests, and political exclusion.

At the same time, Soviet authorities undertook a fundamental reorganization of the South Caucasus. Through negotiations mainly conducted behind closed doors, Sharur and Daralayaz were assigned to Armenia. At the same time, Zangezur and Karabakh were designated as disputed territories. Turkish objections, combined with local resistance, resulted in Nakhichevan being retained under Azerbaijani protection, a status formalized in the 1921 Treaty of Kars. Subsequent administrative decisions in the late 1920s completed the transfer of Zangezur and Ordubad to Armenia, severing Nakhichevan's direct territorial connection with mainland Azerbaijan and fixing borders that would remain sources of contention throughout the Soviet period and beyond.

The most consequential of these decisions concerned Nagorno-Karabakh. At a July 1921 meeting of the Caucasus Bureau, under the influence of Joseph Stalin, it was decided that Karabakh would remain within the Azerbaijan Soviet Socialist Republic while being granted autonomous status. This arrangement was formalized in 1923 with the creation of the Nagorno-Karabakh Autonomous Oblast, whose administrative center was established in Khankendi and later renamed Stepanakert after the Bolshevik revolutionary Stepan Shaumyan.

The structure embedded a fundamental ambiguity. Nagorno-Karabakh was incorporated into Azerbaijan's territorial framework yet retained a distinct political and administrative identity. Autonomy did not resolve competing claims, and instead, it institutionalized them, creating a system in which grievances could be expressed but not settled. Over time, this framework shaped local governance, cultural policy, and demographic patterns in ways that reinforced mutual suspicion rather than integration.

The Soviet era left behind unresolved claims, and divergent historical narratives that outlasted the Soviet Union itself. By carving Nagorno-Karabakh into an autonomous oblast within Azerbaijan while fostering demographic shifts and political dependency, Moscow planted the seeds of disputes setting the stage for the conflict's reemergence once Soviet authority collapsed. What began as administrative decisions in distant Kremlin offices became lived realities for Armenians and Azerbaijanis, shaping how each community remembered the region, often in conflicting ways.

* * *

The story of Karabakh cannot be told solely through Azerbaijan. Armenia entered the Soviet era carrying its own long history of kingdoms and empires, shaped by faith, survival, exile, and diaspora. If Azerbaijan's past was marked by layers of empire and the formation of a Muslim Turkic identity, Armenia's was shaped by the endurance of Christianity, the preservation of a distinct alphabet, and the resilience of a people dispersed across many lands. These two historical narratives developed along parallel yet distinct paths, only to converge and collide as competing claims took shape.

Brief History of Armenia

Armenia's historical narrative, like that of Azerbaijan, reaches deep into antiquity. Armenian identity took shape across the highlands surrounding Lake Van and the Ararat plain, at a crossroads of empires where Indo-European-speaking groups interacted with the legacy of the ancient kingdom of Urartu. Classical authors such as Herodotus and Strabo identified Armenians among the established peoples of the Near East. Armenian historical tradition, preserved by writers such as Moses of Khoren, blended recorded events with legend, linking early kingship to biblical narratives, including the account of Noah's Ark resting on Mount Ararat. While modern scholars continue to debate the precise ethnogenesis of the Armenians, there is broad agreement that Armenia emerged early as a distinct cultural and political community, identified in Persian inscriptions as Armina.

By the first century BCE, Armenia had consolidated from a collection of regional principalities into a recognized kingdom. Its rulers operated within a volatile geopolitical environment, navigating pressure from Persian, Hellenistic, and later Roman powers while seeking to preserve autonomy. The reign of Tigranes II, known as Tigranes the Great, marked the apex of Armenian territorial expansion. During the early first century BCE, his realm briefly extended from the eastern Mediterranean to the Caspian basin. Although this empire was short-lived, its memory assumed enduring significance in Armenian historical consciousness. The legacy of Tigranes's reign later informed nationalist interpretations of the past, including the idea of a "Greater Armenia," understood less as a continuous political reality than as a retrospective symbol of lost sovereignty and ambition.

Ancient Roots of Armenia

By the ninth century BCE, much of the Armenian Highlands had come under the control of the Kingdom of Urartu, a powerful mountain state centered on Lake Van. Urartian rulers constructed fortified cities, irrigation networks, and road systems that transformed the highland plateau into a durable political and economic landscape. For nearly two centuries, Urartu rivaled Assyria as a dominant regional power before collapsing in the early sixth century BCE under pressure from Median expansion. Its fortresses, inscriptions, and hydraulic works survived long after the kingdom itself, and many historians view Urartu as a foundational layer in the later formation of Armenian society.

The emergence of the Armenians as a distinct people followed this collapse and remains the subject of scholarly debate. Classical Greek writers such as Herodotus and Strabo suggested migrations from the west, linking Armenians to Thracian or Phrygian origins. Other interpretations emphasize Iranian or Anatolian connections. Armenian historical tradition, preserved by writers such as Moses of Khoren, blended these developments with biblical genealogy, tracing Armenian lineage to Noah and Mount Ararat. While these narratives differ in emphasis, most scholars agree that Armenian identity took shape through the fusion of an Indo-European language with the cultural and political inheritance of the Urartian highlands.

By the reign of Darius the Great in the Achaemenid Empire, the region was already known as *Armina*, and its inhabitants were incorporated into the Persian imperial system as a satrapy. The Persian influence on Armenia was significant, introducing Zoroastrian religious concepts into local beliefs, enriching the language with Persian vocabulary, and establishing Aramaic as the administrative script. This long period of contact set a pattern that would repeat throughout Armenian history: living under powerful empires while retaining a strong sense of cultural identity.

In the fourth century BCE, the Yervanduni (Orontid) dynasty consolidated much of Armenia under its rule, maintaining a fragile autonomy within the Achaemenid imperial system. This balance ended in 333 BCE, when Alexander the Great defeated the Persian Empire. In the aftermath, Greek and Macedonian elites established new urban centers, introducing Hellenistic art, architecture, and intellectual life to the region. While these influences took hold in cities, much of the Armenian countryside retained its language, social structures, and local traditions. The result was a layered cultural landscape in which Urartian heritage, Persian administration, and Hellenistic forms coexisted. From this synthesis emerged the first distinctly Armenian kingdoms, paving the way for the rise of the Artaxiad dynasty and, eventually, the reign of Tigranes the Great.

Kingdom to Christianity

In the third century BCE, Artashes I founded the Artaxiad dynasty, establishing an Armenian kingdom positioned between two expanding powers: Parthia to the east and Rome to the west. For a period, Armenia maintained a measure of independence. Its aristocracy was conversant in Greek and Persian political culture, while Armenian remained the language of the broader population. The kingdom reached its political height under Tigranes II, known as Tigranes the Great. Through conquest and alliance, he briefly created an empire that extended from the eastern Mediterranean deep into the Near East, bringing Armenia unprecedented influence. His new capital, Tigranokert, embodied this ambition. In 69 BCE, however, Roman legions besieged and sacked the city. Internal dynastic rivalries and sustained Roman pressure soon dismantled Tigranes' empire, and Armenia was reduced to a client kingdom within Rome's eastern sphere of influence.

From the first century CE onward, Armenia became a contested frontier between Rome and Parthia. Capitals were destroyed and rebuilt, and rulers were repeatedly installed and removed as the balance of power shifted.

In 66 CE, Tiridates I of the Arsacid line traveled to Rome, where he was crowned by Emperor Nero, inaugurating the Arshakuni dynasty in Armenia. This period deepened Armenia's dual political and cultural orientation: Greco-Roman artistic and intellectual influences flourished at court, while Parthian models shaped governance, elite culture, and administrative practice.

The rise of the Sassanid Empire in the third century CE drew Armenia more firmly into the Persian sphere of influence. With Zoroastrianism established as the Sassanian state religion, pressure mounted on Armenia to conform religiously and politically. In 252 CE, Shapur I invaded the country and installed his son on the Armenian throne, tightening Persian control. Nevertheless, Armenia resisted complete absorption. This prolonged struggle to preserve autonomy, and identity set the stage for a defining decision: adopting Christianity.

Tradition holds that in the early fourth century, King Tiridates III converted to Christianity under the guidance of Gregory the Illuminator, making Armenia the first state to adopt Christianity as an official religion. While other ancient Christian communities have advanced similar claims, the Armenian conversion marked a decisive turning point. Pagan shrines gradually gave way to churches, monasteries spread across the landscape, and Armenia entered the Christian world as a distinct political and cultural entity. Conversion, however, was neither instantaneous nor uniform. Older beliefs persisted alongside the new faith, and periods of Persian dominance brought renewed religious pressure. At times, churches were destroyed, and Zoroastrian fire temples rebuilt, illustrating how closely religion and imperial politics remained intertwined.

Despite these pressures, Christianity endured. Around 400 CE, the scholar Mesrop Mashtots created the Armenian alphabet. This thirty-three-letter script enabled the translation of scripture into the vernacular. More than a liturgical tool, the alphabet preserved language, fostered literature, and strengthened communal identity, allowing Armenian society to endure conquest and upheaval. By the eve of the Arab invasions in the seventh century, Armenia was no longer merely a buffer between empires, but a society defined by Christianity, a distinct written tradition, and a durable sense of historical continuity.

Arab Caliphate

By mid-century, Arab control was renewed under Turkish commanders who enforced Abbasid authority with fresh vigor. In 847 CE, the general Bugha al-Kabir led campaigns that subdued Armenia, Georgia, and Caucasian Albania, binding the region more tightly to the Caliphate. Local princes continued to govern, but only as vassals. The outcome was not independence but life under a protectorate. Armenian society endured, yet it did so under persistent political, fiscal, and religious pressure.

By the late ninth century, as the Caliphate was distracted by internal struggles, Ashot Bagratuni emerged as the leading Armenian noble, marking the rise of a new dynasty. Balancing diplomacy and force, he secured recognition from Byzantium and revived Armenian statehood under the Bagratuni dynasty. Though Armenia's autonomy remained precarious and often threatened, the Bagratuni marked the beginning of a national revival that stood in contrast to centuries of foreign domination.

The Cilician Kingdom and the Crusades

As Byzantine and Seljuk expansion pressed into the Armenian Highlands, successive waves of Armenians migrated south toward Cilicia, where rugged mountains and fertile valleys offered both refuge and opportunity. There, they joined earlier Armenian communities and gradually established a new political center that evolved from a principality into a kingdom.

This development coincided with the era of the Crusades. Following Pope Urban II's call in 1095, European crusading forces moved through the eastern Mediterranean, and the Armenians of Cilicia, led by the Rubenid dynasty, emerged as crucial regional partners. They supplied provisions, guided armies through rugged terrain, and contributed military support. In return, Armenian rulers gained recognition, protection, and political leverage. The alliance was not without strain, particularly as Byzantine attempts to reassert control periodically threatened Cilicia's autonomy, yet the Armenian polity endured.

Cilicia reached its height under Levon II, who was crowned king with papal recognition in 1198. Under his rule, the kingdom became a formally acknowledged Christian monarchy integrated into the diplomatic world of medieval Europe. Its court reflected this position, combining Armenian institutions with Western influences. Latin and French circulated alongside Armenian, legal practices were modeled on European norms, and cultural exchange shaped elite life. The Armenian Church also strengthened its presence in Jerusalem through monasteries and endowments, though rivalry with Greek Orthodox authorities persisted. For nearly three centuries, the Kingdom of Cilicia functioned as Armenia's Mediterranean anchor, linking the Armenian world to the political, commercial, and religious networks of the Crusader East.

Turkic and Mongol Powers: An Age of Upheaval

Between 1040 and 1045, successive waves of Turkic groups from Central Asia entered the South Caucasus. Under the leadership of Toghrul Beg, the Seljuks established an empire that fundamentally altered the political landscape of Armenia and Azerbaijan. Local rulers, including the Bagratuni kings of Armenia and the Georgian monarchy, found themselves navigating an increasingly unstable environment, balancing between stronger imperial forces while attempting to preserve autonomy.

By the early thirteenth century, a new and more disruptive power emerged from the east. Mongol armies advanced into the Caucasus, bringing Armenia, Georgia, and Cilician territories under their control. Local elites were incorporated into Mongol administrative and military structures, with Armenian and Georgian forces drawn into campaigns far from their homelands. Governance relied heavily on fragmentation and coercion, as Christian and Muslim authorities played against one another to maintain order. The conversion of the Ilkhanid rulers to Islam around 1300 further reshaped the region's political and religious alignments.

Destruction intensified during Timur's campaigns between 1386 and 1403. Armenian cities were repeatedly sacked, population centers disrupted, and established trade routes destabilized. After Timur's death, power fragmented once again. Ottoman forces, the Timurids, the Shirvanshahs, and the competing Turkic confederations, the Aq Qoyunlu and Qara Qoyunlu, vied for control. Although this prolonged instability deepened Armenia's vulnerability, it also marked a transitional phase that preceded the major imperial realignments of the fifteenth century.

The Safavids, the Ottomans, and the End of Medieval Armenia

The sixteenth century marked another decisive turning point. In the east, Shah Ismail I founded the Safavid dynasty in 1501 and proclaimed Shi'a Islam the state religion, reshaping the political and confessional landscape of Iran and the Caucasus. To the west, the Ottomans, emerging from the Seljuk legacy in Anatolia, consolidated power as an expanding imperial state following the conquest of Constantinople in 1453. As these two empires collided, Armenian lands lay directly between them, turning the region into a prolonged zone of warfare.

The Safavid–Ottoman conflicts of the sixteenth and seventeenth centuries had devastating consequences for Armenian society. Large-scale population movements accompanied repeated campaigns. Shah Abbas I forcibly relocated tens of thousands of Armenian families from eastern Armenia into the Safavid interior, resettling many in Isfahan, where their commercial and artisanal skills contributed significantly to the empire's economy while depopulating their regions of origin. In the West, Armenians lived under Ottoman rule, where recurrent wars, taxation, and insecurity produced additional displacement.

By the early modern period, Armenia's political autonomy had disappeared entirely. Demographic shifts gradually reduced Armenians to minorities across much of their historic territory, now dominated by Turkic- and Persian-speaking populations. At the same time, within the Ottoman Empire, Armenians retained their church, alphabet, and communal institutions, sustaining a distinct cultural identity over centuries of imperial rule. In Istanbul and other urban centers, Armenian merchants, financiers, and artisans achieved notable economic influence, at times operating within the highest circles of imperial society.

The 18th Century: Between Empires

The collapse of the Safavid Empire in the early eighteenth century plunged the South Caucasus into renewed instability. Ottoman and Persian forces contested control over Armenian territories, while Afghan incursions from the east compounded the destruction. Lacking independent political institutions, Armenians experienced shifting administrations as authority changed hands according to the fortunes of imperial warfare.

Over time, the traditional nobility lost much of its influence, and leadership within Armenian society increasingly shifted to ecclesiastical figures. The Armenian Church emerged as the primary institutional anchor of communal life, preserving social cohesion in the absence of state structures. Periodic uprisings occurred, often encouraged by Russia's expanding ambitions in the Caucasus. Seeking Christian allies against the Ottomans and Persians, St. Petersburg offered Armenians protection and promises of future autonomy, drawing them further into imperial rivalries.

By the nineteenth century, Armenian political agency had mainly become externalized. Networks of merchants, financiers, clergy, and intellectuals operating across the Russian, Ottoman, and Persian empires, and increasingly within Europe, assumed a central role in shaping Armenian public life. In the absence of sovereignty, these transregional connections sustained identity and advocacy, establishing patterns of diaspora engagement that would profoundly influence Armenian politics well into the modern era.

Russian Expansion into the South Caucasus

At the dawn of the nineteenth century, the Russian Empire moved decisively southward into the Caucasus, seeking to displace both Persian and Ottoman authority. Georgia was annexed in 1801, and Russian forces soon advanced into the Armenian Highlands and neighboring territories. The First Russo–Persian War (1804–1813) concluded with the Treaty of Gulistan, which transferred Karabakh and several adjacent khanates to Russian control. A second conflict followed in 1826–1828 and proved more consequential. Russian armies under General Ivan Paskevich captured Erivan and

Nakhichevan, and the Treaty of Turkmenchay established the Araz River as the new imperial frontier.

For Armenians, these developments marked a profound turning point. In the aftermath of the wars, the Russian authorities facilitated the resettlement of more than 40,000 Armenians from Persia and approximately 90,000 from the Ottoman Empire into the newly annexed territories of the South Caucasus. Within a generation, the Armenian population numbers increased sharply in the Erivan region and in several upland districts of Karabakh. In some towns, Armenians became the largest community. At the same time, Shusha retained a mixed population, and many surrounding rural areas remained predominantly Muslim.

The demographic effects extended beyond Karabakh itself. Armenian migration reshaped urban and social life across the region. Tbilisi emerged as a significant cultural and economic center for the Armenian elite. At the same time, Elizavetpol (Ganja) developed a substantial Armenian population alongside its Azerbaijani residents. These shifts, rooted in imperial policy and population movement, would later acquire political significance as national identities hardened under Russian rule.

Migration, Awakening, and Repression

While Eastern Armenia came under Russian imperial control, the majority of Armenians remained within the Ottoman Empire, which by the late nineteenth century was strained by reform fatigue, nationalist movements in the Balkans, and intensifying rivalry with Russia. The eastern provinces, where Armenians lived alongside Muslim communities, occupied a particularly sensitive position. Russian expansion in the Caucasus encouraged many Armenians to look northward for protection, reform, and political opportunity. At the same time, these connections heightened Ottoman fears of foreign interference, leading authorities to interpret Armenian political activity more through the lens of imperial competition than of internal reform.

From the 1860s onward, petitions and appeals for administrative reform gradually gave way to more assertive forms of resistance. Localized uprisings emerged in mountainous regions, including Zeitun and Van, where communities sought to defend themselves against abuses and assert limited autonomy. During the same period, underground political networks grew among students, merchants, and clergy. By the late nineteenth century, organizations such as the Armenakan, Hnchak, and Dashnaktsutyun transformed social grievances into organized political movements. These movements advocated for security, legal equality, and, in some cases, autonomy. Many of their leaders had studied or lived in Russia and Western Europe, absorbing revolutionary ideas of national self-determination that further unsettled Ottoman officials.

The Ottoman response combined suspicion, repression, and violence. Under Sultan Abdul Hamid II, widespread attacks in the 1890s devastated Armenian villages and towns, destroyed religious institutions, and forced large numbers of people into exile. These events, often described as massacres, deepened communal mistrust and hardened political positions. For many Armenians, expectations of reform within the imperial system collapsed. For Ottoman authorities, unrest reinforced the belief that Armenian political activity was inseparable from foreign manipulation.

The Young Turk Revolution of 1908 briefly raised hopes of renewed coexistence. Armenians participated alongside Muslims in public celebrations of constitutional restoration, believing that civic equality could stabilize imperial life. This optimism proved fragile, and by 1913, the Committee of Union and Progress increasingly embraced a centralized and exclusionary vision of the state, shaped by nationalist doctrines that cast ethnic diversity as a liability. Armenians were progressively redefined from reform partners into perceived threats to national cohesion.

The First World War intensified these dynamics. Armenian subjects of the Russian Empire served in significant numbers within the Russian Imperial Army, including volunteer formations that fought against Ottoman forces in the Caucasus campaign. Their participation reflected both loyalty to the Russian state and the belief that Russian victory might secure Armenian protection or autonomy. Simultaneously, Armenian resistance movements operated within Ottoman territory, while others aligned with Allied forces beyond it. Notably, Armenian volunteers formed units under French command, including the Armenian Legion, which fought alongside French troops in the eastern Mediterranean and Cilicia between 1916 and 1918.

These wartime alignments, shaped by imperial collapse and survival calculations, further reinforced Ottoman suspicions of Armenian collaboration with foreign powers. By the end of the war, political radicalization, mass violence, and mutual fear had transformed long-standing tensions into catastrophe, reshaping Armenian society and leaving legacies that would reverberate throughout the South Caucasus and the broader region for generations.

Breaking Point: 1915

The First World War brought these tensions to a catastrophic conclusion. Ottoman defeats in the Balkans had already driven large numbers of Muslim refugees into Anatolia, intensifying social strain and sharpening hostility toward minority communities. When Enver Pasha's Sarıkamış campaign against Russia collapsed in early 1915, Armenians were widely accused of collaboration with the enemy. Within weeks, Armenian soldiers in the Ottoman army were disarmed, community leaders in Constantinople were arrested on April 24, and mass deportations were initiated.

What followed was a humanitarian disaster on a vast scale. Armenian families were expelled from their homes and forced southward toward the deserts of Syria and Mesopotamia. Many died from hunger, disease, or violence along the routes of deportation; others were resettled under conditions that proved fatal to most. Villages were emptied, churches destroyed, and entire districts depopulated. Although estimates vary, historians broadly agree that more than one million Armenians lost their lives through a combination of killings, famine, exposure, and forced marches.

Armenians remember these events as genocide, understood as a deliberate effort to destroy their people and eliminate their historical presence in Anatolia. Turkish officials, while acknowledging widespread suffering and loss of life, reject this characterization, arguing that the deportations occurred within the context of war, rebellion, and imperial collapse. Between these irreconcilable interpretations lies one of the most enduring and contested legacies of the late Ottoman period.

The consequences of 1915 fundamentally reshaped Armenian existence. Survivors dispersed across the Middle East, Russia, Europe, and the Americas, forming a global diaspora. Cities such as Beirut, Tbilisi, Paris, Boston, and Los Angeles emerged as new centers of Armenian cultural and communal life. As time passed, memory, upheld by churches, schools, literature, and memorials, became a fundamental aspect of collective identity. For many, the feeling of loss supplanted territorial continuity as the defining feature of nationhood.

For the Ottoman state, the events of 1915 deepened isolation and entrenched mistrust toward minorities and external powers. For Armenians, it became both an enduring trauma and a unifying narrative, shaping political consciousness long after the empire itself had vanished. More than a century later, the legacy of 1915 remains a defining rupture in Armenian–Turkish relations. It forged the modern Armenian diaspora, influenced regional politics, and continues to cast a long moral and historical shadow over how both societies understand their past and one another.

Armenians in the Russian Empire

Meanwhile, under Russian rule, Armenians encountered new opportunities for communal consolidation and economic advancement. Large-scale migration following the Russo–Persian wars, particularly after 1828, significantly increased Armenian numbers within the empire. By the late nineteenth century, Armenian populations had grown markedly in Erivan, Tbilisi, and parts of Karabakh. Meanwhile, many Armenians also found success in Baku's rapidly expanding oil economy. After 1915, additional waves of refugees fleeing massacres, deportations, and famine in the Ottoman Empire further reshaped the demographic landscape. Towns and villages across the Erivan and Kars provinces absorbed tens of thousands of displaced families. For the first time in centuries, Armenians approached demographic parity with Muslims across much of the former Erivan Khanate and neighboring districts, forming a modest majority in Erivan.

Russian imperial policies reinforced these changes. The Armenian Church and communal institutions operated with state recognition and relative protection. At the same time, access to education, urban employment, and commercial networks enabled segments of the Armenian population to advance economically. In contrast, much of the Azerbaijani Muslim population remained rural and politically marginalized. These asymmetries, sharpened by imperial favoritism, fostered resentment and mistrust. Tensions erupted violently during the ethnic clashes of 1905–1906 in Shusha, Khankendi, and other towns across the South Caucasus, leaving lasting scars and establishing patterns of communal confrontation that would reemerge in later decades.

The collapse of the Romanov dynasty in 1917 briefly raised Armenian hopes for autonomy as imperial authority dissolved across the Caucasus. These expectations were quickly undermined. The Treaty of Brest-Litovsk transferred contested territories, including Kars and Ardahan, back to Ottoman control. At the same time, Russian forces withdrew from the region. As governance disintegrated and the front collapsed amid revolution and peace negotiations, Armenians were mainly left on their own to defend exposed communities in an increasingly unstable landscape.

The First Republic of Armenia (1918–1920)

Armenia's independence emerged amid an acute crisis. On May 28, 1918, following the collapse of the Transcaucasian Federation and with Ottoman forces advancing toward Erivan, Armenian leaders proclaimed the establishment of a republic. In practice, sovereignty preceded capacity. The new state encompassed roughly 4,500 square miles and a population of approximately 700,000, nearly half of whom were refugees from the Ottoman Empire. Erivan, previously a provincial administrative center, was abruptly transformed into a national capital.

The republic faced structural vulnerabilities from the outset. It was landlocked, economically underdeveloped, and largely devoid of industrial infrastructure. Food shortages, disease, and displacement strained state institutions that barely existed. Armed groups operated beyond effective government control, while unresolved territorial disputes with the Ottoman Empire, Azerbaijan, and Georgia rendered every border contested.

Independence, though formally achieved, was sustained amid scarcity, insecurity, and constant external pressure.

The Ottoman defeat in November 1918 brought only a brief reprieve. Armenian forces temporarily reoccupied Kars and adjacent districts, while exiled political leaders and intellectuals returned to Erivan with renewed expectations of statehood. During the Paris Peace Conference, Armenian representatives proposed a "Wilsonian Armenia," a potential state envisioned under American protection, reflecting broader aspirations for a historical concept of Greater Armenia. Lacking military enforcement or a Western mandate, however, the proposal proved unattainable. Britain prioritized access to Baku's oil fields. It supported Azerbaijan in disputes over Karabakh and Zangezur, while France and other powers declined deeper involvement. On the ground, fragile ceasefires collapsed into renewed violence. Villages were destroyed, populations displaced, and Shusha suffered extensive devastation.

As the Great Powers withdrew from the region, pressure mounted from both west and east. In the west, Turkish nationalist forces under Kazım Karabekir advanced into Kars and Alexandropol, overwhelming Armenia's exhausted defenses. At the same time, Bolshevik Russia sought to secure its southern frontier. Moscow provided Ankara with material support while simultaneously moving to reassert its own influence in the South Caucasus. Caught between Turkish military advances and Bolshevik expansion, the Armenian Republic collapsed. In December 1920, Red Army units entered Erivan, and Armenia was proclaimed a Soviet Socialist Republic, ending its brief experiment with independence.

Armed resistance, however, did not immediately cease. In the mountainous region of Zangezur, Garegin Nzhdeh, a former Imperial Russian Army officer and veteran of the First World War, organized local militias that expanded Armenian control over the territory. Between 1919 and 1921, his forces resisted both Azerbaijani units and Bolshevik troops. While Nzhdeh's campaign occupies a prominent place in Armenian historical memory, it also involved severe violence. His forces carried out reprisals and forced expulsions of Muslim villagers, primarily Azerbaijani and Kurdish, significantly altering the region's demographic composition and entrenching patterns of interethnic division. Earlier, General Andranik Ozanian had conducted similar operations before withdrawing into exile. These campaigns established Armenian control in Zangezur through force, leaving legacies of displacement and grievance that long outlasted the fighting.

The Treaty of Kars, signed in 1921 by Turkey, Soviet Russia, and the South Caucasus republics, formalized the new territorial order. Armenia retained Zangezur but ceded Kars and Ardahan to Turkey and relinquished claims to Ani and Koghb. The borders established by the treaty became the foundation of the modern map of the South Caucasus and marked the consolidation of Soviet rule in the region. Although short-lived, the First Armenian Republic assumed lasting significance in political memory and diaspora discourse, functioning more as a symbol of interrupted statehood than as a governing model.

Armenia in the Soviet Era

The Sovietization of Armenia in 1920–1921 came amid exhaustion and despair. Lenin's New Economic Policy softened the transition, allowing limited private trade. To ease local fears, Bolshevik leaders such as Aleksandr Miasnikian promised gradual reform rather than immediate revolution.

In 1922, Armenia was incorporated into the Transcaucasian Socialist Federative Soviet Republic, which was later absorbed into the USSR. As Soviet authority consolidated, border-making decisions taken in Moscow gave legal form to the territorial realities created by war and revolution. Armenian and Azerbaijani Bolshevik factions competed over Karabakh, Nakhichevan, and Zangezur, but the Communist Party's Caucasian Bureau determined the outcome. The resulting settlement placed Nagorno-Karabakh under Azerbaijani control as an autonomous oblast. It designated Nakhichevan as an autonomous republic under Azerbaijani jurisdiction, while Zangezur, already under Armenian control, was retained within Armenia.

Presented as administrative compromises, these decisions contained structural contradictions that later manifested as open conflict. They also raised issues related to language and naming conventions, demonstrating how Soviet authority redefined both space and identity. Under Soviet rule, the city, long known as Erivan, officially adopted the form *Yerevan*, reflecting the standardization of Armenian-language usage within the Soviet administrative system.

During the early Soviet years, several Armenians rose to influential positions within Moscow's political establishment. They helped shape policies that defined the new union. Among them, Anastas Mikoyan emerged as one of the most prominent and enduring figures. A veteran Bolshevik and close associate of both Lenin and Stalin, Mikoyan held key economic and political posts, including serving as People's Commissar for Trade and later as a member of the Politburo. Though firmly loyal to Moscow, he worked to advance Armenian interests by promoting industrial development, infrastructure investment, and education within the republic, ensuring Armenia maintained a visible place within the Soviet framework.

At home, Armenia remained largely poor and agrarian, but Yerevan expanded rapidly as internal migrants and returning diaspora families settled in the capital. For the first time, Armenian became the official state language, and mass literacy campaigns reached nearly every village, laying the foundations of a modern national culture under Soviet rule.

World War II brought both sacrifice and collective pride. Nearly half a million Armenians served in the Red Army, and commanders such as Hovhannes Bagramyan became national heroes. Armenian losses approached 175,000, leaving lasting social and demographic scars. After 1945, the Armenian Church, briefly suppressed under Stalin, was permitted to reopen, and a state-sponsored repatriation campaign brought more than 100,000 Armenians from the Middle East and Europe. Their arrival revitalized the republic but also generated social tensions; locals often referred to the newcomers as *aghbars* (brothers), a term that carried both solidarity and unease.

By the 1960s and 1970s, Armenian society grew increasingly restless. Petitions and demonstrations called for the protection of language rights and the reconsideration of the status of Karabakh and Nakhichevan. Underground nationalist organizations, such as the National Unity Party, demanded self-determination. In contrast, others framed their activism within the language of human rights, drawing on the Helsinki Accords. Moscow responded with surveillance, arrests, and censorship, but these pressures failed to extinguish dissent,

The decisive rupture came in the late 1980s, when *perestroika* (reconstruction) and *glasnost* (expanded openness in public discussion and media) loosened the mechanisms of Soviet control. In February 1988, the regional council of the Nagorno-Karabakh Autonomous Oblast, formally under Azerbaijan's jurisdiction, passed a resolution requesting unification with Armenia. Though illegal under Soviet law, the decision ignited mass demonstrations in Yerevan and Stepanakert, marking the emergence of the Karabakh movement and signaling the unraveling of Soviet authority in the South Caucasus. What began as a procedural appeal soon evolved into the first sustained challenge to Moscow's control over the region.

***

The long histories of Armenians and Azerbaijanis reveal overlapping experiences under successive empires, while also tracing divergent political and social trajectories that produced distinct national identities. By the early nineteenth century, these identities had hardened under the cumulative weight of foreign rule, historical memory, and religious affiliation. Karabakh lay at the intersection of these trajectories, a region where both peoples established settlements, built fortifications, and sustained cultural traditions. It was here, as Russian imperial authority expanded across the Caucasus, that longstanding coexistence gave way to political competition. The policies, treaties, and population movements of the imperial period transformed Karabakh from a zone of interaction into a contested space, setting in motion the conflict examined in this study.

Map of Azerbaijan. Source: United States Central Intelligence Agency, 1992. Public domain.

The Centuries-Old Roots of the Karabakh Conflict

The histories of Armenia and Azerbaijan show how deeply Karabakh was connected to both peoples long before it became a modern battleground. For Armenians, the region was home to monasteries, villages, and noble lineages that anchored a Christian cultural landscape. For Azerbaijanis, Karabakh occupied a central place within a network of khanates, fortresses, and political traditions shaped by Turkic and Islamic influences. Beneath these later formations lay older historical layers, including the legacy of Caucasian Albania, where early Christianity and Zoroastrian practices had coexisted centuries before Turkic migrations and the spread of Islam reshaped the region's spiritual and political life.

These overlapping inheritances did not, by themselves, produce conflict. It was under nineteenth-century Russian rule that earlier legacies were reconfigured into sharper political and demographic boundaries. Imperial treaties, administrative restructuring, and population movements altered Karabakh's balance and transformed patterns of coexistence into competing claims. The modern struggle over Karabakh begins in this period, when imperial governance recast a shared historical space into a contested territory and laid the foundations for the nationalist narratives that would later dominate regional politics.

Russian Empire Policies and Armenian Migration to the Caucasus

The early nineteenth century marked a decisive turning point for Karabakh and the wider South Caucasus. Russia's victory over Persia and the Treaty of Gulistan in 1813 brought much of the region, including Karabakh, under imperial control, inaugurating a new political order. This shift was confirmed by the Treaty of Turkmenchay in 1828, which transferred the Erivan and Nakhichevan khanates to Russia and established the Araz River as the formal frontier between the Russian and Persian empires.

These agreements were negotiated without the participation of local rulers or the local population. By fixing the border along the Araz, imperial authorities divided a historically interconnected space into northern territories under Russian rule and southern lands remaining within Persia. While Russia possessed the capacity to expand further south, it instead chose to consolidate a frontier it considered administratively manageable, prioritizing strategic control over cultural or historical continuity.

For Azerbaijanis, the new boundary came to symbolize a lasting rupture, separating communities and reordering long-standing social and economic ties. For the Russian Empire, it marked the beginning of a deliberate strategy to stabilize its southern border through administrative restructuring, population management, and the redefinition of political loyalties. These policies would profoundly shape Karabakh's future, transforming it from a regional crossroads into a focal point of imperial governance and, eventually, nationalist contestation.

Before the introduction of Russian resettlement policies, Armenians in the South Caucasus constituted a relatively small minority, living alongside a predominantly Muslim, Azerbaijani-speaking population across Karabakh, Erivan, and Nakhichevan. A central pillar of Russia's imperial strategy was demographic reconfiguration. Imperial officials believed that Christian settlers would prove more reliable subjects and therefore actively encouraged the migration of Armenians from Persia and the Ottoman Empire into newly annexed territories.

Between 1828 and 1831 alone, an estimated 57,000 Armenians were resettled from Persia under the provisions of the Treaty of Turkmenchay. In the following decades, particularly after successive Russo-Turkish wars, an additional 80,000 to 90,000 arrived from Ottoman Anatolia. The demographic consequences were immediate and far-reaching. Whereas Armenians had constituted roughly one-fifth of the population of Eastern Armenia before Russian conquest, by 1832 they accounted for nearly half, due both to inward migration and the parallel departure of tens of thousands of Muslims to Persia and Anatolia.

Karabakh reflected this transformation in microcosm. Russian records from the 1830s counted approximately 19,000 Armenians and 35,000 Muslims in the former khanate. Armenians tended to settle in the mountainous districts, while Muslims remained predominant in the plains and lowlands. Russian authorities facilitated Armenian settlement through land grants, tax exemptions, and, in some cases, by permitting the acquisition of property previously held by Muslims. Although relations between the communities in these early decades were generally stable, perceptions gradually emerged among Muslims that imperial policies favored Armenians, contributing to latent resentment.

Administrative reforms reinforced these dynamics. Following the abolition of the khanates, the region was initially governed under military administration and later reorganized into civilian provinces. By 1867, most of Azerbaijan had been incorporated into the guberniyas of Baku and Elizavetpol. These reforms dismantled the authority of local elites and introduced an imperial administrative order that tended to advantage educated, urbanized groups. Armenians, who had established strong commercial and professional networks, were particularly well positioned within this system.

By the late nineteenth century, the Armenian population of Transcaucasia had grown to more than 1.2 million, bolstered by continued migration and, later, by refugees fleeing violence in Ottoman Anatolia during the 1890s. These shifts were most visible in Baku. Once a modest Caspian port, the city expanded rapidly into a major oil center after the 1870s, its population rising from roughly 14,000 in 1863 to over 200,000 by 1903. Russians,

Armenians, and Muslims formed the city's three largest communities. Economic roles, however, were unevenly distributed. Many Muslims worked as unskilled laborers in the oil fields, while Armenians and Russians were disproportionately represented in managerial, technical, and commercial positions. Urban growth produced increasingly segregated neighborhoods, intensifying economic competition and sharpening social boundaries.

By the turn of the twentieth century, Russian conquest, administrative restructuring, and population policies had fundamentally altered the political and human landscape of the South Caucasus. Armenians consolidated their presence through migration and institutional access, while Azerbaijani Muslims experienced the erosion of traditional authority and relative demographic decline. Karabakh embodied these contrasts with particular clarity, as its plains and highlands became a mosaic of shifting populations and competing loyalties. For several decades, this fragile coexistence persisted despite underlying tensions. In the early twentieth century, however, those tensions would erupt into open violence, marking the first phase of a conflict whose consequences continue to shape the region.

The First Armenian Azerbaijani Clashes (1905–1907)

The first large-scale clashes between Armenians and Azerbaijanis erupted in the early years of the twentieth century, amid a broader crisis of authority within the Russian Empire. The Revolution of 1905, sparked by the shock of Russia's defeat in the Russo-Japanese War and the massacre known as "Bloody Sunday" in St. Petersburg, exposed the fragility of tsarist rule. In the South Caucasus, long-standing social tensions were intensified by economic inequality, competing national movements, and the weakening of imperial control. Communities that had coexisted for generations now found themselves navigating a rapidly shifting political landscape in which coexistence gave way to fear-driven mobilization and growing mutual suspicion.

Armenian nationalist organizations played a prominent role in this escalation. The Hnchak Party, founded in 1887, and the Armenian Revolutionary Federation (Dashnaktsutyun), established in 1890, had by the early twentieth century developed disciplined networks capable of political agitation and armed action. The tsarist decree of 1903, confiscating Armenian Church property, proved a turning point, prompting the Dashnaks in particular to abandon cautious cooperation with imperial authorities in favor of open resistance. Azerbaijani Muslims, by contrast, lacked comparable centralized political or military organizations at the time. Russian officials, rather than acting as neutral arbiters, frequently exacerbated tensions. Weapons circulated widely, rumors spread unchecked, and local authorities often failed to intervene decisively, allowing confrontations to escalate into violence.

The first major clashes broke out in Baku in February 1905, lasting several days and resulting in heavy casualties. Violence soon spread to Nakhichevan, Erivan, Jabrail, Zangezur, and other districts. In August 1905, Shusha, the cultural and administrative center of Karabakh, became a focal point of fighting. Azerbaijani residents mounted organized defenses, while armed Armenian groups sought to assert control. The violence resumed the following summer. In June 1906, Shusha again experienced intense fighting, including bombardment and street battles, amid allegations of official negligence and corruption. Rural areas suffered similarly. In Zangezur, attacks on villages and travelers triggered retaliatory killings, while in Khankendi and Malibeyli, further bloodshed deepened cycles of revenge. By the end of the clashes, more than one hundred Azerbaijani villages and over one hundred Armenian villages had been destroyed, displacing tens of thousands of civilians.

The consequences of the 1905–1907 violence were profound. Among Armenians, the clashes reinforced the belief that organized resistance and armed self-defense were necessary for communal survival. For Azerbaijanis, the experience underscored the perceived need for greater political organization, education, and participation in public life. Both communities emerged with hardened national identities, deepened mistrust, and a growing tendency to interpret events through collective narratives of victimhood and threat. Russian imperial authorities, meanwhile, succeeded in reasserting control only after significant destruction, thereby weakening both communities. Karabakh, and Shusha in particular, stood at the center of this upheaval, remembered as both a site of violence and endurance.

By 1907, widespread exhaustion, the devastation of towns and villages, and the gradual restoration of imperial military authority brought the violence to a halt. The calm that followed was fragile. Neither Armenians nor Azerbaijanis achieved a decisive outcome, and the underlying grievances remained unresolved. What emerged was a tense coexistence shaped by historical context, fear, and competing national aspirations.

The clashes of 1905–1907 did not fade quietly into the past. They demonstrated how quickly coexistence could unravel when imperial authority weakened and political uncertainty prevailed. The pattern established during these years of mobilization, communal violence, and contested authority would reappear decades later during the collapse of Soviet rule. In Karabakh, where these dynamics were especially acute, the early twentieth century left a legacy that continued to shape the region's trajectory well into the modern era.

The March Days of 1918

World War I thrust the South Caucasus into global focus. Baku's oil became one of the empire's most strategically valuable resources. However, the region's Muslims were largely exempt from frontline conscription and instead subjected to special wartime taxation, expected to finance Russia's campaigns without receiving equal recognition as soldiers. Only a small number advanced within the imperial officer corps, most notably Aliagha Shikhlinski and Samed-bey Mehmandarov, whose prominence highlighted both opportunity and structural exclusion.

The collapse of imperial authority in 1917 left Baku politically fragmented and heavily armed. In November of that year, Stepan Shaumyan, an Armenian Bolshevik, assumed the role of Commissar Extraordinary for the Caucasus and emerged as the central figure of the Baku Commune, a fragile coalition of Bolsheviks, Left Socialist Revolutionaries, Mensheviks, and Dashnaktsutyun. Lacking a reliable Muslim base of support and commanding only about 6,000 loyal troops, Shaumyan faced a critical decision: whether to cooperate with the Azerbaijani Musavat movement or to rely on

Armenian Dashnak forces. He chose the latter, securing the support of an additional 3,000 to 4,000 experienced Dashnak fighters. Many had served in the Russian Imperial Army during recent Ottoman campaigns and brought with them not only military experience but also grievances shaped by earlier violence and displacement.

On March 9, 1918, General Talyshinski, commander of Azerbaijani forces in Baku, was arrested along with several senior officers, further inflaming anti-Bolshevik sentiment among the city's Azerbaijani population. Soon afterward, Bolshevik authorities moved to disarm a detachment of Azerbaijani sailors from Lankaran aboard the ship Evelina, docked in the Baku port. The action provoked widespread outrage. Mediation was attempted by the Muslim socialist party Hummet, which proposed taking temporary custody of the weapons. Shaumyan initially agreed to this compromise.

On March 31, when representatives arrived to collect the arms, gunfire erupted in the city. The precise origin of the shooting was never conclusively established. Shaumyan and the Bolshevik leadership immediately accused Musavat of organizing an armed uprising, declared Baku under siege, and ordered operations against Muslim neighborhoods.

Over the following three days, the violence escalated into mass killing. Bolshevik units, operating in coordination with Dashnak armed detachments, shelled Muslim quarters, burned mosques, and carried out widespread executions. Civilians were targeted irrespective of political affiliation. In later accounts, Shaumyan acknowledged that the Bolsheviks had "exploited the opportunity" to eliminate Musavat as a rival political force. Estimates of the dead in Baku range from approximately 3,000 to as many as 12,000. Additional atrocities followed in Shamakha, Guba, Salyan, and Lankaran. In Shamakha, entire districts were destroyed, and thousands of residents were killed. Arrests, property seizures, and large-scale looting accompanied the violence.

The Baku Commune officially portrayed the events as the suppression of counterrevolutionary threats. In practice, its reliance on Dashnak forces introduced a pronounced ethnic dimension to the conflict. Many Armenian fighters, recently engaged in warfare against Ottoman forces, viewed the city's Turkic-Muslim population through the prism of wartime hostility.

Among Azerbaijanis, the March Days became embedded in collective memory as an episode of mass violence and as one of the earliest formative traumas of the twentieth century.

The significance of March 1918 extended well beyond its immediate toll. The events demonstrated how revolutionary instability could rapidly devolve into ethnic violence, dissolving long-standing patterns of coexistence. Although Karabakh was not directly affected, developments in Baku were closely watched. The violence reinforced fears, hardened communal boundaries, and contributed to the erosion of trust between Armenians and Azerbaijanis. In this sense, the March Days marked not only a tragic episode in Baku's history but a turning point in the broader trajectory of interethnic relations across the South Caucasus.

Independence and Escalation

The collapse of the Russian Empire in 1917 plunged the South Caucasus into political uncertainty. The short-lived Transcaucasian Federation quickly fractured as Georgians, Armenians, and Azerbaijanis pursued separate paths to statehood. On May 28, 1918, the Azerbaijani National Council proclaimed the Azerbaijan Democratic Republic (ADR), the first secular parliamentary republic in the Muslim world, while Armenians established their own republic in Erivan. From the outset, relations between the two new states were unsettled, with Karabakh already emerging as a central point of contention.

Seeking security, the ADR turned to the Ottoman Empire, which became the first state to recognize its independence. Ottoman forces under Nuru Pasha, joined by Azerbaijani volunteers, defeated Bolshevik and Dashnak units at Goychay in June–July 1918, opening the route to Baku. The collapse of the Baku Commune followed, replaced by the Centro-Caspian Dictatorship, an unstable coalition of Mensheviks, Socialist Revolutionaries, Dashnaks, and a small British expeditionary force under General Lionel Dunsterville. Stepan Shaumyan and the other Bolshevik commissars fled the city but were later captured and executed by anti-Bolshevik forces in Turkmenistan.

The decisive struggle for Baku unfolded between August and September 1918. Ottoman–Azerbaijani forces advanced on the city, which was defended by British troops and Armenian battalions loyal to the Centro-Caspian regime. After weeks of heavy fighting, British troops withdrew, accompanied by many Dashnak units. Large numbers of Armenian civilians fled as well, some crossing into Iran. On September 15, Ottoman and Azerbaijani forces entered Baku and assumed control. The change in authority was followed by retaliatory violence against Armenian quarters of the city, resulting in widespread killings and mass displacement. Together with the March violence earlier that year, the September events became embedded in communal memory and further deepened mistrust between Armenians and Azerbaijanis.

The victory proved short-lived. The Ottoman defeat in World War I soon forced their withdrawal under the Armistice of Mudros. On November 17, British forces under General William Thomson entered Baku, imposed martial law, and stationed approximately 5,000 troops in the city. The ADR retained formal independence, but its survival increasingly depended on external powers beyond its control.

Meanwhile, conflict spread across Karabakh and neighboring regions. In late 1918, Armenian commander Andranik Ozanian led irregular forces into Zangezur, Nakhichevan, and Karabakh, destroying villages and displacing tens of thousands of Azerbaijani inhabitants. In response, the ADR established a Karabakh governorship in January 1919, appointing Khosrov bey Sultanov with his seat in Shusha. Armenian councils rejected the authority of Azerbaijan and sought unification with Erivan. A fragile dual arrangement followed: temporary agreements offered cultural autonomy to Armenians while affirming Azerbaijani administrative control. In practice, neither side was able to impose stability. Raids, reprisals, and the destruction of villages became a persistent feature of life in the highlands.

By early 1920, the ADR army, numbering nearly 40,000 men but inadequately equipped, regained control of Shusha and halted Armenian advances near Askeran. Internationally, the ADR secured de facto recognition from diplomatic circles in Paris and Washington. Domestically, however, it remained overstretched, confronting Armenian resistance in Karabakh, instability in Zangezur, and growing pressure from the Red Army advancing from the north. Independence rested on an uncertain future, and the struggle over Karabakh had already become central to the republic's fate.

Diaspora Influence and the International Dimension

While Armenians and Azerbaijanis struggled on the ground over Karabakh, Zangezur, and Nakhichevan, their representatives and communities abroad carried the conflict into international diplomatic arenas. The Armenian diaspora, particularly in the United States and Western Europe, emerged as a highly influential actor. At the Paris Peace Conference in 1919, Armenian delegations lobbied intensively for Allied guarantees of a future Armenian state, explicitly presenting Karabakh, Zangezur, and Nakhichevan as integral Armenian territories. In the United States, Armenian organizations mobilized through church networks, relief committees, and advocacy groups, raising funds and submitting petitions directly to Washington. Their efforts found receptive audiences. American officials such as Colonel William Haskell, dispatched to the Caucasus, reported extensively on the humanitarian crisis facing Armenian refugees, lending institutional credibility to diaspora appeals.

President Woodrow Wilson briefly considered the possibility of an American mandate over Armenia, including parts of the South Caucasus. Although Congress ultimately rejected the proposal in 1920, the inclusion of Karabakh in such deliberations highlighted the extent to which diaspora advocacy shaped Western perceptions of the conflict. Armenian activism extended beyond political lobbying. Diaspora organizations raised substantial humanitarian aid, financing orphanages, schools, and food relief across Armenia and neighboring regions. For a society devastated by war and mass displacement, this support reinforced the diaspora's dual role as both a material lifeline and an international political voice, foreshadowing the transnational activism that would later become central to modern Armenian identity.

Azerbaijani representatives also appeared on the international stage, though under more constrained circumstances. Led by Alimardan bey Topchubashov, the Musavat delegation sought diplomatic recognition of the

Azerbaijan Democratic Republic. It argued that Karabakh and Zangezur were inseparable parts of the Azerbaijani territory. Their efforts secured de facto recognition of the ADR by several powers in 1920, albeit too late to ensure the republic's survival. Unlike the Armenians, Azerbaijanis lacked a large, well-established diaspora capable of sustained lobbying abroad. Nonetheless, their representatives articulated Azerbaijan's territorial integrity in Western capitals and secured formal recognition of their claims.

The imbalance in diaspora influence meant that Armenian perspectives resonated more strongly in Washington and Paris. However, both communities succeeded in internationalizing their competing narratives. From the earliest stages of the Karabakh dispute, arguments made far from the Caucasus helped shape how the region was understood and contested. This early globalization of the conflict would return with far greater intensity in the late twentieth century.

Soviet Rule and the Karabakh Question (1920–1923)

By 1920, both of the young republics were overstretched, engaged in border conflicts, facing large waves of refugees, and dependent on external support from various sources, including Britain, the remnants of the Ottoman Empire, and fluctuating Western allies, whose commitment was quickly waning. Into this void stepped the XI Red Army. In April 1920, Soviet forces entered Baku while much of the army of the Azerbaijan Democratic Republic was still occupied in Karabakh and Zangezur. As a result of military pressure and political ultimatums, power shifted dramatically. The national army was disbanded, and resistance in Ganja and Karabakh was quelled through severe reprisals. Although Soviet rule promised class equality, achieving this goal proved challenging in a region divided by ethnic tensions and unresolved territorial disputes.

Between 1920 and 1921, borders were redrawn through a combination of force and treaty. In Zangezur, the consolidation of Armenian control, shaped by earlier campaigns led by figures such as Nzhdeh, contributed to the depopulation of Azerbaijani villages and, crucially, severed Azerbaijan's direct overland connection to Nakhichevan, leaving the corridor question to be settled by treaty. At the same time, Nakhichevan was anchored to Azerbaijan by the Moscow Treaty of March 1921 and the Treaty of Kars in October 1921, under Turkish guarantee. Only the highland region of Karabakh remained unresolved, its status suspended between competing claims and Moscow's shifting priorities as it sought to balance relations between Baku and Yerevan.

These territorial decisions were not merely cartographic. They altered settlement patterns, uprooted communities, and reshaped family histories across the region, including those of individuals who would later play prominent political roles. Heydar Aliyev, who would become a central figure in Azerbaijani politics, was born into a family that had relocated from villages in what is now Armenia's Syunik Province to Nakhichevan. His father's family came from Comardlı (present-day Tanahat), and his mother from Vorotan. Such relocations were common during the early 1920s, as violence, shifting borders, and the consolidation of Soviet rule displaced populations before political identities had fully hardened.

The Kavburo's decision of July 1921 settled the remaining issue administratively. Nagorno-Karabakh was retained within Soviet Azerbaijan, a choice justified by considerations of regional stability and the oblast's economic ties to the surrounding lowlands. Moscow pledged autonomy and, in 1923, established the Nagorno-Karabakh Autonomous Oblast. Although its population was at times predominantly Armenian, the oblast was placed under Azerbaijani jurisdiction and lacked a direct land connection with Armenia. Khankendi was designated as its capital and later renamed Stepanakert, after Bolshevik leader Stepan Shaumyan.

By 1923, the basic contours of the Karabakh dispute were firmly in place. Years of war, population violence, and treaty-making had reshaped the region's political and demographic landscape. Armenians and Azerbaijanis each advanced historical claims to Karabakh, while Soviet administrative decisions formalized its inclusion within Azerbaijan. Soviet authority ended open fighting, but it did not reconcile these competing narratives.

The creation of the Nagorno-Karabakh Autonomous Oblast was presented as a pragmatic compromise, combining limited Armenian self-administration with centralized control from Baku. While this arrangement imposed a measure of stability under Soviet rule, it failed to secure political acceptance, particularly among Armenian elites. The grievance was not resolved but suspended, carried forward by institutions and narratives that would resurface once Soviet authority weakened.

Illusion of Peace

Economic Growth and Transformation, 1923–1945

For many who lived in Karabakh during the Soviet decades, the period evokes nostalgia for a time of stability and genuine friendship. Schools operated, industries expanded, and Armenians and Azerbaijanis lived side by side in peace. Families intermarried, neighbors celebrated holidays together, and both communities held positions in local administration. They fought for the Soviet Union in the Second World War against a common enemy. In everyday life, the divisions of the past seemed distant, even forgotten.

However, this peace rested on the firm grip of the Soviet system. The creation of the Nagorno-Karabakh Autonomous Oblast in 1923 granted Armenians limited cultural recognition while keeping the region within Soviet Azerbaijan, an arrangement never entirely accepted in Yerevan, and beneath the surface of official fraternity, political elites and nationalist circles quietly preserved older grievances, portraying Azerbaijanis as "Turks" and as long-standing adversaries, while asserting that Karabakh was inherently Armenian. Karabakh thus became a space of coexistence sustained by Soviet control, while Armenian political grievances over the region's status remained unresolved.

When the Nagorno-Karabakh Autonomous Oblast was created in 1923, it was a poor, war-scarred land. Shusha, once a bustling regional hub, had seen its economy collapse in the turmoil of 1918–1920. Across the countryside, farms were small and unevenly distributed; more than half of households worked less than half a hectare, and many were so poor that they were exempt from taxes. Agriculture remained the backbone of life, but production was low, irrigation scarce, and herds modest.

The Soviet authorities recognized both the region's poverty and its potential. From the mid-1920s, Baku and Moscow funneled subsidies into Karabakh, financing canals, electrification, and collective farms. The Uzuntal, Talish, and Madagiz canals were built to irrigate fields. Collectivization swept through villages, and by the late 1930s, most households had been absorbed into kolkhozes (collective farms) and sovkhozes (state-owned farms). At the same time, wealthier farmers were deported in the waves of dekulakization. Still, surviving communities gained access to tractors, machinery, and cooperative structures that re-shaped rural life.

Traditional industries were also revived. Carpet-weaving and silk production, devastated by earlier violence, were restored with state support. A silk combine began operating in Stepanakert in the early 1930s. At the same time, dozens of small wineries and distilleries processed the region's grapes and mulberries. Woodworking and furniture-making appeared in new workshops, and the first power stations lit up towns and factories.

The numbers told the story. By the end of the first two Five-Year Plans, Karabakh's industrial output had risen more than 40-fold from 1923. In 1938 alone, production reached nearly 100 million rubles. Forty-two new enterprises had been established before the Second World War, from hydroelectric plants in Madagiz to wine factories and limestone quarries. Karabakh had been transformed from a neglected agrarian province into a contributor to the USSR's silk, wine, and building materials.

By the eve of the war, Karabakh had become an integral part of the Soviet system, industrialized, educated, and rebuilt. These transformations, however, did not eliminate earlier disputes. As Soviet authority weakened, a generation raised within the Soviet order drew on long-standing grievances, bringing unresolved historical claims back into political life.

World War II

The Second World War drew Karabakh deeply into the Soviet struggle for survival. Approximately 45,000 people from the oblast were mobilized into the Red Army, and nearly 22,000 never returned. Conscription reflected the region's demographic composition, with Azerbaijanis serving alongside Armenians. Their absence placed immense strain on civilian life. Women, the elderly, and adolescents assumed responsibility for vineyards, fields, and workshops, sustaining production with minimal equipment under strict rationing.

Local industry was rapidly redirected toward the war effort. The silk combine produced fabric for parachutes, wineries distilled medicinal alcohol, and workshops repaired machinery for the front. Despite chronic shortages, Karabakh, like the rest of the Soviet Union, remained integrated into the collective wartime economy.

Victory left the region battered but resolute, as the wartime sacrifices of Armenians and Azerbaijanis, entered Soviet memory as symbols of endurance and shared struggle. For a time, this experience muted ethnic divisions, reinforcing the Soviet narrative of an ordinary people forged by hardship and triumph. Yet the war's toll was severe. Heavy losses and postwar migration altered the oblast's demographic balance, and the Nagorno-Karabakh Autonomous Oblast entered the postwar years burdened by reconstruction and lingering social strain.

Economic Expansion and Integration, 1945–1985

Postwar reconstruction quickly evolved into expansion. Veterans returned not only with medals but with the conviction that their sacrifices bound them to the Soviet project. The oblast was no longer a marginal district; it was presented as evidence that Soviet planning could transform even a mountainous borderland into a productive part of the Union.

Vineyards spread across the foothills, and by the 1970s, Karabakh had become one of Azerbaijan's leading wine-producing regions, turning out nearly two million decaliters annually. Cognac production followed, with shipments reaching Moscow, Kyiv, and other major cities. The Stepanakert silk combine revived a traditional craft and, at its peak, supplied nearly a quarter of Azerbaijan's silk thread. A shoe factory made the oblast the republic's second-largest footwear producer, while the electrotechnical plant, opened in the 1960s, exported lighting equipment across the USSR and abroad. By the early 1980s, more than fifty enterprises operated in the oblast, roughly one-third of them established after the war.

Agriculture modernized alongside industry. Collective and state farms were consolidated, vineyards expanded, and mechanization raised yields. The completion of the Sarsang hydroelectric station in 1976 symbolized this transformation, providing electricity to mountain settlements and irrigation to the surrounding lowlands. Household plots continued to play a vital role, supplying much of the region's meat, dairy, and vegetables and illustrating how private labor complemented official production targets.

Trade patterns highlighted the oblast's integration. Despite later political claims, most of Karabakh's output moved through Baku and other Soviet republics rather than through Armenia. Wine, silk, footwear, and electrical goods circulated primarily within Azerbaijani and all-Union markets, while raw materials and machinery arrived through the same channels. By the late 1970s, the structure of the oblast's economy closely resembled that of Azerbaijan as a whole, centered on food processing and light industry and embedded in Soviet supply chains.

For ordinary residents, these decades brought stability and modest prosperity. Employment was steady, wages predictable, and towns expanded with new housing, schools, and cultural institutions. Many later recalled factory parades, evenings at the cinema, and weddings that brought Armenian and Azerbaijani families together. At the same time, the system's limits became increasingly visible. Investment frequently lagged behind plans, projects stalled, and the region's dependence on viticulture left it exposed to decisions made in Moscow.

By the mid-1980s, these weaknesses were fully exposed. Gorbachev's anti-alcohol campaign slashed vineyard output by nearly half and idled thousands of workers. Shortages, strikes, and declining confidence followed. Karabakh entered the era of perestroika not as a neglected periphery but as a developed Soviet district, integrated, dependent, and vulnerable to shocks beyond its control. Economic strain intersected with unresolved political grievances, creating conditions for conflict to reemerge.

Forced Migration and Population Engineering, 1940s–1950s

The aftermath of the Second World War brought renewed demographic upheaval to the South Caucasus. While Karabakh itself remained within Azerbaijan, Soviet Armenia became the focal point of one of Stalin's most consequential population policies: the removal of Azerbaijanis from Armenia and the resettlement of Armenians from abroad.

In 1926, Azerbaijanis constituted nearly 10 percent of Soviet Armenia's population, numbering approximately 85,000. By 1939, their number had grown to more than 130,000, reflecting natural population increase despite wartime losses. By the 1959 census, however, following a decade of state-directed relocations, the Azerbaijani population had fallen to fewer than 108,000. This decline was not demographic in origin but the result of deliberate policy.

Stalin's administration, with the support of the Armenian party leadership, increasingly viewed Azerbaijanis in Armenia as a potential security liability in the event of renewed conflict with Turkey. In the late 1940s, as Moscow advanced territorial claims against Turkey's provinces of Kars and Ardahan, Armenians abroad were actively encouraged to repatriate to Soviet Armenia. To make room for these arrivals, Azerbaijani families were ordered to relocate. In December 1947, Stalin approved Resolution No. 4083, authorizing the transfer of up to 100,000 Azerbaijanis from Armenia to the Kura–Araz lowlands of Azerbaijan. Armenian party secretary Grigory Arutinov and Azerbaijani leader Mir Jafar Baghirov formally oversaw the policy. In practice, the policy was frequently implemented by Armenian officials at the republican and local levels.

Although presented as voluntary, the resettlement was coercive in practice. Families were promised housing, livestock, and limited financial assistance, yet archival records and personal accounts describe widespread resistance and appeals to remain. Between 1948 and 1953, an estimated 45,000 to 53,000 Azerbaijanis were forcibly relocated from Armenia. Their vacated homes and villages were rapidly resettled by Armenians arriving from Syria, Lebanon, France, and the United States.

The consequences were profound on both sides of the border. Many relocated Azerbaijanis struggled to adapt to the harsh conditions of the Kura–Araz steppe, an area marked by limited infrastructure, inadequate housing, and persistent public health challenges. For the Armenian SSR, the policy strengthened its strategic position along the Soviet–Turkish frontier and accelerated a shift toward demographic consolidation. For Azerbaijanis, it meant displacement from long-established settlements and a sharp contraction of their cultural and historical presence in much of Armenia.

These deportations hastened the de-Azerbaijanization of Armenia, contributing to its transformation into one of the most ethnically homogeneous republics of the Soviet Union. Azerbaijan, by contrast, remained markedly multiethnic, with cities such as Baku and Sumgait retaining substantial Armenian, Russian, and Jewish populations throughout the Soviet period. The asymmetry produced by these policies widened demographic and social contrasts across the border, reshaping the region's ethnic landscape in ways that would reverberate long after the Stalinist era had ended.

Demographic Shifts and Migration in the Soviet Era

These forced relocations were part of a broader demographic transformation unfolding across the South Caucasus. From the late 1940s through the 1970s, Soviet industrialization created powerful centers of attraction for internal migration. Armenians from Karabakh and the Armenian SSR moved in large numbers to Sumgait, Mingachevir, Dashkasan, and especially Baku, where the Armenian population nearly tripled between 1926 and 1979.

Within Nagorno-Karabakh itself, population growth was steady but uneven. Between 1970 and 1979, the oblast's population increased by approximately 12,000 people, of whom about 10,000 were Azerbaijanis and only 2,000 Armenians. Higher Azerbaijani birth rates, combined with migration from surrounding districts, gradually altered the demographic balance. At the same time, many Armenians continued to gravitate toward urban centers, both within Azerbaijan and beyond its borders.

Despite these demographic shifts, the oblast's political structure remained essentially unchanged. Armenians retained near-total control of local party and administrative institutions. In the late Soviet period, they accounted for more than 90 percent of deputies in oblast councils and dominated the administration in Stepanakert. Azerbaijanis, despite their growing share of the population, remained consistently underrepresented in decision-making bodies.

Political Campaigns over Nagorno-Karabakh (1945–1950s)

After the Second World War, Armenian political leaders renewed efforts to change the status of Nagorno-Karabakh. The creation of the Nagorno-Karabakh Autonomous Oblast in 1923 had long been regarded in Yerevan as a compromise rather than a settlement. Although the region remained within Azerbaijan, autonomy was widely viewed as a provisional arrangement that left the possibility of unification with Armenia open.

In 1945, amid renewed Soviet pressure on Turkey over Kars and Ardahan, the "Armenian question" reentered high-level policy discussions in Moscow. Within this context, Armenian Communist Party leader Grigory Arutinov submitted a proposal to transfer Nagorno-Karabakh to Armenia, asserting that such a move would reflect the preferences of the oblast's population and facilitate its development.

Azerbaijan's leader, Mir Jafar Baghirov, rejected the proposal outright. He reminded Moscow that Nagorno-Karabakh shared no border with Armenia and was surrounded by Azerbaijani districts. Any attempt to alter this arrangement, he warned, would destabilize the republic. Baghirov further argued that if Karabakh were to be transferred, then Armenian districts with substantial Azerbaijani populations should be reassigned to Azerbaijan in return. Unwilling to entertain territorial exchange, the Armenian leadership withdrew the initiative.

With the transfer blocked, Armenian leaders adjusted their strategy. Rather than pressing for immediate border changes, they emphasized the mass "repatriation" of Armenians from abroad. As noted in the previous section, this policy unfolded at the expense of tens of thousands of forcibly displaced Azerbaijani families removed from Armenia. Formal territorial claims were set aside, but the demographic objective remained clear: to reduce the Azerbaijani presence within the Armenian Republic.

After Stalin's death, the political climate eased, allowing Armenian elites to revive demands for the transfer of Nagorno-Karabakh. Intellectuals and activists within the oblast began organizing petitions addressed directly to Moscow, bypassing Baku altogether. In 1963, a letter signed by approximately 2,500 Armenians from Karabakh and neighboring districts was submitted to Nikita Khrushchev, calling for either "reunification" with Armenia or direct incorporation into the Russian Federation. Diaspora organizations echoed these appeals through parallel campaigns abroad.

Moscow publicly ignored the petitions, but Azerbaijani authorities followed them closely. KGB reports described Armenian teachers, writers, and cultural figures in Karabakh as disseminating what officials termed "provocative narratives," often linked, rightly or wrongly, to Dashnak networks overseas. Surveillance intensified, and several activists were placed under monitoring. When Anastas Mikoyan privately raised the possibility of transferring Karabakh, Khrushchev responded dismissively, remarking that he could "send twelve thousand army trucks and relocate the Armenians of Karabakh to Armenia in a single day." The message was unambiguous: Soviet borders in the Caucasus were not open to revision. Yet the persistence of these campaigns revealed a deeper reality—many within Karabakh's Armenian leadership regarded integration into Azerbaijan not as a settled outcome, but as a temporary and reversible condition.

The removal of Nikita Khrushchev and the rise of Leonid Brezhnev in 1964 gave Armenian claims renewed momentum. In 1965, Moscow permitted public commemorations in Yerevan for the first time, marking the fiftieth anniversary of the events of 1915. For Armenians, this was widely interpreted as a tacit acknowledgment of genocide, even though Soviet authorities avoided the term and maintained official silence on legal or political implications. Among Azerbaijanis living in Armenia, the demonstrations generated deep unease. Letters sent to Moscow warned of growing tensions;

one described the republic as a "ticking bomb," vulnerable to violence at the slightest provocation.

The unrest soon extended into Nagorno-Karabakh. In June 1965, the Armenian writer Bagrat Ulubabyan, with the support of local party officials, submitted a petition to Moscow calling for the transfer of the oblast to Armenia. Youth groups circulated clandestine leaflets, and by 1966, nearly two thousand members of the Armenian intelligentsia had signed an appeal declaring that "Karabakh is Armenia by territory, culture, and spirit." The campaign reached the highest levels of the Armenian Communist Party, which sought to frame the demand as an act of "historical justice" rather than territorial revisionism.

Azerbaijani authorities responded forcefully behind the scenes. Heydar Aliyev, then deputy chairman of the Azerbaijani KGB, later recalled that Moscow briefly considered convening a joint discussion between the Armenian and Azerbaijani party leaderships. "It meant," Aliyev observed, "that the fate of Azerbaijan was being placed in Armenia's hands." Brezhnev ultimately shelved the issue, siding with Baku and making clear that the Soviet leadership would not reopen the border question. While the immediate challenge was contained, the episode reinforced a pattern: Armenian political activism around Karabakh resurfaced during moments of perceived liberalization, only to be suppressed without resolution.

✳✳✳

For most of the Soviet period, Karabakh was a relatively stable region where Armenians and Azerbaijanis lived side by side. Many villages had mixed populations, and daily life followed familiar Soviet routines: work, schooling, family life, and shared public celebrations. Weddings, birthdays, and community events often brought people of different backgrounds together. Mixed marriages were common, and friendships frequently crossed ethnic lines. On the ground, political questions about borders or sovereignty rarely intruded into everyday life. Most residents were far more concerned with livelihoods, education, and family than with abstract debates over autonomy or unification.

At the same time, political discourse followed a very different path at the elite level. In Yerevan and among segments of the Armenian intelligentsia, the idea of "reunification" with Karabakh was quietly preserved. These efforts remained confined to petitions sent to Moscow, private discussions, and cultural or academic circles. They were never aired in the Soviet press or openly debated in public forums. As a result, most Azerbaijanis and many Armenians were largely unaware of these initiatives. They experienced daily life without sustained ethnic tension or hostility.

Karabakh during these decades reflected broader Caucasian traditions of hospitality, cooperation, and local interdependence. Its stability rested less on ideology than on shared habits, mutual reliance, and the routines of ordinary life. That equilibrium, however, depended on the constraints of the Soviet system itself. With the advent of perestroika and glasnost in the mid-1980s, censorship weakened, and long-suppressed nationalist narratives reemerged. Themes that had circulated quietly within intellectual and political circles now entered public discourse. In this environment, Azerbaijanis were increasingly described as "Turks" in Armenian nationalist rhetoric, not as an ethnolinguistic classification, but as a political label that associated them with historic Ottoman adversaries. This framing recast contemporary neighbors as extensions of an older, unresolved conflict, hardening perceptions on both sides.

What had once remained contained within archives and private conversations moved into the open. The social fabric of coexistence, long sustained by silence and stability, was suddenly exposed to competing historical claims and mobilized identities. This shift laid the ideological groundwork for the confrontation that followed, transforming Karabakh from a space of everyday coexistence into the focal point of a renewed and far more volatile conflict.

Nagorno-Karabakh, 1993. Source: United States Central Intelligence Agency (CIA). Public Domain

Perestroika

In 1985, Mikhail Gorbachev came to power as the youngest Soviet leader in decades, chosen by an aging Politburo in the hope that generational change might rescue a system paralyzed by economic stagnation and political inertia. Raised in a provincial farming region and shaped by postwar Soviet life, Gorbachev believed that socialism could be renewed through openness, accountability, and administrative reform rather than repression. Fluent in English and at ease with Western leaders, he quickly became a symbol of change abroad, admired for his accessibility and willingness to engage in dialogue.

At home, however, his strengths proved less suited to the challenges he faced. Gorbachev entered office with limited experience managing the Soviet Union's complex internal politics, a state composed of dozens of nationalities, regions, and economic systems held together by centralized authority. While he articulated reform convincingly, he lacked a coherent and enforceable long-term financial strategy to stabilize a deteriorating command economy.

Perestroika promised restructuring, but in practice it relied heavily on improvisation, shifting priorities, and experimental policies rather than on precise mechanisms for growth, investment, or fiscal discipline. In a country as vast and diverse as the Soviet Union, reform required not only openness but careful sequencing, economic clarity, and sustained institutional control. Instead, political liberalization advanced more rapidly than economic reform, widening the gap between public expectations and the state's capacity to govern and deliver stability. That imbalance would prove increasingly difficult to contain.

Perestroika did more than loosen economic controls. It dismantled long-standing restraints on political expression, allowing ethnic grievances that had been kept out of public view for decades to resurface. Gorbachev later acknowledged that the leadership in Moscow understood the consequences of this opening. "In just three years," he recalled, "the Central Committee received 500 letters about Nagorno-Karabakh. Perestroika (the restructuring of the Soviet political and economic system) set great internal forces in motion. Old wounds opened, national feelings revived, and with them, nationalism." What had changed was not the existence of grievance, but the space to express it. For the first time since the 1920s, demands to alter Azerbaijan's borders were voiced openly, framed in the emerging language of democracy, rights and self-determination.

Armenian leaders and activists seized the moment. In 1987 alone, more than 70,000 signatures were gathered in Karabakh on a petition calling for unification with Armenia. Writers such as Zori Balayan and historians such as Sergey Mikoyan used newspapers and diaspora outlets abroad to advance the cause, operating within the new political space created by *glasnost* (expanded openness in public discussion and the media). That autumn, the movement received its boldest signal yet. Abel Aganbegyan, one of Gorbachev's top economic advisers, told a group of Armenians in Paris, "I would welcome it if Nagorno-Karabakh were returned to Armenia… I believe their ties to Armenia are stronger than to Azerbaijan." Published in *L'Humanité* and rebroadcast by diaspora radio from Paris to California, the remarks spread quickly, energizing Armenians worldwide and catching many in Azerbaijan by surprise. For Armenian activists and intellectuals, the Karabakh question was suddenly back on the global stage.

For many in Baku, the moment was one of disillusionment. Azerbaijani leaders had long relied on the Soviet system to enforce stability, believing that Moscow would curb Armenian territorial claims as it had in 1945, 1965, and 1977. This time, the familiar pattern did not hold. Gorbachev's silence following Aganbegyan's remarks suggested that the Kremlin was no longer the unquestioned arbiter it once had been.

Inside Karabakh, the atmosphere shifted rapidly. KGB reports documented the arrival of emissaries from Yerevan, the spread of underground groups, and the circulation of Zori Balayan's book *Ochag* (*The Hearth*), which openly called for unification with Armenia under the slogan of *miatsum* (reunion). As one local officer later recalled, by February, everything was clear. If it had not erupted in Sumgait, violence would have broken out elsewhere." By the end of 1987, the question of Karabakh was no longer confined to archives or closed meetings. It had become public, political, and urgent, set loose by the very reforms intended to preserve the Soviet Union and soon to emerge as the first major ethnic crisis of its collapse.

From Petition to Movement

The Karabakh campaign was driven by segments of the Armenian intelligentsia, including writers, historians, and academics, who interpreted perestroika's call for openness as an opportunity to revive territorial claims. Through essays, speeches, and petitions, these figures advanced narratives of Karabakh's "ancient Armenian heritage." They recast Stalin's 1921 decision as a historic injustice, arguing that the region had been improperly assigned to Azerbaijan. Such arguments aligned with the broader Soviet reassessment of Stalinism, but in Karabakh they acquired a sharper political edge, providing the ideological foundation for an emerging separatist movement.

In 1988, the movement entered mass politics. Local party officials in Stepanakert openly resigned from the Communist Party to form new organizations, including Krunk, Karabakh, and the Armenian National Movement (AOD). These were not marginal dissidents but administrators and officials who had previously enforced Soviet rule. Their defection lent the movement visible legitimacy, and their calls for miatsum echoed across the oblast. Arrests only amplified their standing, turning them into symbols of resistance.

Armenian advocacy framed the conflict in both cultural and economic terms. Activists pointed to the growth of the Azerbaijani population in Karabakh, portraying it as deliberate demographic "pressure." In practice, this trend reflected higher birth rates and routine migration from neighboring districts. Economically, claims of neglect and discrimination were also advanced, despite Soviet data suggesting otherwise. By the 1980s, living standards in Karabakh often exceeded the Azerbaijani average, with more schools, hospitals, and cultural institutions per capita than in surrounding regions.

Moscow misread the nature of the crisis. The Kremlin treated the unrest primarily as an economic problem and responded with subsidies rather than political engagement. On March 24, 1988, the Central Committee and the Council of Ministers launched a special development program for Karabakh, promising new investment, supplies, and infrastructure. The core demand, however, was political rather than material, and no financial package could resolve it.

By the summer of 1988, both the Armenian SSR and the Karabakh regional council passed resolutions demanding union with Armenia. In July, the Supreme Soviet of the USSR convened a special session and, on July 18, ruled decisively against altering borders, declaring that the territorial division between Armenia and Azerbaijan was permanent under Soviet law.

Exodus from Armenia: 1988–1990

As Armenians mobilized around the call for miatsum, a parallel tragedy unfolded across the border. Beginning in late 1987, the final and most consequential expulsion of Azerbaijanis from Armenia took place. Over the next three years, the process advanced at a rapid pace and with finality. Unlike the deportations of the late 1940s, this wave coincided directly with Armenia's territorial claims against Azerbaijan and unfolded with the involvement and acquiescence of local administrative and law enforcement structures. Officials justified removals as part of a "historical restoration" of lands they asserted had always been Armenian.

The process became visible in the autumn of 1987, when interethnic violence in Armenia's southern Kafan district forced Azerbaijani families to flee. By January 1988, trainloads of displaced villagers began arriving in Baku. Women, children, and the elderly arrived bruised, frightened, and carrying little more than what they could hold. Refugees described intimidation, night raids, and explicit warnings that they could no longer be protected if they remained. Homes, fields, orchards, and burial grounds were abandoned under pressure rather than choice.

One Azerbaijani refugee from the Kafan district recalled the collapse of everyday coexistence in a public oral-history interview recorded in 2024:

"In Kafan, we once lived without locks on our doors. Armenian and Azerbaijani neighbors drank coffee together, and children played freely in the courtyards. Then people began saying, 'Turks must leave.' At first, it was taunts, then stones, and then night raids. By 1987, armed men came to our village, and the police told us, 'We cannot protect you. Leave before it is too late.' We packed what we could, left behind our animals and orchards, and boarded buses under guard. When we arrived in Sumgait, people listened to our stories about beatings, homes burned, and families torn apart. I will always remember the expressions on their faces: a mix of anger, disbelief, and fear. We lost not just our houses, but the earth where our grandparents were buried. To leave was like tearing out our own root."

As the expulsions accelerated, delegations of displaced Azerbaijanis appealed directly to Moscow. Letters poured into the offices of the Communist Party and Soviet ministries, pleading for intervention and guarantees of safe return. These appeals were largely ignored. The Kremlin responded either with silence or with limited disciplinary measures against individual local officials, avoiding engagement with the crisis's political nature.

By December 1988, the Azerbaijani Council of Ministers reported that more than 78,000 refugees had crossed into Azerbaijan. The 1989 Soviet census still recorded 84,860 Azerbaijanis living in Armenia. Within a year, almost none remained. By 1990, virtually the entire Azerbaijani population of Armenia, estimated at approximately 250,000 people, had been displaced. What began as sporadic intimidation had become a systematic erasure of long-established communities from towns and villages across Armenia.

Most of those expelled were rural residents, farmers and shepherds, uprooted from mountain villages, valleys, and pastures that had sustained their families for generations. Others came from towns such as Kirovakan, Spitak, and Yerevan, where Azerbaijanis had long formed part of the urban population. Many spoke Armenian fluently and had lived alongside Armenian neighbors for decades. As nationalist rhetoric hardened, however, Azerbaijanis were increasingly recast as outsiders. The term "Turk," once a neutral ethnolinguistic designation, came to function as a pejorative and a marker of enmity.

The scale of displacement produced a humanitarian crisis that Moscow failed to grasp. Rather than confront the expulsions directly, the Kremlin adhered to a doctrine of "equal responsibility," treating Armenian and Azerbaijani grievances as symmetrical. In practice, this meant overlooking the one-sided removal of Azerbaijanis while assigning equal blame to both republics. The result was paralysis. Refugees continued to arrive in Azerbaijan, and many were resettled in tent camps, abandoned factories, and public buildings.

Beyond statistics, displacement reshaped daily life in visible ways. One of my classmates in Baku arrived in 1988 as a refugee from Yerevan. At the time, he was simply a new student, one among many children whose lives had been abruptly uprooted. Only later did I understand what his presence represented.

Zaur had grown up in Yerevan in what he remembered as an ordinary Soviet childhood. Armenian was his first spoken language. He attended a regular Soviet school and lived in a mixed neighborhood where ethnic identity rarely defined daily interactions. That sense of normalcy began to unravel in 1987, as nationalist slogans appeared openly and Azerbaijani families were increasingly singled out. At school, he was called "Turk," a label that shifted quickly from description to insult. Teachers offered no protection. Police warnings made clear that safety could no longer be guaranteed. By early 1988, harassment escalated into violence. Zaur and his brother were beaten for refusing to join chants demanding Karabakh's transfer from Azerbaijan to Armenia. His family barricaded their apartment at night as threats became routine.

In May 1988, after being advised by officials to leave "before it was too late," the family fled Yerevan under security escort. They crossed into Azerbaijan through the Qazakh district and resettled in Baku. Zaur was eleven years old. Like thousands of others, he became displaced by forces far beyond his control. Such experiences were not isolated. Across Azerbaijan, the arrival of displaced families transformed social and political perceptions. Accounts of violence, expulsion, and official inaction circulated rapidly, reinforcing a growing belief that existing institutions could no longer guarantee security or justice. The Karabakh question, once framed as a distant administrative issue, came to be understood as an immediate matter of collective vulnerability.

By the end of 1990, the fate of Azerbaijanis expelled from Armenia was clear. Their displacement was irreversible. Villages that had once been Azerbaijani were emptied or resettled, while the communities that sustained them vanished. What endured were memories of homes, fields, places of worship, and burial grounds carried by families now forced to rebuild their lives inside Azerbaijan as displaced people. The influx of refugees became not only a humanitarian challenge but a formative force in Azerbaijan's political and social transformation on the eve of independence.

When the first buses of refugees arrived in Sumgait, the crisis took on a local, immediate dimension. Stories of beatings, expulsions, and official indifference spread quickly, heightening fear and resentment. Tensions that had been building for months came to a head. Within weeks, the situation crossed a threshold, and violence followed.

Sumgait, 1988

The violence erupted at night on February 27, 1988, in the industrial city of Sumgait, roughly twenty miles from Baku. For many residents, it came as a profound shock. Such acts disrupted the city's established multiethnic social order, in which Azerbaijanis, Armenians, Russians, and Jews lived and worked alongside one another. When unrest broke out, it was not spontaneous. Small groups moved deliberately through Soviet-era housing complexes, targeting Armenian families whose addresses were already known. Over two nights, apartments were looted and set ablaze, and residents were beaten or killed as they attempted to flee. Police and emergency services, understaffed and unprepared, were quickly overwhelmed. Many Azerbaijani neighbors intervened, sheltering Armenian families or helping them escape, though the disorder spread faster than such efforts could contain it. As in other episodes of the conflict, individual acts of protection across ethnic lines coexisted with collective violence, revealing how quickly shared civic life could fracture under pressure. For a city long defined by coexistence, the events marked a sharp rupture.

Sumgait, however, was not an isolated eruption. In the months preceding February 1988, Azerbaijani communities in southern Armenia had already been uprooted, and displaced families began arriving across the border. Their accounts of intimidation, expulsion, and official inaction circulated in private conversations rather than in public reporting, as Soviet media remained silent and state institutions avoided acknowledging them. By early 1988, Sumgait had absorbed a growing number of these displaced families. Their arrival introduced stories of violence and abandonment into an already strained industrial city facing overcrowding and deepening economic hardship. While this background neither explains nor excuses the violence that followed, it helps illuminate the volatile atmosphere in which weakened authority and accumulated grievance created conditions for unrest.

Sumgait altered that dynamic. It was the first episode of mass violence to breach the Soviet system of silence and reach a national and international audience. Images of burned apartments and panicked civilians circulated widely, transforming what had previously been a concealed pattern of ethnic expulsions into an unmistakable political crisis. The name Sumgait quickly became synonymous with the breakdown of Soviet authority in the Caucasus and the collapse of the assumption that coexistence would endure.

Investigators dispatched to the city later described armored patrols, military checkpoints, and hundreds of security personnel sent to restore order. Among them was senior prosecutor Vladimir Kalinichenko, who emphasized that the official investigation confirmed twenty-seven Armenian men and women killed during the pogrom, a figure far lower than the numbers circulating in rumor and foreign press. He acknowledged, however, that many more were beaten, assaulted, or driven from their homes. Kalinichenko also recorded instances in which Azerbaijani neighbors hid Armenian women and children in their apartments, helping them survive the violence. For him, Sumgait revealed both the brutality of collective violence and moments of restraint and solidarity, alongside clear indications that the unrest was fueled by organizers who were never fully identified or held to account.

Soviet and Western media coverage focused overwhelmingly on the bloodshed. Acts of rescue and assistance received little attention, as they did not fit the dominant framing of ethnic confrontation. The public instead encountered images of burning buildings and enraged crowds, while stories of individuals who risked themselves to protect neighbors largely remained outside the narrative.

Within Armenian nationalist circles, Sumgait appeared to confirm a long-held conviction that Azerbaijanis, often conflated rhetorically with the Ottoman Turks of earlier memory, were inherent adversaries, violent and untrustworthy. Televised reports and survivor interviews, widely broadcast in Western media, reinforced this perception, shaping international opinion long before Soviet investigations were completed. The tragedy became central to a nationalist narrative that portrayed Armenians as perpetually unsafe among Muslim neighbors. The language of genocide resurfaced in slogans and statements, now linked explicitly to accounts of pogroms. Across Armenia and the diaspora, Sumgait became a rallying cry: a moral justification for nationalist ideology and an emotional appeal for foreign sympathy. Within Armenia and Karabakh, the same rhetoric provided ideological cover for continued expulsions and attacks against Azerbaijani civilians, further deepening mistrust and violence as Moscow struggled to reassert control.

Among Azerbaijanis, Sumgait was both a tragedy and a trap. The violence shocked a society that had long viewed itself as tolerant and cosmopolitan. Yet the actions of a few were projected onto an entire people. In both Soviet and Western media, Armenia appeared primarily as the victim, while Azerbaijan was cast as the aggressor. For many Azerbaijanis, this framing was experienced as a profound injustice: the crimes of mobs eclipsed the suffering of tens of thousands of Azerbaijani families already expelled from Armenia and parts of Karabakh. The events dealt a lasting blow to Azerbaijan's international reputation and would shadow its public image for decades. Subsequent clashes, diplomatic disputes, and refugee crises were repeatedly interpreted through the prism of Sumgait, which Armenian leaders and diaspora organizations continued to invoke as evidence and justification in advancing long-standing claims against Azerbaijan.

Azerbaijan in Turmoil: From Leadership Crisis to Mass Protest

In May 1988, Secretary Kamran Bagirov was replaced by Abdurrahman Vazirov, a career diplomat and personal ally of Mikhail Gorbachev. Vazirov had spent much of his career abroad, serving as the Soviet ambassador to Pakistan and later to Nepal. Returning to Baku after years away, he was unfamiliar with local politics and detached from the social realities of a republic in turmoil. At a moment when Azerbaijanis looked for a strong and decisive leader to defend national interests and speak directly to the people, they were met instead with a man shaped by Soviet ideals, an official of the old order at a time that demanded a new kind of politics. Loyal to Moscow and steeped in Gorbachev's internationalist rhetoric, Vazirov avoided expressions of national sentiment or empathy. In more stable times, his restraint might have been tolerated, but in 1988, it proved disastrous.

By mid-1988, Azerbaijan was entering a combined social and political crisis. The steady influx of refugees from Armenia had become a permanent feature of public life in Baku, bringing with it firsthand accounts of violence and expulsion that circulated widely across the city. Their presence intensified anti-Armenian rhetoric and sharpened interethnic tensions within Azerbaijan. At the same time, their unresolved status exposed the paralysis of the Azerbaijani leadership, which continued to minimize the crisis rather than confront Moscow directly. Vazirov appeared detached and uncertain, acting as though no serious conflict existed. His cautious appeals for calm, delivered in the familiar language of party slogans, failed to resonate with a frustrated public. Lacking both a clear strategy and credible communication, his administration left a political vacuum that was quickly filled by nationalist rhetoric and emerging grassroots activism.

By May, demonstrations had spread across Baku and the provinces, giving rise to new opposition figures whose rhetoric resonated with public sentiment and quickly elevated them to national prominence. In October 1988, these disparate voices coalesced under a single banner with the formation of the Azerbaijani Popular Front (APF). Conceived as a broad national platform for political renewal, the Front sought to channel popular discontent into organized political action. Intellectuals and activists such as Abulfaz Elchibey, Etibar Mammadov, and Ali Karimli provided the movement with ideological direction and credibility, translating abstract grievances into a coherent political program. The APF rapidly emerged as the leading force of opposition, combining demands for democratization with the defense of Azerbaijan's territorial integrity and growing calls for sovereignty within the Soviet Union.

On November 17, 1988, reports about the Topkhana Forest became the catalyst that transformed Azerbaijan's unrest into a nationwide movement. News spread that Armenians linked to the Yerevan Aluminum Plant were clearing land in the protected forest near Shusha. For many Azerbaijanis, the incident was understood as a challenge to sovereignty and dignity, touching a landscape long associated with Karabakh and national identity. Within days, hundreds of thousands assembled in Baku's Lenin Square, later renamed Azadlıq (Freedom) Square, a space that soon became known simply as the Meydan, to protest what they perceived as another step toward the erosion of Azerbaijan's control over Karabakh, compounded by the indifference of both Moscow and local authorities. What began as a reaction to a single incident quickly expanded into a broader expression of national awakening and disillusionment with Soviet rule. The demonstrations marked an open challenge to the Communist Party's authority. For eighteen consecutive days, tens of thousands gathered daily, demanding protection for Azerbaijanis in Armenia and Karabakh, an end to governmental paralysis, and greater national sovereignty.

The leaders of the demonstration came from various backgrounds. On one side were radical nationalists from the organization *Varlıq*, led by Neimat Panakhov, whose fiery speeches drew large crowds. On the other hand, there were intellectuals like Zardusht Aliza-de, Leyla Yunus, Eldar Namazov, and Tofik Qasimov who sought reform through dialogue. Their meeting with party leader Abdulrahman Vazirov, however, revealed the limits of cooperation. Vazirov held fast to Soviet internationalist ideals and refused to acknowledge the growing demand for change. Disillusioned, segments of the intelligentsia began organizing a civic movement outside the Communist Party's structures.

However, on December 5, Soviet authorities imposed a state of emergency and deployed troops to disperse the demonstrators. By that point, the Communist Party's legitimacy had already eroded beyond repair. Karabakh transformed from a mere territorial dispute into a significant political tool. Opposition leaders used it to channel public anger toward the ruling elite, while the regime attempted, unsuccessfully, to restore authority through propaganda and coercion. The Meydan rallies of 1988 marked a decisive turning point, signaling the rise of a mass national movement and the beginning of the end of Soviet rule in Azerbaijan.

Events moved rapidly. In January 1989, Moscow imposed a system of "special administration" in Nagorno-Karabakh under Arkady Volsky, effectively sidelining Azerbaijani authority in the region. For many in Azerbaijan, the move confirmed a growing fear that the republic was losing control over its own territory. Protests surged once more, with demonstrators demanding the dissolution of Volsky's committee, the legal recognition of the Popular Front, and a fundamental change in the republic's political course.

In September, amid mounting pressure, the Supreme Soviet of Azerbaijan convened an emergency session. After heated debates, conducted under the gaze of crowds gathered outside the parliament, it adopted the Constitutional Law on the Sovereignty of the Azerbaijani SSR. One month later, the Popular Front was officially registered as a political organization. By late November, Moscow retreated, dissolving Volsky's special administration. On paper, it marked Azerbaijan's first symbolic victory over the central authority in Moscow.

That autumn, events along the Soviet–Iranian border further exposed the fragility of imperial control. Along the Araz River, families separated for decades by Soviet border fences briefly reunited as barriers were torn down and border troops largely stood aside. The scenes invited comparisons to the fall of the Berlin Wall and revealed the contradictions of perestroika. While Germans were celebrated for pursuing reunification, Azerbaijanis were condemned for similar aspirations. The same Kremlin that praised "new thinking" in Berlin denounced the movement in Baku as nationalist extremism, underscoring the selective limits of Soviet reform.

For Moscow, this was the final warning. At a Politburo meeting on January 2, 1990, KGB chief Vladimir Kryuchkov warned that the situation was slipping beyond control, reporting to Moscow that "power in Jalilabad had passed to the so-called Popular Front. The state border is collapsing. The army must assist the border guards." Gorbachev had promised to guide the USSR through perestroika without civil war. Within weeks, that promise would be shattered.

The Baku Pogroms: January 1990

By early 1990, Baku was under intense social and political pressure. The continued arrival of refugees from Armenia had reshaped daily life in the capital, intensifying public resentment as both the local Communist leadership and Moscow failed to assert effective control. With institutional channels for redress effectively closed, frustration accumulated as Soviet authorities hesitated, uncertain and unwilling to impose a clear course: Refugee families crowded into dormitories, schools, and public buildings, their visible hardship a daily reminder of violence beyond the republic's borders. In this charged atmosphere, the remaining Armenian community in Baku, already reduced after waves of departures since 1988, became increasingly vulnerable. For many Azerbaijanis, the continued presence of Armenian families who had not fled appeared as a painful contrast to the suffering of displaced Azerbaijanis, reinforcing perceptions of injustice, abandonment by the state, and unresolved violence in Armenia and Karabakh.

On January 13, another mass rally in Lenin Square escalated into violence. Radical figures within the Popular Front openly called for retaliation, drawing stark contrasts between the suffering of Azerbaijani refugees and the continued presence of Armenians in the city. By evening, groups broke away from the demonstration and moved through residential districts, looting apartments and attacking Armenian residents. Subsequent investigations by Human Rights Watch indicated that the violence was not entirely spontaneous. In several instances, attackers appeared to possess lists identifying Armenian households. Soviet troops and internal security forces, though present in Baku, did not intervene to stop the attacks; instead, they concentrated on the protection of government buildings as the violence spread across the city.

I witnessed firsthand how quickly rhetoric turned into violence. I was in the seventh grade when a mob surged into our four-story apartment building in a central Baku neighborhood where an elderly Armenian couple lived. Across the street, a bus filled with Soviet soldiers in riot gear remained stationary, its occupants observing but not intervening. As the crowd moved through the stairwell, my father and a neighbor from the ground floor rushed to the couple's apartment and positioned themselves in the doorway. They told the men that the residents were Jewish, not Armenian. The crowd lingered in the stairwell, arguing before slowly backing away, weighing the possibility of returning. The intervention was just enough to disrupt the attack's momentum and protect the couple for now. Fearing the mob might return, the couple left the building immediately and sought shelter elsewhere.

Others had no such protection. Survivors were escorted by soldiers to the Caspian docks and placed on ferries to Turkmenistan. Within days, most of the remaining Armenian community in Baku, once among the largest in the Soviet Union and long integral to the city's social fabric, fled or were evacuated, effectively ending the centuries-long Armenian presence in the city. Many contemporaries later questioned whether the violence was truly spontaneous. Witnesses described individuals who appeared to coordinate the movement of crowds, while security forces remained largely inactive. The pattern that emerged suggested targeted intimidation rather than uncontrolled chaos, though the scale and intensity varied across neighborhoods.

The events exposed the particular vulnerability of Azerbaijani–Armenian mixed families, who had long navigated the boundaries between their communities. Within these households, Azerbaijani surnames sometimes reduced the likelihood of being targeted. In contrast, relatives bearing Armenian names faced a greater risk. Numerous accounts indicate that violence was often carried out by organized groups or individuals arriving from outside specific neighborhoods rather than by long-time residents, some of whom intervened to conceal identities or provide protection. Families endured a period of acute uncertainty as they sought to safeguard one another while confronting the possibility of separation. In many cases, Armenian relatives were compelled to leave while Azerbaijani family members remained. Over time, however, numerous mixed families chose to resettle in Russia or farther abroad to ensure safety and preserve family unity. Their experiences underscored the extent to which Baku's communities had been socially intertwined before the violence fractured those ties.

Internationally, the violence in Baku was often interpreted through the framework established by Sumgait, reinforcing an already hardened narrative about Azerbaijan. Within the city, however, January 1990 carried a broader significance. It marked not only the near disappearance of Baku's Armenian community but also a decisive erosion of trust between neighbors and between society and a Soviet state that appeared either unwilling or unable to prevent the breakdown of order.

Black January: The Point of No Return

In the aftermath of the violence, Baku remained tense and unstable. Soviet troops, conspicuously inactive during the attacks, now prepared to intervene. Their purpose, however, was not to investigate the killings or restore public trust, but to contain unrest and reassert Moscow's authority over a rapidly mobilizing society. The republican leadership, headed by Abdulrahman Vazirov, appeared immobilized, caught between a furious population and mounting pressure from Kremlin envoys dispatched to take control of the situation.

Even within the Popular Front, unity began to fracture as the crisis deepened. Some leaders urged restraint, warning that continued mobilization risked provoking a crackdown similar to the bloodshed in Tbilisi in April 1989. Others argued that hesitation would only invite further losses and pressed for escalation. On January 13, these tensions crystallized in the formation of a National Defense Council, which began collecting funds under the banner of "defending Karabakh." Soviet security services closely monitored the council, forwarding detailed assessments to Moscow's envoys, who adopted a dual-track strategy. While publicly negotiating with Popular Front figures and offering assurances that troops would not be deployed, they simultaneously prepared the ground for military intervention.

As the crisis deepened, barricades spread across Baku. Heavy construction trucks and decommissioned buses were positioned at the city's main entrances, near military garrisons and other strategic points, blocking major roads. Volunteers, mostly unarmed civilians, took shifts guarding the barriers, convinced that their presence could deter Soviet troops from entering the capital. In total, twenty-six barricade points were established along Baku's access routes. When the assault came, however, these improvised defenses proved no match for advancing armored units and offered little resistance.

On the night of January 19–20, 1990, Soviet forces launched Operation Udar (Strike) under direct orders from Defense Minister Dmitry Yazov and KGB chief Vladimir Kryuchkov. Around 26,000 troops, including units of the 4th Army, interior troops, and special forces, entered Baku to "restore constitutional order" and suppress the growing influence of the Azerbaijani Popular Front. Tanks and armored personnel carriers advanced along key routes from the outskirts, breaking through the civilian barricades and seizing control of government buildings and broadcast centers. Gunfire erupted in several districts as troops encountered unarmed civilians on the streets. By morning, dozens lay dead and hundreds were wounded, while the city remained under curfew and military control.

This massacre became known as Black January (*Qanlı Yanvar*). It was the bloodiest crackdown of the perestroika era, leaving more than 130 people dead and over 700 wounded. The assault laid bare the Soviet Union's willingness to employ lethal force against its own citizens to preserve authority. For Azerbaijanis, Black January marked a point of no return, the moment when reconciliation with Moscow ceased to be imaginable.

Two days later, on January 22, more than a million people filled the streets of Baku in a funeral procession without precedent. Bodies wrapped in white burial shrouds were carried on biers for kilometers, as the city became a landscape of mourning and restrained defiance. The victims were laid to rest on the city's highest ground, in what was then Kirov Park, later renamed the Alley of Martyrs (*Shahidler Khiyabani*), a site that would come to symbolize sacrifice and national loss. In protest against the assault, forty-day strikes were declared across the republic. Communist Party membership cards were publicly burned, and the walls surrounding Azadliq Square filled with stark slogans: "Tbilisi, Baku—who will be shot next?" and "Gorbachev, you are a butcher and a liar."

For many Azerbaijanis, Black January was experienced not only as a political rupture but as a personal trauma. I remember those days clearly. On the night of January 20, I was awakened by unusual movement in our apartment building. The entrance door stood open, and neighbors had gathered in the stairwell, speaking in low, urgent voices about what they had heard and seen outside. Despite the late hour, nearly two in the morning, no one seemed to be asleep. Adults moved from window to window, glancing out briefly before closing the curtains again. I was told to return to bed, and the door was shut behind me, though it was clear that the night was not an ordinary one.

By morning, armed soldiers were patrolling the nearby streets in full combat gear, metal helmets, bulletproof vests, and Kalashnikov rifles. Armored vehicles and at least one tank was stationed at intersections, even though our building stood away from the main avenues and government sites where the shooting had occurred. The show of force extended well beyond the immediate zones of violence.

School was canceled, and regular television programming was suspended, replaced by continuous mourning music. On the day of the funerals, tens of thousands of people passed near our building in silence, moving toward the burial grounds under the watch of armed soldiers positioned along the route. The procession was broadcast nationwide.

In the days that followed, amateur VHS recordings began circulating privately among families. At my grandfather's apartment, we watched footage from the aftermath, including scenes of many deceased bodies being prepared for burial and testimonies from the relatives of those who were killed. The images were stark and unlike anything I had encountered before. Overwhelmed, I fainted.

In the weeks that followed, everyday life did not resume. When I returned to the Dinamo youth sports facility where I trained, it was closed. The city's premier sports complex, a multi-story institution that had trained generations of athletes, including world champions, was converted into temporary barracks, its halls and former training facilities lined with rows of bunk beds for deployed soldiers. Spaces once devoted to ordinary routines had been absorbed into the military presence that now defined the city. It was a quiet but unmistakable sign that everyday life had been suspended, replaced by a permanent sense of occupation and uncertainty.

The Soviet authorities imposed a strict information blockade. Local newspapers were silenced, television was cut off, and even national editions of *Pravda* or *Izvestia* distributed in Baku were censored, stripped of reports that elsewhere justified the assault. Information nevertheless continued to circulate beyond official controls. On January 21, Heydar Aliyev, a former Politburo member sidelined under Gorbachev since 1987, appeared at Azerbaijan's permanent mission in Moscow. In a dramatic speech, he denounced the attack as "inhuman, anti-democratic, and unconstitutional," laying the blame squarely on the Soviet leadership. His statement, broadcast by foreign radio and relayed by international correspondents, reverberated far beyond Moscow.

For many Azerbaijanis, Aliyev's words gave voice to an anger that had found no official acknowledgment. In Moscow, they also marked his return to public political life, a reentry that would later alter the republic's course. For Gorbachev's perestroika, Black January carried a different meaning. It revealed the point at which reform gave way to coercion and made clear that Soviet authority in Azerbaijan had fractured beyond repair. From that moment, the relationship between Baku and Moscow entered an irreversible phase of estrangement.

The End of Soviet Era

By 1990–1991, the Karabakh conflict had moved beyond petitions, rallies, and Moscow's tentative interventions. What had begun as a dispute over autonomy was now unfolding alongside the rapid disintegration of the Soviet Union itself. The framework of Communist authority, weakened by Black January, continued to erode as central control diminished. At the same time, public confidence in the Communist Party collapsed. Political movements that had emerged earlier gained strength and mass support, as large segments of society turned away from party institutions and toward alternative national and civic organizations. Each republic charted its own course: Azerbaijan clung to Moscow in hopes of regaining Karabakh, Armenia marched toward independence with new leaders at its helm, Karabakh has become a militarized zone with checkpoints, curfews, and OMON (Special Task Police Unit) raids, as newly formed armed groups assert control on both sides. The following period marked a decisive turning point, shaped by Operation Ring, the August Coup, and the declarations of independence, as the Soviet structure finally collapsed and the path toward full-scale war became irreversible.

After January 20: Shifting Grounds in Baku

The blood of January 20 had not yet dried when Azerbaijan awoke to a new political reality. The Soviet tanks that crushed Baku also left behind a vacuum of authority. On January 24, Ayaz Mutalibov, a cautious career bureaucrat with a background in industry, was installed as First Secretary of the Azerbaijani Communist Party. Moscow appointed him to maintain order, signaling a preference for stability and centralized control over political reform. Compared to the discredited local party leadership, he was younger, administratively capable, and regarded as a reliable figure able to reassert authority without further inflaming public unrest. For many Azerbaijanis, the appointment raised hopes for concrete action and some reforms after Vazirov's removal. While public sympathy for the Popular Front deepened after January, the movement itself was temporarily constrained by arrests, internal divisions, and the shock of the violence, limiting its ability to act openly.

However, on July 28, representatives from more than twenty opposition groups gathered in Baku to form the Democratic Bloc, a coalition meant to challenge Communist dominance in the September elections to the Supreme Soviet. The results exposed the imbalance of power. Of 360 parliamentary seats, only 30 went to Bloc candidates; the rest were secured by the Communist machine, backed by emergency rule and the full weight of the state. Although small in number, the opposition's presence in parliament gave it an influence far greater than its size. Televised parliamentary sessions showed Democratic Bloc deputies speaking sharply in Azerbaijani, openly criticizing government failures and exposing corruption. Their language was direct and accessible, standing in clear contrast to Mutalibov's cautious Soviet phrasing. This style resonated with a public increasingly impatient with the old order. Azerbaijan was entering a phase of open political confrontation. Mutalibov retained formal control of the state, but his credibility and public authority were steadily eroding.

From Soviet Republic to Independent Armenia

Across the border, Armenia was moving in the opposite direction. In the May 1990 elections, the Armenian National Movement (ANM) secured a majority in the Supreme Soviet, the first time Communists were displaced in any Soviet republic. On August 4, Levon Ter-Petrosyan, a scholar of Oriental Studies and the son of a repatriate family that moved from Aleppo, Syria, to Soviet Armenia in 1947, was elected speaker of parliament and became the republic's de facto leader, while Vazgen Manukian was appointed prime minister. Ter-Petrosyan's rise symbolized the ascent of a new generation of intellectuals, shaped by both diaspora memory and the Soviet academic elite. Just three weeks later, on August 23, Armenia declared sovereignty. Lenin's statue was removed from Yerevan's central square, signaling a decisive break with Soviet authority.

This shift alarmed Moscow on two fronts: the erosion of Communist control in Armenia and the rise of irregular armed groups operating outside state authority. Militias such as the Armenian Army of Independence (AAI) and the Armenian National Army (ANA), numbering perhaps two thousand fighters, had already clashed with Soviet troops in Yerevan. Gorbachev's July decree banning illegal armed formations was aimed squarely at Armenia. Ter-Petrosyan's government moved quickly to dissolve one militia and rebrand the other as a political party, but the fighters did not disappear. Many instead gravitated toward Karabakh, where the struggle was intensifying.

By autumn, the hills and villages of the enclave were filling with new units calling themselves *fedayin*, reviving a term once associated with Armenian nationalist armed groups a century earlier. They ambushed convoys, seized railway checkpoints in Zangezur to halt train traffic, and launched assaults on Azerbaijani positions. Officially, Yerevan reassured Moscow that it posed no threat to the Soviet Union. On the ground, Armenia was simultaneously constructing the institutions of a new state and organizing its military forces.

Karabakh Escalation in Nagorno-Karabakh, 1990

In early spring 1990, violence spread beyond Karabakh itself. Before dawn on March 24, several vehicles carrying armed men crossed from the Armenian border village of Baganis. They attacked the Azerbaijani settlement of Baganis-Ayrum in the Qazakh district. The assault occurred during the Novruz holiday, the traditional spring New Year celebration observed across Azerbaijan and the wider region, catching residents asleep. Armed with shotguns and assault rifles, the attackers set fire to nearly twenty homes and shot villagers as they fled. Eight civilians, including three women and an infant, were killed, though some accounts place the death toll as high as eleven. Soviet Interior Ministry troops arrived only after the attackers had withdrawn.

The attack on Baganis-Ayrum marked a significant escalation, demonstrating that the conflict had expanded beyond Karabakh and into internationally recognized Azerbaijani territory. In Azerbaijan, it deepened doubts about Moscow's ability, or willingness, to secure the borders, and strengthened the Popular Front's argument that central authority could no longer guarantee public safety. Armenia increasingly came to be perceived not as a neighboring Soviet republic but as a direct adversary within a widening conflict.

In Armenian narratives, the incident was later framed as part of a broader cycle of retaliatory violence linked to Karabakh, reflecting the emergence of a self-reinforcing logic of escalation that increasingly justified violence on both sides. In attempt to restore order and tighten control, Soviet authorities-imposed emergency rule across Nagorno-Karabakh. Civilian life came under strict regulation: public gatherings were banned, cultural institutions such as theaters and cinemas were closed, and local media were placed under censorship. Travel between settlements required special permits, and soon transport restrictions caused shortages of food, fuel, and medicine. Rail traffic between Azerbaijan and Armenia was suspended, and flights to Yerevan were limited to a few military or emergency charters. At one-point, Soviet troops blocked Stepanakert's runway with armored vehicles to prevent civilian departures. In response, Armenians built a makeshift dirt airstrip near Martakert for small AN-2 planes, which was destroyed by Azerbaijani forces in May 1990.

As tensions escalated in Nagorno-Karabakh, Moscow intensified its security campaign. A decree issued on July 25, 1990, banning "illegal armed formations," gave formal cover for a new wave of raids across the region. That year alone, Soviet internal troops and Azerbaijani law-enforcement units, including police and OMON detachments, carried out more than 160 operations, most of them in Armenian-populated areas of Karabakh. Moscow described these as efforts to disarm militants and restore order. Armenian and diaspora media depicted the events as acts of persecution. This framing was quickly echoed in Western coverage, where the Armenian interpretation came to dominate. On July 27, 1990, *The New York Times* published an open letter signed by 133 intellectuals, including Elie Wiesel and Jürgen Habermas, urging Soviet authorities and the international community to condemn what the authors described as "anti-Armenian pogroms," lift Azerbaijan's blockade, and prevent what they warned could become "a second genocide." The letter framed the Karabakh conflict primarily as a moral and human rights issue, reinforcing Western sympathy for Armenian claims and contributing to perceptions of Azerbaijan as the principal aggressor.

Clashes escalated through the summer of 1990, pushing the confrontation closer to open war. On August 10, a passenger bus traveling from Tbilisi to Aghdam was destroyed by an explosive device near Khanlar (today Goygol). At least fifteen people were killed, and dozens more were wounded. Azerbaijani investigators identified the perpetrators as two ethnic Armenians linked to the underground group Vrezh, which had already been associated with earlier bombings along transit routes between Georgia and Azerbaijan. The attack shocked the public and underscored that the struggle was entering a broader and more dangerous phase.

Days later, on August 16, two Armenian militants opened fire on a police checkpoint near the Azerbaijani border village of Baganis-Ayrum, the same settlement that had been attacked earlier that spring, when eleven residents were killed. When one assailant was captured, Armenian commanders reportedly threatened to destroy nearby villages unless he was released. On August 19, Armenian militias launched a coordinated assault on Baganis-Ayrum and Upper Askipara, using mortars, rockets, and grenades.

Azerbaijani civilians were killed and wounded, homes were burned, and survivors fled. Soviet Internal Troops under General Yuri Shatalin intervened with tanks and helicopters to restore control.

By late summer, the line between sporadic violence and organized war had all but vanished. The borderlands of the Qazakh district, where Armenian and Azerbaijani villages once stood side by side, had become an open battlefield, signaling transition to the full-scale war.

Operation Ring: Spring 1991

By the winter of 1990–1991, the lines of confrontation had hardened. In Baku, Mutalibov's government relied heavily on Moscow for political and military support in Karabakh. Armenia, meanwhile, had moved decisively toward sovereignty, with institutions that remained Soviet in form but were increasingly nationalist in content. At the center of these opposing trajectories was Karabakh, now administered directly by Viktor Polyanichko's Organizing Committee and reinforced by Interior Ministry troops under General Safonov. Curfews were imposed, and OMON units, known as the "Black Berets," established checkpoints and took control of Khojaly Airport. At the same time, Azerbaijani authorities began resettling refugees expelled from Armenia in depopulated and underutilized areas. Armenian officials and media portrayed these resettlements as deliberate demographic pressure, embedding the issue of population movement directly into the political struggle over the region.

By early 1991, Mutalibov warned Moscow that unless Armenian armed formations were disarmed, Azerbaijan risked sliding into a wider confrontation. The Kremlin, facing the accelerating erosion of central authority, moved to reassert control. On March 17, Azerbaijan participated in the all-Union referendum on preserving the USSR, with more than 93 percent voting in favor, while Armenia boycotted the vote entirely. The contrasting outcomes underscored the widening political divide between the two republics and shaped Moscow's response.

In April, Soviet Interior Ministry forces, operating jointly with Azerbaijani police units, launched a coordinated campaign in and around Karabakh.

Soviet and Azerbaijani officials presented Operation Ring as a law-enforcement effort aimed at disarming illegal armed formations and restoring administrative control. During the operation, armed groups withdrew from several villages, which were subsequently emptied of their Armenian inhabitants. Armenian sources and later Western analyses characterized this outcome as the forced removal of civilians.

The first phase of Operation Ring began in late April 1991 in the villages of Getashen (Chaykand) and Martunashen (Karabulagh), located in the wooded hills of the Khanlar (Goygol) District west of Ganja. These settlements were identified by Soviet and Azerbaijani authorities as centers of armed resistance. The operation involved Soviet Internal Troops units 5477 and 5478, supported by tanks from the 4th Army and Azerbaijani OMON detachments. Field command was exercised by Lieutenant Colonel Igor Mashkov, operating under the oversight of Interior Minister Mammad Asadov and Prosecutor General Ismet Gayibov.

On April 23, electricity and water supplies to Chaykend (Getashen) and Martunashen (Karabulagh) were cut off, and the surrounding area was sealed. Loudspeakers broadcast demands for the villagers to surrender their weapons. On April 30, Soviet Internal Troops and Azerbaijani OMON units advanced toward Chaykend as part of the disarmament operation. When an armored convoy entered the village center to negotiate the surrender of arms, the situation escalated into a firefight with local defenders. The defense was led by Tatul Krpeyan, a schoolteacher from Yerevan who had organized armed resistance in the village. During the confrontation, Lieutenant Colonel Igor Mashkov and thirteen Soviet servicemen were taken hostage, and an Azerbaijani civilian guide accompanying the unit was killed. On May 1, Soviet forces launched clearing operations. Several Armenian defenders were killed, including Krpeyan, who was posthumously awarded the title of National Hero of Armenia. Parts of the village were damaged by shelling and fire, and the hostages were eventually released. Most residents agreed to surrender their weapons in exchange for assurances of safe passage. Between May 4 and May 8, approximately 3,000 villagers were evacuated. Women and children were transported by helicopter to Stepanakert and Yerevan, while men were taken by bus to Ijevan.

In a parallel operation, resistance in Martunashen (Qarabulaq) was organized by the "Arabo" detachment, a volunteer unit named after the nineteenth-century Armenian fedayi Arabo and associated with Dashnaktsutyun networks in Armenia. The group was led by Simon Achiggozyan, a Romanian-born geologist whose family had resettled in Soviet Armenia. As joint security forces advanced into the village, Achiggozyan's fighters resisted with small arms and a single rocket-propelled grenade launcher, reportedly disabling one armored personnel carrier. The response escalated quickly. Tanks and heavy machine guns were brought in to suppress the defenders. After several hours of fighting, Achiggozyan and several members of the detachment were killed. Much of Martunashen was left heavily damaged in the aftermath of the assault.

The operation soon expanded southward. In the Hadrut District, joint security units carried out operations in more than a dozen Armenian-populated villages, including Aghbulag, Dolanlar, and Arakyul. In the Shusha District, security forces entered multiple settlements and detained large numbers of residents during weapons searches. One notable incident involved the capture of a helicopter carrying armed personnel from Armenia, near the border, which Soviet authorities cited as evidence of cross-border support for local militias.

Moscow and Baku justified these actions as law-enforcement measures aimed at restoring state authority, disarming illegal armed groups, and reasserting control over areas slipping beyond Soviet jurisdiction. Armenian interpretations, however, focused less on the stated objectives than on the cumulative effects on the ground. In practice, the operations resulted in the removal of Armenian villagers from settlements near Azerbaijani-controlled towns and transport routes, particularly in mixed or strategically sensitive areas. Many of these vacated villages were later resettled by Azerbaijani refugees forcibly displaced from Armenia in earlier waves of violence, as well as by Meskhetian Turks who had fled renewed unrest in Central Asia. The arrival of multiple displaced populations further reshaped the demographic composition of these regions. The gap between official justification and lived outcome proved decisive. What Soviet authorities described as security operations increasingly came to be understood, especially by Armenian communities, as instruments of demographic transformation. Operation Ring thus marked a turning point: coercive policing blurred into population displacement, and law enforcement was no longer perceived as neutral but as part of a widening struggle over territory, control, and ethnic balance.

As fighting persisted in Karabakh, the third phase extended operations beyond the enclave. Raids were carried out along Armenia's northern border in the Noyemberyan–Ijevan–Tavush region. Artillery and helicopter fire struck several villages, including Voskepar, Paravakar, and Kirants. Near Voskepar, an Armenian police bus was ambushed, killing fourteen officers. Parallel actions took place in southern Armenia, near Goris and Tegh, where OMON units operating under the Soviet Interior Ministry detained twenty-five militia officers suspected of aiding armed groups in Karabakh. The Armenian enclave of Artsvashen (Bashkend), located within Azerbaijan, surrendered its weapons following an ultimatum. The extension of these operations onto the territory of the Armenian SSR marked a turning point, provoking political backlash and enabling the Armenian government to frame the events more effectively in international reporting and diplomacy.

By mid-May, operations expanded deeper into Karabakh. Azerbaijani OMON and Internal Troops entered multiple villages in Martuni (Khojavand) and Mardakert (Aghdara) districts. In Martuni, about seventy people were detained, including the town's mayor and the district prosecutor. In Mardakert, security forces raided Kichan, Karmiravan (Giziloba), Seysulan, and Talysh, seizing weapons and arresting local administrators. Several villages, including Mets Shen, received written orders to prepare for relocation. Operations in the Askeran District followed the same pattern.

Escalation and International Response

International criticism brought the campaign to a brief pause in June, exposing the limits of Moscow's ability to manage both the conflict and its global image. On July 4, the Kremlin lifted the state of emergency in Karabakh and withdrew the Internal Troops, which had often acted as a buffer between opposing forces. The withdrawal immediately altered the balance on the ground. Within days, Azerbaijani OMON units attempted to enter the villages of Erkech, Manashid, and Buzlug without armored support and were repelled, suffering casualties.

The setback prompted renewed concern in Moscow. Interior Minister Boris Pugo informed the Supreme Soviet that many Armenian villages in Karabakh had been extensively fortified and that local armed groups remained intact. On July 9, operations resumed with significantly greater force. This phase was supported by elements of the 23rd Motorized Rifle Division and air power, signaling a shift from police-style actions to overt military engagement. By July 12, the targeted villages had been taken, and their inhabitants were moved to Armenia. Additional encirclement operations followed in Yukhari Aghjakend, Gulistan, and Garachinar, though several were left incomplete due to persistent resistance.

The escalation did not restore control. On July 20, Armenian fighters armed with rocket-propelled grenades shot down three Soviet helicopters near Buzlukh. Ten days later, an attack on Zamzur (Khojavend district) left two dead and several taken captive. These incidents underscored Moscow's waning authority on the ground, where military force increasingly replaced political management yet failed to restore stability. While the July campaign achieved its immediate military objectives, it further entrenched a militarized logic that would shape the conflict going forward.

The conflict also moved rapidly beyond the battlefield. Armenia and its diaspora mobilized an international campaign portraying Operation Ring as a state-directed persecution of Armenians. Russian deputies denounced the operation as a Soviet war against civilians, and in May, the U.S. Senate passed a resolution condemning the actions of Soviet and Azerbaijani forces. The Armenian leadership appealed to the United Nations and Western governments, frequently invoking the memory of 1915, while leading Western media outlets reported allegations of mass deportations.

Moscow countered with data indicating that between March and May 1991, Soviet authorities recorded 235 armed clashes: 150 attributed to Armenian forces, 82 to Azerbaijani forces, and over one hundred directed at Soviet Internal Troops. These statistics were ignored mainly outside the USSR. Within Russia, liberal newspapers and the RSFSR leadership under Boris Yeltsin increasingly echoed Armenia's framing of the conflict.

Azerbaijan's domestic opposition also criticized Mutalibov's handling of the campaign. Leaders of the Popular Front of Azerbaijan condemned the operation as politically disastrous. Though Operation Ring achieved a tactical victory, it proved a strategic failure: it restored short-term control but persuaded much of the world that Azerbaijan and Moscow were enforcing a punitive campaign.

Operation Ring ended abruptly after the failed August 1991 coup (often referred to as a *putsch*) in Moscow, which disrupted political authority across the Soviet Union. As tanks entered the capital and Gorbachev was placed under house arrest, uncertainty spread to Baku. Mutalibov, still closely tied to Moscow, responded cautiously and delayed taking a clear position. The Popular Front, by contrast, immediately denounced the coup, aligning itself with the democratic opposition in Russia.

When the coup collapsed on August 21, the Communist Party's authority vanished overnight. Across the USSR, offices were ransacked and banners torn down. Interior Minister Boris Pugo's suicide and Viktor Polyanichko's departure left Azerbaijan without central backing. On August 30, 1991, the Supreme Soviet of Azerbaijan declared the restoration of state independence. Mutalibov remained in power, but his close alignment with Moscow increasingly limited his political room for maneuver. At the same time, the Popular Front, weakened earlier by arrests and curfews, began to regain visibility and influence.

Declarations and Escalation

Events now accelerated rapidly. On August 30, Azerbaijan declared independence. Two days later, Karabakh's Armenian deputies proclaimed their own Nagorno-Karabakh Republic. The duel of sovereignties was now explicit, each side asserting legitimacy while undermining the other. Clashes escalated. Armenian detachments tried to retake villages emptied during Operation Ring. At the same time, Azerbaijani OMON and local forces bombarded Stepanakert with artillery and Alazan rockets. On September 20, a helicopter carrying twenty-three senior Azerbaijani officials, along with Russian and Qazakh mediators, was shot down near Karakend (Khojavend district) , killing all on board. The incident shocked the republic and hardened attitudes in Baku. On November 26, Azerbaijan's Supreme Soviet revoked Nagorno-Karabakh's autonomy and reinstated Stepanakert's historical name, Khankendi. Moscow condemned the move as illegal, but its authority no longer carried weight.

December brought the dissolution of Soviet power. Azerbaijan formed its National Army, while Karabakh Armenians held their own independence referendum. Boycotted by local Azerbaijanis and unrecognized internationally, the vote was nonetheless symbolically decisive for the separatist movement. Days later, on December 29, Azerbaijanis voted overwhelmingly for state independence, following the signing of the Alma-Ata accords that formally dissolved the Soviet Union.

By the end of 1991, the Soviet state had ceased to exist. Russian forces withdrew from Karabakh, abandoning bases and stockpiles that were swiftly claimed by both sides. Azerbaijan and Armenia emerged as independent states, each asserting sovereignty over Karabakh and each increasingly convinced that the other posed an existential threat. Local clashes escalated into organized violence. Villages were emptied, civilians came under fire, and political language hardened into military command. What was previously considered a Soviet "internal matter" has now escalated into an international conflict between two sovereign nations. Armenia and Azerbaijan became embroiled in a war that would be known as the First Karabakh War.

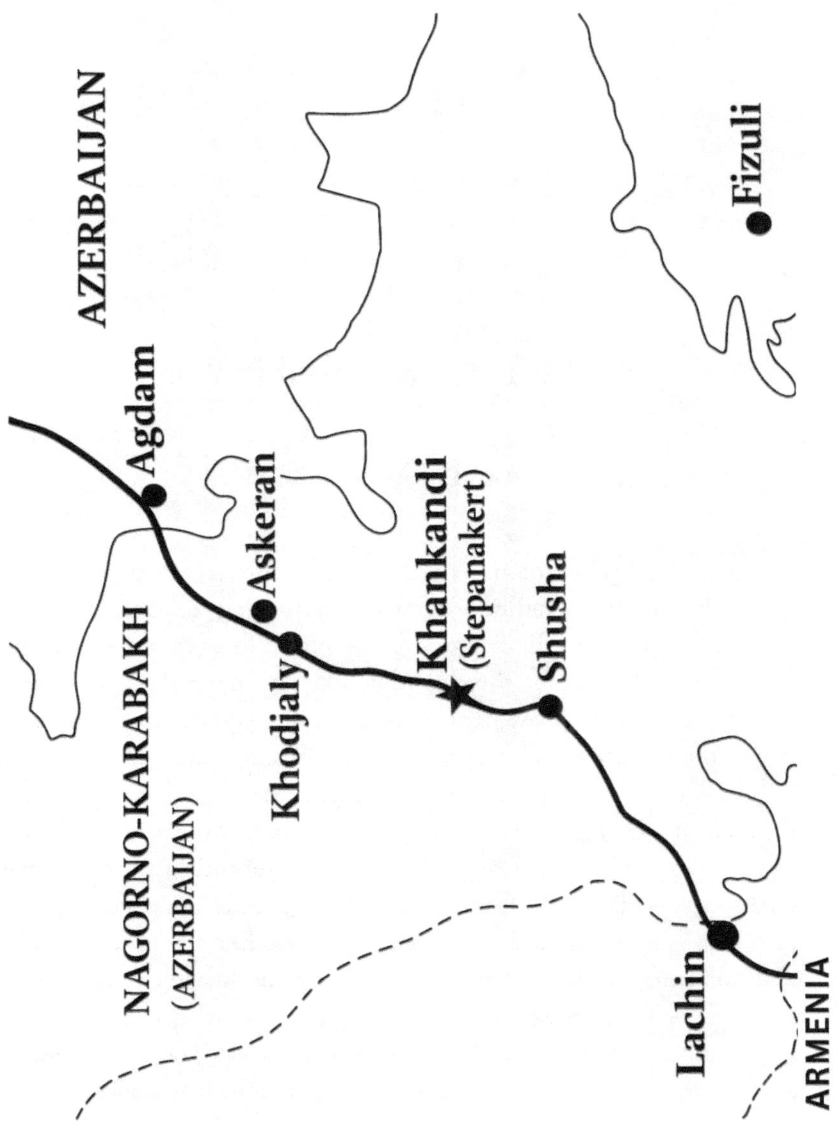

Transit Route through Azerbaijan to Armenia via Nagorno-Karabakh
(Soviet Period)

The First Karabakh War

With the Soviet Union gone, the conflict entered a new phase marked by the absence of any authority capable of restraining violence. In December 1991, Soviet Interior Ministry troops completed their withdrawal from Nagorno-Karabakh, leaving the region without any external authority capable of enforcing order. The departure removed the last buffer and shifted control of the battlefield to local armed formations, militias, and newly formed state forces. From that moment, decisions were made on the ground, and the logic of war began to govern events. Karabakh Armenians now assumed direct control of armed formations, no longer subordinated to Moscow or entirely answerable to Yerevan. Armenia itself, newly independent and fragile, tried to walk a careful line: offering military-technical support, volunteers, and humanitarian aid, but officially avoiding the image of direct involvement. In practice, however, weapons, money, and men flowed across the border. Local Karabakh commanders became the war's decision-makers, organizing their own defense and launching operations that would reshape the region.

Meanwhile, the inheritance of Soviet military arsenals began. No part of the South Caucasus was more heavily militarized than Azerbaijan. On its territory stood the Soviet 4th Army, comprising four motorized rifle divisions, three air defense brigades, a special forces brigade, four air force bases, and elements of the Caspian Flotilla. To this were added massive stockpiles of ammunition: the strategic depot at Kilyazi, regional stores in Aghdam and Nasosnoye, divisional warehouses scattered from Gyuzdek to Ganja, Lankaran, and Nakhichevan. In total, these depots contained an estimated eleven thousand wagonloads of ammunition, an arsenal vast enough to sustain years of fighting. By 1992, the disbandment of the Soviet 4th Army and the transfer of equipment from the 49th placed much of this military hardware under Azerbaijani control. The process, however, was far from orderly. As Soviet units withdrew to Russia, Azerbaijani forces seized weapons and equipment directly, stripping departing garrisons and, in some cases, appropriating assets from the 19th Air Defense Army before its departure.

Armenians also moved to secure weapons as Soviet forces withdrew. In Stepanakert, Armenian fighters seized part of the armory of the 366th Guards Motor Rifle Regiment of the Soviet 23rd Division, which had been slated to transfer its equipment to Azerbaijani control. Stationed in Karabakh since 1988, the regiment had become increasingly entangled in the conflict. By 1991, roughly 50 of its 300 personnel were ethnic Armenians, including the commander of the 2nd Battalion, Major Seyran Ohanian. Born and raised in Shusha, Ohanian had graduated from a military school in Baku and previously served in Ganja, reflecting the integrated Soviet career paths that were now fracturing along national lines. Within the regiment, officers based in Stepanakert increasingly sympathized with Armenian forces, while commanders in Ganja remained aligned with Azerbaijani authority. What had once functioned as a unified Soviet unit was, by the end of 1991, divided by the same conflict consuming the region.

The regiment's stockpiles quickly became a strategic asset. Its ten tanks, the only heavy armor stationed in Karabakh, were at times temporarily transferred to Armenian fighters and used in assaults on Azerbaijani villages. Some officers engaged in the informal sale of weapons, fuel, or artillery support, often in exchange for cash or alcohol. Others permitted the use of equipment under ad hoc arrangements described as "loans." For many Armenians in Karabakh, the presence of former Soviet units became a crucial source of material support. Among Azerbaijanis, these practices deepened the belief that any neutral authority no longer governed the conflict and would be decided by force rather than mediation.

For the rank-and-file soldiers of the 366th Motor Rifle Regiment, loyalty had lost mainly meaning. By early 1992, the unit was effectively isolated at its base in Stepanakert, cut off from reliable command, short of food, fuel, and water, and surrounded by escalating violence. Azerbaijani forces shelled positions from Shusha, while Armenian fighters operated in proximity on the ground. The regiment no longer functioned as a coherent military force. With the central authority collapsed, any transparent chain of command had dissolved. Some officers aligned themselves with Armenian forces, negotiating access to weapons and armored vehicles. Most conscripts, however, were trapped. Hunger, confusion, and constant exposure to fire defined their daily existence. In this sense, the regiment became a microcosm of the Soviet collapse itself: a disintegrating army caught between two emerging states, no longer neutral yet no longer controlled. In March 1992, the unit was formally withdrawn and disbanded, and the remaining conscripts were evacuated from Karabakh, leaving behind both weapons stockpiles and unresolved accusations.

In Armenia proper, the division of Soviet military property was more orderly but far less generous. The republic had hosted fewer Soviet units than its neighbors, leaving it with a modest inheritance: two divisions of the 7th Guards Army, the 15th and 164th, and roughly five hundred wagonloads of ammunition. Even so, this material, supplemented by captured weapons and clandestine supply routes, provided Yerevan with the foundations of a national army. Unlike Azerbaijan, Armenia would soon retain a permanent Russian military presence on its territory. This factor would shape the postwar balance but did not yet determine the course of the fighting.

The skies were divided as well. In early 1992, Azerbaijan inherited fourteen Mi-24 attack helicopters and nine Mi-8 transport helicopters from the Sangachal base near Baku. Armenia acquired thirteen Mi-24s from the 7th Helicopter Regiment outside Yerevan. These Soviet-built aircraft would soon dominate the highlands of Karabakh, delivering firepower that transformed localized clashes into sustained military operations.

By the dawn of 1992, the battlefield was fully stocked, and the principal actors were armed. The mechanisms that had once enforced Moscow's authority had vanished, replaced by local militias, emerging national armies, and irregular formations competing for territory. Armenia and Azerbaijan now confronted one another directly as rival states, fighting with the inherited arsenals of a collapsed empire rather than under the constraints of Soviet central authority.

The First Battles: January–February 1992

The beginning of 1992 marked a significant shift from sporadic violence to ongoing military confrontation. As the conflict increasingly took on the characteristics of a war, remnants of Azerbaijani state authority continued to function within the Armenian-controlled regions of Karabakh. OMON units and police posts remained active in and around Stepanakert, a residual feature of the Soviet administrative order that had not yet entirely disintegrated. This uneasy overlap between formal security structures and emerging armed formations created an unstable environment in which escalation was both rapid and unpredictable.

On January 1, Azerbaijani forces launched an operation against the Armenian village of Khramort (Pirlar) in eastern Karabakh. Units from the Aghdam Battalion, commanded by Yakub Rzaev, entered the settlement with armored support. Although the assault did not alter territorial control, it marked a vital escalation. Heavy military equipment that had previously remained under Soviet custody was now being employed directly by local forces. In the days that followed, additional armed units moved into the area along the same axis, consolidating positions and accelerating the transformation of the confrontation into a fully militarized front.

On January 6, Armenian representatives in Nagorno-Karabakh issued a declaration of independence, formalizing a political rupture that had already taken shape on the battlefield. Stepanakert ceased to recognize Baku's authority, even as Azerbaijani police units remained stationed in the city. Within days, the conflict escalated further. On January 13, Azerbaijani forces for the first time employed multiple-launch rocket systems against the Shaumyan district, causing widespread destruction.

Control over Stepanakert itself became increasingly contested. On January 21–22, Armenian forces overran a key Azerbaijani OMON base inside the city. After heavy fighting, the remaining police personnel withdrew toward Aghdam. The loss underscored the vulnerability of Azerbaijani security positions operating deep inside Armenian-dominated territory without reliable reinforcement.

A further escalation occurred in the air. On January 28, an Azerbaijani civilian helicopter flying from Aghdam to the besieged city of Shusha was shot down by a surface-to-air missile. Dozens of passengers, including women and children, were killed. The attack widened the conflict beyond the ground front, introducing civilian air traffic into the war and triggering a surge of public outrage across Azerbaijan. Within days, the fighting intensified. On January 31, Azerbaijani forces launched another offensive employing heavy weaponry, reflecting mounting pressure to reverse losses on the ground. By February, the violence had spread into villages with catastrophic consequences. Armenian forces seized Karadagly in the Martuni district and Agdaban in Kelbajar, killing at least ninety-nine civilians and wounding many more. Survivors described expulsions, executions, and homes burned to the ground.

On February 9, Armenian fighters dropped leaflets over Malibeyli, urging residents to evacuate through a designated "safe corridor" if they surrendered their weapons. The offer was ignored. On February 10, the village fell after fighting, and its population was expelled. For Azerbaijan, these military setbacks were compounded by deepening political and institutional disarray at home. The government in Baku struggled to assert effective authority amid rivalry between the presidency, the Popular Front, and competing power centers within the security apparatus. Opposition groups organized their own armed units, often operating independently of, or in defiance of, central command. Rather than consolidating authority amid external pressure, politics in the capital became marked by internal competition and mistrust. As a result, Azerbaijan's armed forces entered the conflict fragmented, with regular army units, OMON detachments, and volunteer battalions operating without coherent coordination or unified strategic direction.

Meanwhile, both sides increasingly relied on irregular forms of warfare. Fighting was often improvised, localized, and personal, frequently involving former neighbors and residents of nearby villages. The boundaries between conflict and survival blurred. Despite ongoing hostilities, communication across front lines did not cease. Informal trade networks persisted, with food, fuel, and alcohol exchanged between opposing sides through intermediaries and local arrangements. At the same time, hostage-taking became a common practice. Civilians and fighters were detained for use in exchanges, whether for prisoners, bodies of the dead, or material supplies. Violence also acquired a symbolic dimension. Acts such as mutilation and the removal of body parts were used to intimidate opponents, strip the dead of dignity, and reinforce group cohesion among fighters. These practices illustrated both the brutality of the conflict and the erosion of norms that had previously limited violence.

In many respects, the conflict retained the character of a neighbors' war. Armenians and Azerbaijanis often spoke one another's languages, maintained social ties, and in some cases had intermarried and lived side by side for decades. Along the front lines, fighters sometimes intercepted opposing radio communications and recognized familiar voices issuing commands. On occasion, this recognition led to brief moments of restraint or to warnings exchanged before an attack. More often, however, it deepened the sense of loss, as violence unfolded between people who, only recently, had lived for decades within the same urban and social fabric.

By mid-February, Azerbaijan had begun to consolidate limited air capabilities. On February 14, its forces seized seven helicopters, forming the basis of an improvised helicopter unit. Within days, former Soviet pilots were conducting combat sorties against Armenian positions near Karagaly. These developments marked a further step in the transformation of the conflict, as increasingly organized and mechanized operations replaced the earlier, more fragmented fighting. By the end of the month, the conflict had shifted into a new phase defined by expanded offensives and increasing risks to civilians. One of the most consequential episodes unfolded at Khojaly.

Khojaly

By the winter of 1991–1992, Khojaly had become a strategically exposed town at the center of the Karabakh conflict. A settlement of roughly 6,000 Azerbaijanis in the heart of the region, it held particular importance as the site of Karabakh's only airport. For months, Khojaly endured siege conditions. Roads were cut, the town was shelled regularly, and electricity, water, and gas were unavailable. Civilians survived under subzero conditions on limited supplies delivered intermittently by helicopter. Its defense rested on a small local militia of approximately 160 lightly armed men, commanded by Major Alif Hajiyev, a native of Khojaly, with only sporadic support from nearby Aghdam.

On the night of 25–26 February 1992, Armenian forces launched a coordinated assault on Khojaly, supported by armored vehicles and personnel linked to the 366th Guards Motor Rifle Regiment stationed in Stepanakert. By evening, the town was fully encircled. Artillery fire struck residential areas, houses were set ablaze, and the limited defensive positions collapsed rapidly. With resistance no longer sustainable, local authorities ordered the evacuation of civilians. By that point, fewer than forty defenders remained in Khojaly. Poorly equipped, they were tasked primarily with covering the withdrawal rather than mounting organized resistance. As the assault progressed from various directions, Major Alif Hajiyev coordinated the evacuation, which remained the only viable option.

Throughout the night, civilians moved in small groups along the Gargar River valley toward open ground near the village of Nakhchivanli, hoping to reach Azerbaijani-held positions outside Aghdam. In the early hours of February 26, these groups, consisting primarily of women, children, and elderly residents, along with retreating militiamen, came under fire. Survivors later recounted hearing gunfire erupting in the darkness and deep snow. Many were killed at close range, while others died from exposure as they struggled to escape.

Survivor testimony corroborates this account of the evacuation's collapse. One witness recalled that as shelling intensified, families initially hid in makeshift bunkers before realizing that the town was under coordinated attack from multiple directions. When residents gathered in the village center, it became clear that no secure escape route remained. Groups then attempted to flee through forests and along the Gargar River valley, crossing icy water and deep snow while under fire.

Contrary to later claims of a protected corridor, civilians encountered gunfire at multiple points along different escape routes. Those not killed outright often succumbed to cold and exhaustion or were captured. The witness described days of wandering through snow-covered terrain, bodies scattered along forest paths, and eventual capture after mistaking an Armenian village for a place of safety. Such accounts indicate that the violence unfolded across a wide area and that civilian deaths occurred not at a single location, but along fragmented routes of flight.

According to Azerbaijani records, 613 civilians were killed, including 63 children, 106 women, and 70 elderly people. Hundreds were wounded, 1,275 individuals were taken captive and later exchanged, and the fate of approximately 150 remains unknown. Eight families were entirely wiped out. Among those killed was Major Alif Hajiyev, who was posthumously awarded the title of National Hero of Azerbaijan. While escorting civilians across open ground, he was shot and killed during an exchange of fire while attempting to reload his weapon. Of the approximately forty defenders present in the town that night, only ten survived.

The events at Khojaly marked a watershed in the war. They demonstrated the collapse of remaining restraints on violence and the extreme vulnerability of civilians caught between advancing forces. International organizations, including Human Rights Watch and Memorial, documented the killings and described them as unconscionable acts of violence against civilians. While acknowledging that armed men were present among those fleeing, Human Rights Watch concluded that nothing could justify the scale of indiscriminate fire directed at the civilian population. Investigations confirmed the participation of troops from the 366th Guards Motor Rifle Regiment, including personnel under the command of Major Seyran Ohanyan, who later became Armenia's defense minister.

Journalistic documentation further cemented Khojaly's place in public consciousness. Azerbaijani journalist Chingiz Mustafayev filmed the aftermath in the valley near Aghdam, capturing evidence of widespread civilian deaths. Russian reporter Victoria Ivleva later entered Khojaly itself and witnessed lines of captured civilians, including mothers with infants, being marched away under guard. International journalists who visited Aghdam described mass burials, the arrival of wounded survivors, and a population in shock.

Media coverage across Russia, Europe, and the United States gave Khojaly immediate international visibility, prompting condemnations from foreign officials and appeals by human rights advocates for civilian protection and accountability. In Azerbaijani legal and political discourse, the events at Khojaly came to be framed as genocide. Several national and sub-national bodies abroad adopted resolutions describing the killings as a massacre or, in some cases, as genocide. At the same time, other institutions avoided legal classification but condemned the violence and loss of civilian life.

Visibility, however, did not ensure narrative balance. In Russian national media, Azerbaijani civilian testimony often struggled to be heard on its own terms. One revealing episode occurred in 1992, when Ulvi Mammadov, a nineteen-year-old survivor of the Khojaly massacre, was invited to Moscow to appear on a live Channel One broadcast at the Ostankino television center, alongside an Armenian participant. Mammadov later recalled that he expected to speak about the massacre and the fate of his family. Instead, he was repeatedly interrupted and denied the opportunity to present his account.

The program took a confrontational turn when the host, Vladimir Posner, brought two revolvers onto the stage. One was placed in Mammadov's hand, while Posner raised the other toward Mammadov's forehead as he positioned himself in front of the Armenian girl. The gesture was unmistakably symbolic. Posner cast himself as a defender and the Azerbaijani survivor as a potential aggressor, converting testimony into spectacle.

The provocation failed. Mammadov did not raise the weapon or react emotionally, refusing to perform the role assigned to him. Yet the visual message had already been delivered. As Mammadov later noted, the episode was less an attempt to understand the violence of the First Karabakh War than a public assignment of moral roles. Azerbaijani suffering appeared suspect and reactive, while Armenian vulnerability was framed as requiring protection. The encounter illustrated how Russian television could transform civilian testimony into symbolic reenactment, reinforcing inherited narrative hierarchies through performance rather than inquiry.

Armenian officials later argued that a "free corridor" had been offered for civilians to escape and claimed that gunfire occurred because Azerbaijani fighters were interspersed among the fleeing population. Some went further, suggesting that the scale of the killings had been exaggerated or politically manipulated. These claims were rejected by Human Rights Watch, which stated clearly that Armenian forces bore direct responsibility for the civilian deaths.

Some Armenian participants and observers later acknowledged that Khojaly represented more than a conventional military engagement. In his wartime writings, later compiled and edited by his brother Markar Melkonian, Monte Melkonian stated that the operation carried an element of retribution, with some units acting beyond formal orders. Years later, Serzh Sargsyan, who would go on to become Armenia's president, remarked that the events at Khojaly had "broken the stereotype" that Armenians would refrain from targeting civilians, underscoring the moral and psychological threshold the conflict had crossed.

For Azerbaijan, Khojaly was not merely a military loss but a profound national trauma. The killings eliminated any hope that the conflict could be managed without significant civilian casualties. Khojaly became a focal point of collective memory and political mobilization, shaping demands for accountability and justice in the years that followed. At the same time, the episode exposed the vulnerabilities of a fragmented state, in which divided authority, poor coordination, and delayed decision-making left civilians insufficiently protected despite mounting indications of an impending assault. Militarily, the capture of Khojaly and its airfield secured Armenian forces a critical logistical position, strengthening their operational reach within Karabakh and accelerating the war's escalation.

The Political Fallout in Baku

The massacre at Khojaly had a profound impact on Azerbaijani politics. Images of murdered civilians began circulating widely, provoking mass outrage in Baku. Crowds filled the streets demanding accountability from the country's leadership, while public willingness to volunteer for the front expanded sharply. For many Azerbaijanis, the Karabakh conflict, previously distant or abstract, became immediate and personal. Central to this shift was the work of independent journalist Chingiz Mustafayev, who documented the aftermath of the massacre under active fire. Flying aboard a military helicopter to the snow-covered fields near Aghdam, Mustafayev filmed hundreds of civilian bodies, women, children, and the elderly, left exposed across the terrain. His footage confronted the public with the human scale of the violence in a way no official statement could. Responsibility for the tragedy was widely placed on President Ayaz Mutalibov. On March 3, parliament convened amid mounting pressure. Opposition deputies demanded that Mustafayev's footage be screened for the chamber. As images of frozen bodies, torn by gunfire, appeared on the screen, the hall fell silent. Those ten minutes of film, one observer later remarked, "changed the history of the country."

Three days later, amid mass demonstrations outside parliament and growing opposition within it, Mutalibov resigned. Yaqub Mammadov, a professor of medicine with no independent political base, assumed the presidency on an interim basis. The Popular Front quickly moved to consolidate its influence, securing key appointments, including Rahim Gaziev as minister of defense and Tair Aliyev as minister of internal affairs. Its leadership also extended control into the provinces, replacing local officials with loyalists. Rather than entirely subordinating the various volunteer battalions to a centralized command, the Popular Front divided its attention between military operations and the approaching June presidential election. Political maneuvering increasingly overshadowed efforts to build a disciplined army. Critics later accused The Popular Front of exploiting military losses for political advantage, characterizing the period as a "civil war within a war."

The political struggle reached another turning point on May 14, 1992, when the Communist-dominated Supreme Soviet reversed course, formally exonerating Mutalibov of responsibility for Khojaly and restoring him to the presidency. Within twenty-four hours, Popular Front militias seized parliament and state television, forcing Mutalibov into exile in Moscow. Parliament was dissolved, Isa Gambar became acting president, and Abulfaz Elchibey soon emerged as the leading presidential contender. Within three months of the Khojaly massacre, Azerbaijan's political landscape had been radically reshaped. A new leadership took power with revolutionary zeal but lacked experience in governance and the military. On the battlefield, volunteer battalions continued to operate in a fragmented and improvised manner.

As political authority shifted in Baku, the spring of 1992 brought a series of military setbacks that ushered in the war's most violent phase.

The Siege of Stepanakert

In March 1992, Moscow ordered the withdrawal of the 366th Guards Motor Rifle Regiment from Karabakh after confirming reports of its involvement in the Khojaly operation. The decision marked the effective end of any remaining Soviet military authority in the region. A ground convoy was dispatched to oversee the regiment's departure, but Armenian forces blocked key routes, preventing the unit from removing much of its heavy equipment and weapons stockpiles. As a result, significant armaments were left behind, and the remaining personnel were evacuated by helicopter. Major Seyran Ohanyan remained in Karabakh and joined Armenian forces, along with several Russian officers who chose not to withdraw, further blurring the boundary between former Soviet units and the emerging local armies.

At the same time, Stepanakert entered one of the war's most destructive phases. With approximately fifty-five thousand residents cut off from Armenia by the loss of road access, the city lay exposed to sustained fire from Azerbaijani positions on the heights of Shusha. Beginning in February, Azerbaijani forces deployed Grad multiple-launch rocket systems on the surrounding cliffs. Designed for area saturation rather than precision targeting, the launchers allowed entire districts to be struck at once. From mid-February into the spring, hundreds of rockets fell on Stepanakert, killing and wounding civilians, destroying apartment blocks, and forcing much of the population to shelter in basements for weeks at a time. Some Azerbaijani officers later acknowledged that launches were occasionally conducted without precise coordinates, amplifying the indiscriminate effects of the bombardment.

The escalation extended beyond artillery exchanges. On March 3, a Russian Mi-26 transport helicopter on its way to Yerevan was shot down near the village of Gulistan, resulting in the deaths of sixteen passengers, many of whom were women and children. A brief ceasefire followed on March 21, but it collapsed within days. On March 28, Azerbaijani forces launched their largest offensive of the year against Stepanakert. The operation opened with attacks on Armenian positions overlooking the city's outskirts. The following day saw the heaviest bombardment to date. The airport at Khojaly was struck, craters torn into its runway, while civilian neighborhoods across the city absorbed the brunt of the fire.

By the evening of March 29, Azerbaijani units had advanced to the outskirts of Stepanakert. Armenian defenders counterattacked from the surrounding heights, pushing them back. As casualties mounted on both sides, a ceasefire took effect in the early hours of March 30. That same day, in the buffer zone near Aghdam, the largest prisoner exchange of the war up to that point took place under the supervision of the International Committee of the Red Cross. Fifteen Azerbaijani hostages and seven bodies were returned in exchange for ten Armenian captives, offering a brief moment of coordination amid continuing hostilities. Within days, however, the siege resumed. Rocket, artillery, and sniper fire again struck Stepanakert throughout April.

On April 8, a notable escalation occurred when Azerbaijani pilot Vagif Qurbanov hijacked a Su-25 attack aircraft from a Russian airbase, marking Azerbaijan's first independent use of combat aviation. Two days later, Azerbaijani forces launched an assault on the Armenian village of Maragha (also known as Leninavan or Shikharkh), near Tartar. The village was briefly taken before Armenian units recaptured it the following day. In May, Armenian forces extended the fighting beyond Karabakh by striking targets in the Azerbaijani exclave of Nakhichevan, prompting retaliatory Azerbaijani shelling of Armenian territory.

On May 8, Qurbanov carried out a series of low-altitude air strikes in support of Azerbaijani operations near Shusha, Lachin, and Askeran. These raids disrupted Armenian defensive positions and supply routes but also caused significant damage to nearby settlements, underscoring the growing reach and risks of aerial warfare.

At this stage, control of Shusha had become central to the strategic balance. Stepanakert had already suffered extensive destruction after weeks of bombardment, and Karabakh's Armenian leadership openly acknowledged that as long as Azerbaijani forces controlled the heights above the city, the capital remained exposed. Capturing Shusha, therefore, became a strategic imperative for the Karabakh forces, viewed not merely as a tactical objective but as a prerequisite for securing Stepanakert itself.

Shusha

By early 1992, Shusha had become a central focal point of the conflict over Karabakh. Perched approximately 600 meters above Stepanakert, the historic fortress town gave Azerbaijani forces both natural defenses and a commanding vantage point. Its elevation placed Stepanakert well within artillery range, making Shusha a critical military position. Azerbaijani units controlled the town under the command of Elbrus Orujev, supported by artillery, armored vehicles, and a mix of regular forces and volunteer detachments. Among the latter were fighters from the North Caucasus, including a contingent led by Shamil Basayev, later known as a prominent Chechen militant commander.

On paper, Shusha appeared highly defensible. Steep cliffs protected three sides of the town, supply routes ran westward toward Lachin, and its defenders enjoyed both numerical strength and control of the high ground. In practice, however, the garrison was deeply fragmented. Several battalions had been withdrawn or placed on leave in the weeks preceding the battle, and Sumgait OMON units deserted their positions; coordination among the remaining forces was weak. These internal fractures would prove decisive when the assault began.

Shusha represented a strategic necessity for Armenian forces rather than a conventional military objective. Under the overall command of Arkady Ter-Tadevosyan, with Gurgen Dalibaltayan serving as chief of staff, planning intensified throughout March and April 1992. Recognizing that a frontal assault against fortified positions would be costly and unlikely to succeed, Armenian commanders devised an alternative plan: Operation "Wedding in the Mountains," built on mobility, deception, and encirclement rather than numerical superiority. The plan divided the attacking force into four main strike groups advancing from the north, east, south, and northeast, with a fifth unit held in reserve. Its aim was to stretch Azerbaijani defenses, sow confusion through diversionary actions near Kosalar, and sever the Lachin–Shusha Road, cutting off reinforcements and supplies.

In the early hours of 8 May 1992, close to a thousand Armenian fighters moved into their assigned positions. At approximately 2:30 a.m., artillery fire opened against Azerbaijani strongpoints around the fortress, while the four assault groups advanced under cover of darkness and low visibility along narrow mountain routes. By dawn, Armenian units had penetrated surrounding villages and were pressing toward Shusha's defensive perimeter. The Azerbaijani defense initially held firm. Forces under Elbrus Orujev repelled the first assaults and launched counterattacks with tanks, heavy machine guns, and BM-21 Grad rocket fire against the mountain approaches. However, coordination among the defenders soon deteriorated. Radio communications failed, units became isolated, and centralized command broke down, leaving small detachments to fight independently in ravines and on exposed ridgelines. On the northern axis, one of the battle's most noted engagements occurred when an Armenian T-72 tank commanded by Gagik Avsharyan was destroyed by a direct hit from an Azerbaijani tank operated by Albert Agarunov, a Jewish Azerbaijani officer, who later became one of the battle's most remembered defenders.

As the day progressed, Armenian units advanced methodically through the defensive belt surrounding Shusha. Diversionary attacks fixed Azerbaijani forces in place, while maneuver elements succeeded in cutting the Lachin road, severing the town's final supply and reinforcement route. One after another, Azerbaijani strongpoints were overrun. By evening, several Grad multiple-rocket launchers had been destroyed or captured, and observation posts along the fortress perimeter were neutralized by sustained fire. Fires broke out across sections of the town as the defensive system unraveled. Inside Shusha, command cohesion rapidly collapsed. Although individual units continued to resist, the absence of effective coordination and a functioning central command proved decisive. By the early hours of May 9, Armenian forces had penetrated the town center, signaling the end of Azerbaijani control over the fortress city.

By the afternoon of 9 May, Azerbaijani defenders began a disorganized withdrawal down the steep roads toward Lachin, which came under fire from Armenian units controlling the high ground. Trucks and armored vehicles jammed mountain turns; some were struck and exploded, blocking passage for others. Small groups tried to break out through forest paths but were ambushed or lost in the fog. Among those covering the retreat was Albert Agarunov, who held a key approach with his tank until it was disabled by enemy fire. He was killed in action and was posthumously awarded the title of National Hero of Azerbaijan.

By dawn Shusha was in Armenian hands. The remaining defenders withdrew or were captured. The cost was heavy. Azerbaijani sources report 480 soldiers killed, nearly 1,900 wounded, and 22,000 civilians displaced. At least 193 civilians were killed, 102 were left disabled, and dozens of captives remain missing. Armenian casualties were lower but still significant, with estimates of more than 100 dead. In the chaos that followed, parts of the city were looted and burned, fueled by rage after months of bombardment from its heights.

The loss stunned Azerbaijan. Shusha was not only a fortress but also the cultural heart of Karabakh, the birthplace of poets, musicians, and composers. Its fall came the same day Azerbaijani leaders were in Tehran signing an Iranian-brokered ceasefire with Armenia, an agreement rendered irrelevant overnight. Opposition leaders in Baku, including defense minister Rahim Gaziev, had vowed that the city would never fall. When it did, many interpreted the defeat as evidence of betrayal, while others pointed to chronic disorganization, poor coordination, and failures of command. In retrospect, Shamil Basayev offered a stark assessment, rejecting conspiracy theories and attributing the collapse to a simpler cause: the defenders, he said, "abandoned their positions."

In Turkey, this loss sparked public outrage. Newspapers condemned the Armenian advances and called for intervention. Prime Minister Suleyman Demirel, facing domestic pressure to support Azerbaijan, refrained from sending troops, cautioning that direct involvement could escalate into a broader Christian–Muslim conflict. Instead, Ankara increased its arms supplies, training programs, and political support for Baku while emphasizing the need for a diplomatic resolution to the conflict.

In Armenia, the capture of Shusha was celebrated as the most significant victory of the initial phase of the war. This victory ended the siege of

Stepanakert, allowed for the opening of the Lachin corridor a few days later, and created the first secure land connection between Karabakh and Armenia.

The Lachin Corridor

With Shusha secured, Armenian forces shifted their focus westward to the final obstacle separating Karabakh from Armenia. While the fall of Shusha had neutralized the immediate threat to Stepanakert, Lachin represented a far more consequential objective. Control of this narrow mountain corridor would end Karabakh's isolation by establishing a direct land bridge to Armenia, enabling sustained movement of supplies, reinforcements, and civilians for the first time since the conflict's escalation.

On May 18, 1992, Armenian units captured Lachin, overwhelming the Azerbaijani garrison and taking control of the town. The seizure of the corridor marked a decisive strategic breakthrough. In its aftermath, widespread destruction and looting followed. Journalists on the ground reported columns of trucks and civilian vehicles moving toward Armenia, loaded with furniture, livestock, and household goods, as fires spread through abandoned neighborhoods. Some Armenian fighters openly described the looting as retaliation for earlier Azerbaijani attacks on surrounding villages. The town's Azerbaijani population fled in panic, becoming internally displaced almost overnight as their homes burned.

The collapse of Azerbaijani control during the retreat from Lachin was captured on camera by journalist Chingiz Mustafayev, whose footage circulated widely inside Azerbaijan. In one widely viewed sequence, Mustafayev confronted Azerbaijani soldiers retreating in armored vehicles, demanding to know who had ordered the withdrawal and accusing them of abandoning their positions. The exchange, raw and unscripted, became emblematic of the confusion, anger, and sense of betrayal that followed the loss of Lachin. It exposed not only a military setback but also the absence of clear command and accountability at a critical moment of the war. For many Azerbaijanis, the images from Lachin carried the same shock as those from Khojaly months earlier. They underscored that the conflict had entered a new phase, one in which territory was being lost irreversibly, civilian displacement was accelerating, and the state appeared unable to control events on the ground.

With Lachin captured, Armenian forces achieved what had once seemed impossible, a direct overland corridor between Armenia and Karabakh. Supplies that once had to be flown in by risky helicopter missions could now move by road, and volunteer fighters from Armenia and abroad reached the front in greater numbers. After months of siege, supplies began to arrive in Stepanakert, including food, fuel, and medicine. Lachin lay in ruins, with its Azerbaijani and Kurdish residents expelled. The town came under the administration of the self-proclaimed Republic of Artsakh and was gradually repopulated by Armenians from Armenia, diasporas abroad, and some refugees from Baku and nearby villages. Even years later, observers noted that the town never regained its prewar vitality, as many of the new settlers confronted sustained economic hardship and social dislocation.

The capture of Lachin was a strategically devastating blow. Within ten days, Azerbaijan lost both its mountain fortress and the only road that could have kept Karabakh isolated. These defeats ended any hope of keeping the conflict confined to the enclave. Karabakh forces were no longer surrounded; they were now securely connected to Armenia.

The Azerbaijani defenses were thrown into confusion when Armenian units briefly crossed into Nakhichevan. In response, Turkish leaders publicly warned that such a situation, created by force, is unacceptable. Meanwhile, Russian commanders quickly cautioned that Turkish intervention could lead to a wider regional conflict. The episode underscored how quickly a local battlefield development could escalate into a broader geopolitical confrontation. In later years, Abulfaz Elchibey candidly reflected on these defeats. He acknowledged that Azerbaijan entered the war unprepared, lacking adequate ammunition, coordination, and discipline. Frontline commanders often operated in isolation, cut off from Baku by failed communications and the absence of a functioning central command. Political turmoil in the capital compounded these problems. Shifting alliances and internal rivalries weakened morale, while orders frequently arrived late or contradicted one another. Elchibey dismissed claims of betrayal and attributed the losses to systemic disorganization: an army still in formation, directed by a government struggling to assert effective control. In his assessment, the fall of Shusha and Lachin was more than a military defeat; it revealed a fractured state unable to wage war as a unified force.

By May 1992, the First Karabakh War had entered a more dangerous phase, one in which military reversals and political instability became inseparable, and the boundary between the front and civilian life narrowed sharply.

Weeks later, on June 15, journalist Chingiz Mustafayev was killed while filming combat near the village of Nakhichevanik. Mortar shrapnel severed a major artery, and he died before reaching medical care. His final moments were recorded by the camera he carried. He was posthumously awarded the title of National Hero of Azerbaijan in recognition of the role his footage played in documenting the human cost of the First Karabakh War. His death followed that of Salatin Asgarova, who had been killed in January 1991 when the vehicle in which she was traveling came under fire along the Lachin–Shusha highway. She died at the scene, along with three accompanying Soviet Army officers.

Elchibey

In the wake of the collapse of the frontline, Azerbaijan entered a period of acute political instability. Amid the crisis, new leadership began to take shape. Following Ayaz Mutalibov's departure, Isa Gambar, the speaker of parliament, assumed the role of acting head of state. However, the political momentum shifted as the Azerbaijani Popular Front gained prominence, driven by public outrage over the Khojaly massacre and the subsequent losses of Shusha and Lachin.

That momentum culminated in June. Abulfaz Elchibey, a historian, philologist, and former Soviet dissident who had worked as an Arabic translator in Cairo and been imprisoned for "anti-Soviet propaganda," was elected in Azerbaijan's first competitive presidential election. He presented himself as a decisive break from the Soviet-trained elite. Openly nationalist and Pan-Turkist in outlook, Elchibey described himself as a "soldier of Ataturk" and called for Azerbaijan's complete emancipation from Moscow's political and psychological legacy. To supporters, he embodied independence and a long-awaited political rupture with Soviet rule. To critics, however, he appeared ill-suited to wartime leadership: a civilian intellectual without military or executive experience, heading a government dominated by academics and activists at a moment when the state faced an existential security crisis.

In contrast, Armenia's political trajectory during this period was marked by greater institutional continuity. Levon Ter-Petrosyan remained in office in Yerevan, and his government maintained a coherent leadership structure capable of directing war policy with relative consistency. While Azerbaijan's parliament was rocked by rapid political turnover, Armenia's state institutions projected stability. This asymmetry carried direct consequences on the battlefield. Azerbaijani forces were constrained by limited resources, fragmented command structures, and weak coordination between political and military leadership. Karabakh Armenian forces, by comparison, operated with greater organizational cohesion, benefiting from unified political direction from Yerevan and sustained financial, logistical, and moral support from the Armenian diaspora.

Elchibey's election was widely celebrated as a moment of national renewal, but it also sharply raised expectations. The Popular Front–Musavat alliance now bore responsibility not only for constructing an independent state but also for reversing a rapidly deteriorating military situation. Despite his popularity, Elchibey took office during a time when the war was escalating beyond the ability of any new leadership to contain it quickly.

The Summer Battles: Martakert and the Struggle for the Corridor

By the summer of 1992, Baku sought to reverse its battlefield losses through a large-scale offensive aimed at reasserting control over Nagorno-Karabakh. The operation, later known as the Goranboy campaign, became Azerbaijan's most ambitious military effort to date and, at least in its opening phase, its most successful. Approximately 8,000 Azerbaijani troops took part, supported by additional battalions, nearly ninety tanks, some seventy armored personnel carriers, and several Mi-24 helicopter gunships.

The offensive began on June 12, when Azerbaijani forces launched coordinated attacks that broke through Armenian defensive lines in the Shaumyan district and parts of Martakert and Askeran. After intense fighting, Azerbaijani units captured a series of villages, including Nakhchivanli, Dovshanli, Pirjamal, Dahraz, and Aghbulag, consolidating control over much of the district. On June 13, formations under the command of Suret Huseynov advanced further toward Goranboy, where Armenian volunteer detachments had constructed fortified positions.

The assault unfolded over several days and relied on sustained artillery fire and armored advances that overwhelmed local defenses. After approximately fifteen hours of continuous combat in key sectors, Armenian forces withdrew, abandoning dozens of settlements. Civilian populations evacuated the area in large numbers. On July 4, Azerbaijani troops entered Agdare, the region's largest town, marking the high point of the summer campaign.

The speed and scale of the advance stunned Yerevan. Within weeks, Azerbaijani forces had regained control over large portions of northern Nagorno-Karabakh, forcing Armenian units to withdraw southward and regroup around Stepanakert and the Sarsang Reservoir. The offensive triggered significant civilian displacement, with an estimated 30,000 Armenian residents fleeing advancing Azerbaijani positions. On June 18, the Armenian leadership in Karabakh declared a state of emergency.

By mid-August, Armenian authorities initiated a rapid reorganization of their military structures. A newly established State Defense Committee of the self-proclaimed Nagorno-Karabakh Republic, headed by Robert Kocharyan and Serzh Sargsyan, oversaw emergency reforms. Partial mobilization was announced for men aged 18 to 40, reserve officers up to 50, and women with prior military training. More than 15,000 recruits were assembled, allowing previously fragmented volunteer units to be consolidated into a centralized Defense Army of Artsakh.

Azerbaijan's initial success, however, proved short-lived. By late July and August, Armenian forces mounted coordinated counterattacks along the Martakert front. Fighting concentrated around villages such as Sirkhavend and Kichan, where Armenian units employed ambush tactics against advancing Azerbaijani armor, destroying and capturing several tanks and armored vehicles. As casualties mounted, the Azerbaijani advance lost momentum.

At the same time, the balance in the air began to shift. Reinforced Armenian air defenses downed several Azerbaijani aircraft, including a Su-25 ground-attack jet and, later, a MiG-25 interceptor flown by a Russian pilot. Helicopter strikes against Azerbaijani columns further disrupted offensive operations. Reports also indicated that some tank crews, including individuals identified as Russian servicemen from the 104th Guards Airborne Division stationed in Ganja, were killed during these engagements.

Through August and September, ground and aerial combat continued, but the front gradually stabilized. Armenian forces regained several positions lost earlier in the summer and threatened key Azerbaijani supply routes. By the onset of autumn, Azerbaijan's offensive momentum had dissipated, marking the end of the most successful phase of its campaign.

The June 1992 counteroffensive, remembered as Operation Goranboy, represented the high point of Azerbaijan's military fortunes. Its rapid gains, however, also exposed profound structural weaknesses. The campaign relied heavily on inherited Soviet equipment and loosely organized volunteer battalions operating with limited coordination. Rivalries among commanders undermined discipline, while Defense Minister Rahim Gaziyev faced growing accusations of reckless planning and operational mismanagement. Politically, President Elchibey's government struggled to assert authority. Volunteer units frequently ignored central directives, corruption spread within key ministries, and Azerbaijan remained diplomatically isolated, lacking reliable external support.

On the Armenian side, developments followed a different trajectory. The opening of the Lachin corridor fundamentally altered the balance of the war, enabling a steady flow of weapons, ammunition, food, medical supplies, and reinforcements. This logistical breakthrough transformed Armenian defensive capacity and allowed sustained operations that Azerbaijan could not effectively counter. By late 1992, momentum on both sides had stalled, setting the stage for renewed political turmoil in Baku.

The Political Gambit of Elchibey

In Baku, Abulfaz Elchibey sought to fulfill his promises of democratic renewal and a decisive break with the Soviet past, a commitment reflected in his cabinet appointments. Key posts were filled by intellectuals and former dissidents with little experience in state administration: a mathematician was appointed minister of defense, a physicist became foreign minister, and the state security service was headed by a pathologist. These appointments, while symbolizing renewal, also exposed the new leadership's limited institutional capacity and managerial competence. As battlefield losses mounted and hopes for a swift victory waned, the challenges of war overwhelmed state institutions, corruption spread, and the machinery of governance struggled to function effectively.

Political cohesion unraveled almost as quickly as the front lines, as former allies fractured into open rivals. Etibar Mammadov and the National Independence Party emerged as Elchibey's most persistent critics, using televised parliamentary sessions to attack the government's failures. The Popular Front fragmented into competing factions locked in struggles for influence and control.

Elchibey's foreign policy further compounded Azerbaijan's difficulties. His uncompromising nationalist stance left the country increasingly isolated. Parliament refused to ratify Azerbaijan's entry into the Commonwealth of Independent States, a symbolic assertion of sovereignty that excluded Baku from negotiations dominated by Moscow. Elchibey's Pan-Turkist rhetoric unsettled Iran, while his openly anti-Russian posture alienated the Kremlin. Isolation deepened in October, when the U.S. Congress adopted Section 907 of the Freedom Support Act, suspending American government assistance to Azerbaijan while aid to Armenia continued. The brief optimism surrounding Elchibey's election had vanished, leaving the state once again confronting a crisis of authority and survival.

Campaigns of Attrition

By September, the operational impact of the Lachin corridor had become evident on the battlefield. Azerbaijani commanders identified the Lachin corridor as a strategic priority and mounted repeated armored assaults toward it under the command of Suret Huseynov. The corridor's mountainous terrain, dense forests, and narrow roads constrained maneuver and neutralized the advantages of heavy armor. Armenian forces, entrenched along elevated positions and sustained by uninterrupted supply lines, exploited these conditions through coordinated ambushes, anti-tank fire, and artillery strikes. Several Azerbaijani helicopters were lost during the fighting. Despite sustained pressure, control of the corridor remained in Armenian hands. After absorbing significant losses and facing fuel shortages, Huseynov withdrew his remaining units from Agdare and redeployed them to Ganja to regroup and resupply at the former Soviet base.

By October, the failure of armored ground operations pushed the conflict decisively into the air. Azerbaijani aircraft carried out repeated strikes on Armenian positions and command infrastructure in and around Stepanakert, seeking to compensate for stalled ground advances. Armenian forces responded by strengthening their air defenses with newly acquired systems, sharply increasing the risks of aerial operations. By the end of October, Azerbaijan had lost two Su-25 ground-attack aircraft and several Mi-24 helicopters. Air superiority, once a critical Azerbaijani advantage, was increasingly contested, further narrowing Baku's military options.

On November 17, Armenian forces launched a coordinated offensive along the Kichan–Vaguas line. Fighting was intense, with control of several villages shifting repeatedly as Azerbaijani armored units were ambushed in the wooded terrain. Armenian detachments captured or disabled approximately ten tanks and armored vehicles, inflicting heavy casualties and forcing Azerbaijani units to withdraw. By late December, much of the territory Azerbaijan had seized earlier in the Martakert sector was slipping back under Armenian control. Losses mounted on both sides, and defensive lines hardened as winter set in. Trenches froze into the landscape, signaling the transition from mobile offensives to a war of attrition, with both sides conserving dwindling fuel, electricity, and supplies.

In Armenia, the military stalemate coincided with a deepening economic crisis. The closure of the Metsamor nuclear power plant severely reduced electricity generation, while ongoing conflicts in Georgia's Abkhazia and South Ossetia disrupted critical transport corridors. Sabotage along oil and gas pipelines linking Armenia to Russia further compounded the shortages, leaving entire towns without reliable heating or power. The winter of 1992–1993, following an already harsh year, intensified these pressures. Across Armenia and Karabakh, civilians endured prolonged cold with limited fuel, electricity. The Armenian diaspora mobilized to alleviate the hardship. Fund-raising drives across Europe and the United States financed humanitarian shipments to the homeland. In December, two American cargo vessels delivered more than 33,000 tons of grain and 150 tons of baby food to Armenia via the Georgian Black Sea port of Batumi. The following February, the European Economic Community allocated 4.5 million European Currency Units in emergency aid. Iran, Armenia's southern neighbor, also became a critical economic lifeline, supplying electricity and consumer goods. In contrast, relations between Tehran and Baku deteriorated. President Elchibey's repeated promotion of the "Greater Azerbaijan" concept, which implied unification with Iran's own Azerbaijani provinces, alarmed Iranian leaders and cooled diplomatic ties.

Economic conditions in Azerbaijan were no less severe. Tens of thousands of refugees and internally displaced persons were living in makeshift camps established by the government, with limited external assistance. In December, the International Committee of the Red Cross distributed blankets and food rations to mitigate the deepening humanitarian crisis. The country's oil sector, long the backbone of the republic's economy, was in marked decline. Aging Soviet-era extraction and refining infrastructure, compounded by wartime instability, discouraged Western investment at a critical moment. Oil production, which had peaked at 21.5 million tons in 1965, had fallen to around 18 million tons by the late 1980s and dropped further amid the disruptions of war. Refineries in Baku operated well below capacity, constrained by shortages of spare parts, technical expertise, and reliable supply chains. By early 1993, the war had stalled, and Azerbaijan's internal political crisis intensified.

Nakhchivan: Heydar Aliyev's Political Return

Heydar Aliyev's reemergence on the political stage began far from the capital, in Nakhichevan. In the aftermath of the Soviet military intervention in Baku in January 1990, Aliyev traveled from Moscow to his native region, where he was received as a figure of authority amid a deepening national crisis. Later that year, he was elected to the Supreme Soviet of both

Azerbaijan and the Nakhichevan Autonomous Republic, marking the first concrete step in his return after years of political marginalization. By 1991, Aliyev had become chairman of the Supreme Assembly of Nakhichevan, placing him at the head of an exposed and strategically vulnerable exclave bordered on three sides by Armenia.

As the Karabakh war escalated, Nakhichevan itself came under intermittent artillery fire, heightening fears in Baku that the conflict might expand beyond Karabakh into a second front. Aliyev moved quickly to stabilize the region, asserting local authority and cultivating direct channels with Moscow, Ankara, and Tehran. In contrast to the turmoil in the capital, Nakhichevan under Aliyev projected discipline and continuity.

In the spring of 1992, Armenian artillery shelled villages in Nakhichevan along the Armenian border, reinforcing concerns about regional escalation. Aliyev's response was pragmatic. He opened direct communication with Yerevan, speaking frequently with Ashot Manucharian, the Armenian president's security adviser, to contain incidents and prevent wider fighting. While some in Baku interpreted this restraint as weakness, it functioned as a calculated effort to shield Nakhichevan from the violence engulfing Karabakh.

In May, Aliyev secured a critical lifeline from Turkey. Invoking Ankara's obligations under the 1921 Treaty of Kars, Turkey opened a land corridor that enabled convoys of food and fuel to reach Nakhichevan. Aliyev framed the move as both a practical necessity and a diplomatic success, emphasizing Turkey's support for Azerbaijan amid regional isolation. The corridor not only sustained the enclave but also enhanced Aliyev's political standing. As Baku descended into factional struggle and administrative paralysis, Aliyev projected steadiness and control. He cultivated ties with Turkey, maintained working channels with Moscow, and preserved a disciplined local administration insulated mainly from the disorder of volunteer battalions and rival commanders.

In November 1992, Aliyev further consolidated his position by founding the New Azerbaijan Party in Nakhichevan, creating an alternative center of political gravity at a moment when Elchibey's government was faltering amid military reversals and internal division. By year's end, Nakhichevan stood apart as a rare zone of administrative order within a rapidly fragmenting state. Aliyev's authority there contrasted sharply with the volatility in

Baku, reinforcing perceptions that he alone possessed the experience and discipline required to restore stability. As winter settled over the Caucasus, Azerbaijan entered 1993 politically fractured and militarily exhausted. The army was strained, the central government unstable, and effective authority unevenly distributed across the country. From Nakhichevan, Aliyev remained outside the immediate crisis, consolidating his position as the balance of power quietly shifted.

Dashalti village, 2015. Photo by Adam Jones.

Road toward Shusha through Dashalti, with the massive rock formation supporting the city rising ahead, 2021. Photo by Asgarov Ruslan.

Azerbaijani refugees from Karabakh, 1993. Photo by Ilgar Jafarov.

Azerbaijani refugee camp, 1993. Photo by Ilgar Jafarov.

Memorial Complex to the Fallen of World War II in Shusha, 2022.
Photo by Aykhan Zayedzadeh.

Armenian protests in Martuni, Nagorno-Karabakh, 1988.
Photograph by Armenian Museum of Photo and Video Materials, via Wikimedia Commons, licensed under CC BY-SA 2.0

Soviet armored column in Baku, 1990. Photo by Ilgar Jafarov.

A Crashed civilian car during Soviet military operations in Baku during (Black January), 1990. Photograph: Azerbaijan State News Agency.

Ruins of Shusha, 1920. Unknown Russian photographer.

Ruins of the Ashagi Govhar Agha Mosque, Shusha, 2017. Photograph by Julian Nyca.

Ruins of Aghdam following the First Karabakh War, 2020.
Photo by Stepan Lohr.

New residential construction in Aghdam, 2025. Photograph from the official
website of the President of the Republic of Azerbaijan.

Azerbaijani military conscripts during the First Karabakh War, 1990. Photo by Ilgar Jafarov.

Azerbaijani environmental protesters facing a Russian peacekeeping post on the Lachin road, 2023. Photo by Mahammad Turkman.

Key West Peace Talks, 2001. Official U.S. Department of State Photo.

The signing of the Armenia–Azerbaijan declaration at the White House, August 8, 2025. Official White House Photo.

Collapse of Authority

In January and February 1993, fighting along the Karabakh front took the form of sustained pressure rather than decisive offensives. Armenian detachments probed Azerbaijani positions along the Martakert axis, testing defenses hastily erected during the previous summer's counteroffensive. Strategic attention was no longer limited to holding Nagorno-Karabakh itself. It shifted westward toward the Kalbadjar District, a rugged mountainous region separating Karabakh from Armenia's northern frontier. Control of Kalbadjar promised a second, more secure land corridor between Armenia and Karabakh, while simultaneously opening a new front against Azerbaijan's northwestern defenses. Throughout the winter, Armenian commanders stockpiled ammunition and quietly prepared for an operation in the highlands.

In contrast, Azerbaijan entered the new year under increasing pressure. Public declarations continued to invoke renewed offensives, but realities at the front told a different story. Ammunition and food supplies were tightening, morale varied sharply across units, and many volunteer battalions that had advanced rapidly in 1992 proved unwilling or unable to sustain prolonged combat. In Baku, the political atmosphere darkened. Parliamentary sessions devolved into televised confrontations, and Elchibey's government appeared increasingly reactive and overwhelmed. Rather than recovery, the winter of 1993 brought a succession of military and political setbacks that exposed the fragility of the state's wartime footing.

Kalbadjar

By early 1993, the fragile equilibrium on the Karabakh front was nearing collapse. Kalbadjar had emerged as a strategic objective of the first order. Its seizure would not only secure Armenia a second land connection to Karabakh via the north but also protect the Martakert sector and place key mountain passes under Armenian control. For Azerbaijan, Kalbadjar functioned as a critical buffer zone and was home to approximately 60,000 civilians, including a substantial Kurdish population.

With the onset of the late-March thaw, fighting resumed across the front. Near the Sarsang Reservoir in the Tartar District, Azerbaijani artillery struck Armenian positions, signaling the end of the uneasy winter pause. In response, Armenian forces under the command of Monte Melkonian secured the lower Qaraglukh area and began preparing for a westward advance toward Kalbadjar. The maneuver highlighted the campaign's changing focus and increased concerns in Baku about an impending offensive.

Anticipating a broader Armenian push, President Abulfaz Elchibey declared a two-month state of emergency and ordered a nationwide mobilization. The measure reflected the depth of Azerbaijan's military crisis: untrained civilians were rushed to the front to compensate for weak planning, fragmented command structures, and chronic shortages of weapons and supplies. The mobilization unfolded chaotically. In Baku, security patrols used commandeered city buses near major transit hubs and metro stations to detain men at random, checking documents and transporting them directly to recruitment centers on the outskirts of the city. Public spaces emptied as fear spread, and many avoided public transportation altogether. Although students were often exempt, others were taken without prior notice, dispatched within days to frontline positions with minimal training and, in some cases, without adequate equipment or ammunition. The process underscored the extent to which the state had lost the capacity to mobilize its population in an orderly or sustainable manner.

The Armenian offensive commenced on 27 March 1993. Coordinated detachments advanced along multiple axes, including from Vardenis in Armenia proper, from southeastern Karabakh, and across the snowbound ridges of the Murov Mountains. Azerbaijani defenses were critically weakened by the withdrawal of Suret Huseynov's brigade, which had been assigned to hold the high ground but redeployed to Ganja following a dispute with political authorities in Baku. The departure left key positions exposed at the outset of the operation. Local Azerbaijani units, reinforced by small contingents of Chechen and Afghan volunteers, mounted determined resistance at Charektar and surrounding villages, but without reinforcements or unified command, they were steadily overwhelmed.

By 31 March, Armenian forces had effectively encircled the district center, and by dawn on 1 April, they launched a coordinated assault across several mountain passes. More than two thousand troops, supported by armor and heavy artillery operating from the Armenian side of the border, crossed into the Tartar River basin in a pincer movement. Azerbaijani border detachments at Soyudlu, Dikyurd, Yellice, and Ayrim resisted fiercely but were heavily outnumbered and forced to withdraw after sustaining significant losses. Only at Zeylik did Azerbaijani forces manage to stabilize their line temporarily, delivering sustained artillery fire against advancing units and positions in the adjacent Basarkechar area, firing nearly two hundred shells over the course of two days.

Kalbadjar city fell on April 3 after Azerbaijani defenses, strained by shortages, internal fragmentation, and the absence of effective command, failed under sustained pressure. The advance was accompanied by widespread destruction and the mass displacement of the civilian population. Within a week, Armenian forces had secured control over the entire district. For the first time in the war, Armenian units had advanced well beyond the boundaries of Nagorno-Karabakh itself, establishing a continuous land connection between Armenia and Karabakh across occupied territory.

The humanitarian toll was catastrophic. Tens of thousands of civilians fled into the mountains in subzero conditions as Armenian forces advanced across the district. The only viable escape route, the Omar Pass, remained buried under late-season snow. Families fled with what they could carry, shouldering bags and small suitcases as they walked along snow-covered, frozen roads through steep terrain, often carrying children for long stretches. Many did not reach safety. Some were taken captive as Armenian units secured the mountain valleys. Survivors later described entire families frozen on the slopes, while overloaded helicopters evacuating civilians crashed or came under fire.

Video footage from the Kalbadjar operation documented acts of intimidation against civilians. One widely circulated recording depicts Armenian soldiers on a tank, laughing and taunting an elderly Azerbaijani woman who pleads for her grandchild to be returned, as he had been placed on the tank. Survivor testimony indicates that the woman was shot and killed shortly thereafter, before the unit withdrew. In separate footage from the same period, an Armenian soldier uses a loudspeaker to address Azerbaijani civilians in the Azerbaijani language, ordering them to leave the area within ten hours. Monte Melkonian is visible standing nearby among the group of armed fighters surrounding the speaker. After the announcement, short bursts of gunfire are fired into the air, and several members of the group, including Melkonian, are seen laughing. Human rights observers later cited such recordings as evidence of intimidation tactics used against the civilian population during the Kalbadjar offensive.

Such images became emblematic of the human dimension of the operation and reinforced accounts of abuses committed during the advance. Human Rights Watch later documented multiple violations of the laws of war during the Kalbadjar offensive, including the forced displacement of civilians. By the end of April, more than 60,000 people, Azerbaijanis and Kurds alike, had been displaced, making Kalbadjar one of the gravest humanitarian disasters of the conflict. The international response was swift but largely ineffectual. Turkey closed its border with Armenia in protest, and the United States issued formal condemnations. On 30 April, the United Nations Security Council adopted Resolution 822, demanding the withdrawal of occupying forces from Kalbadjar. However, the resolution produced no immediate change on the ground. Armenia retained control of the district, while Azerbaijan's defeat hastened the breakdown of political authority in Baku.

The Collapse in Baku

Following the loss of Kalbadjar, Elchibey's government moved to contain the fallout by reshuffling the cabinet and dismissing Defense Minister Rahim Gaziyev. These measures failed to restore public confidence. The army was fragmenting, discipline was collapsing, and field commanders increasingly operated as autonomous power brokers rather than as instruments of the state.

At the center of the crisis stood Suret Huseynov, commander of the powerful 709th Brigade. Defying orders to return to Baku, he entrenched himself in Ganja with his forces and heavy equipment, fueling suspicions that he was preparing a challenge to the government, possibly with Russian backing. In early June, Elchibey authorized a desperate attempt to reassert control. Operation Typhoon dispatched government forces to seize Huseynov's base and place him under arrest. The assault failed. Huseynov's men repelled the attack, shelled government units, and captured senior officials, decisively shifting the balance of power.

Emboldened by victory, Huseynov prepared to advance on Baku, drawing on weapons and heavy equipment abandoned by Russia's 104th Airborne Division. Panic spread through the capital as ministers resigned, opposition groups mobilized, and rumors of an impending coup circulated widely. Within days, Elchibey had effectively lost control of both his government and the war.

As Huseynov's forces moved toward Baku, parliament turned to Heydar Aliyev of Nakhichevan, one of the most experienced political figures in Azerbaijan and the wider post-Soviet space. For many deputies, he appeared to be the only individual capable of imposing authority and averting a further breakdown of the state. His return to the capital offered a prospect of stabilization, but it also carried political risk, reopening unresolved divisions from the Soviet past. Azerbaijan now faced not only military defeat at the front, but the real possibility of internal armed confrontation.

Heydar Aliyev's Return to Power

Heydar Aliyev arrived in Baku on 9 June 1993 as the capital prepared for the possibility of civil war. Within days, he traveled to Ganja to meet Suret Huseynov, the renegade commander whose advance toward the capital had brought the republic to the edge of internal armed confrontation. The talks were tense but decisive. Aliyev secured Huseynov's agreement to suspend his advance, defusing a crisis that threatened to erupt into fratricidal violence. For many Azerbaijanis, the episode offered the first concrete indication in years that political authority might once again impose limits on the use of armed force.

On 15 June, parliament elected Aliyev as its chairman, placing him at the center of state authority. Shortly thereafter, President Abulfaz Elchibey left Baku and returned to his native village of Kalaki, effectively relinquishing control of the government. The Popular Front's brief experiment in power had come to an end. It was replaced by a leader whose legitimacy derived from long experience at the highest levels of the Soviet political system rather than from revolutionary rhetoric. Aliyev's first weeks in power underscored the depth of the crisis he inherited. In the south, local elites openly discussed separatist scenarios, while Huseynov was appointed prime minister as part of a political compromise aimed at stabilizing the capital. The armed forces, however, remained fractured, divided among rival commanders and personal power networks. Even so, Aliyev's presence restored a measure of order in Baku, reassured foreign diplomats, and projected an image of continuity at a moment when state collapse had appeared imminent.

Political stabilization in the capital had little effect on the situation at the front. Azerbaijan's efforts to stabilize political authority coincided with renewed Armenian military calculations. Preparations intensified for a major summer offensive. Within weeks, the towns of Agdam, Fuzuli, Jabrail, and Zangilan would fall, triggering another mass displacement and opening the most destructive phase of the war.

The Armenian Summer Offensive

On 12 June 1993, as Azerbaijan was consumed by a political crisis in Baku, Armenian forces in Karabakh launched a coordinated offensive toward Aghdam and Agdare (Mardakert). Approximately 6,000 troops took part, supported by tanks, heavy artillery, including self-propelled guns, and Mi-24 attack helicopters. Initial assaults were accompanied by diversionary maneuvers designed to stretch Azerbaijani defenses across multiple sectors.

Azerbaijani brigades mounted counterattacks and temporarily stabilized sections of the front, retaking several villages north and south of Aghdam. Later that day, near the village of Marzili, Armenian field commander Monte Melkonian was killed in a brief firefight with Azerbaijani forces after the main engagement had concluded. He was posthumously awarded the title of National Hero of Armenia. His death was widely mourned and carried substantial symbolic weight within Armenian society, but it did not alter the operational momentum of the offensive.

After encountering resistance along the central Aghdam axis, Armenian commanders shifted focus toward Agdare, attacking from both the north and south to unhinge Azerbaijani positions along the Tartar Canal. On 27 June, Agdare fell. The front stabilized along the Sugovushan–Levonark–Tartar Canal line, allowing Armenian forces to consolidate gains and redeploy strength against Aghdam while further straining Azerbaijan's already weakened logistics. To pin Azerbaijani reserves, diversionary attacks were launched against Fuzuli and Jabrail in early July, temporarily breaching defensive lines.

By early July, Armenian forces were preparing to encircle Aghdam. The strike group consisted of several infantry regiments, tank battalions, artillery units, and helicopter support. The operational logic mirrored earlier successes: seize surrounding high ground, cut supply routes, and compress defenders into isolated pockets. On 3 July, Armenian units launched a renewed push, capturing villages north and south of Aghdam and threatening the Aghdam–Barda highway. Azerbaijan rushed reinforcements from the 709th Brigade to support the 708th, but on 4 July, sustained artillery bombardment devastated much of the city, forcing the evacuation of civilians and frontline units. Between 5-7 July, Azerbaijani counterattacks briefly recovered limited ground, easing pressure but failing to reverse the overall course of the campaign.

A brief pause followed on 12 July during a visit by the OSCE Minsk Group delegation led by Mario Raffaelli. Fighting temporarily subsided, but the lull exposed the depth of Azerbaijan's internal collapse. In Aghdam, a local armed faction overthrew the district administration and seized government offices, underscoring the erosion of central authority. Once the delegation departed, Armenian forces resumed operations. Key elevations at Shahbulag, Yeddikhirman, and Bozdag were captured, tightening the ring around Aghdam. Although Azerbaijani units still held positions on the outskirts, control of the surrounding heights effectively sealed the city.

After days of sustained artillery fire, Armenian forces launched coordinated ground assaults from the Askeran and Khojavend directions. Within forty-eight hours, Aghdam's remaining supply routes were cut, leaving Azerbaijani defenders with little choice but to withdraw in small groups to avoid encirclement. Armenian units entered the city soon afterward, encountering only sporadic resistance before taking complete control. In the aftermath, Aghdam and its surrounding settlements were systematically looted and burned, leaving behind a landscape of near-total destruction. Limited Azerbaijani counterattacks in early August near Novruzlu briefly reached the airport road but quickly collapsed amid low morale and poor coordination. Another ceasefire brokered through the Minsk process between 25 and 28 July proved short-lived as Armenian operations continued southward.

Throughout the campaign, Armenian forces augmented their capabilities with captured Azerbaijani armor and artillery, while Azerbaijan's heavy weapons were depleted, redeployed, or rendered inoperable. Superior organization and logistical cohesion allowed Armenian units to maintain operational tempo and complete the encirclement.

The fall of Aghdam represented more than a battlefield loss. Human Rights Watch later documented widespread hostage-taking, indiscriminate fire, and forced displacement during and after the takeover. Entire neighborhoods were torched or deliberately demolished, reducing the city to ruins. An estimated 128,600 residents, nearly 85 percent of the district's prewar population, were displaced. Azerbaijani sources place military losses during the broader campaign at roughly 5,000 killed, compared to approximately

1,500 on the Armenian side. Armenian commanders characterized the destruction as retaliation for the earlier razing of Martakert. For Azerbaijanis, Aghdam became one of the war's enduring symbols of loss and displacement.

With Aghdam's loss, Azerbaijan surrendered control of the closest major route to Khankendi, while Armenian forces established a broader defensive buffer around Karabakh. The advance did not stop there. In August, Armenian armored units moved into the lowlands of Fuzuli, employing encirclement tactics that left civilians a single escape route. Tens of thousands fled in panic. Fuzuli fell on 22 August, followed by Jabrail days later. By early September, Gubadli also collapsed after Armenian forces shot down an Azerbaijani Mi-24 helicopter over the town.

By the end of the summer of 1993, Azerbaijan had lost four districts in rapid succession. Its armed forces were fragmented, civilian displacement had reached massive proportions, and the central government remained immobilized by internal power struggles. For Armenian troops, the campaign produced strategic depth and a chain of territorial buffers. For Azerbaijan, it marked the war's lowest point: the intersection of military breakdown, political paralysis, and a widening humanitarian catastrophe.

As Azerbaijan's military and political authority unraveled, the meaning of these gains was being articulated on the Armenian side in increasingly explicit terms. The summer of 1993 marked not only a phase of battlefield consolidation but also a moment of rhetorical clarification, as wartime outcomes were framed as historical necessity rather than contingent violence. In remarks delivered around the time of the capture of Aghdam, President Levon Ter-Petrosyan characterized the results of the Karabakh movement and the actions of Yerkrapah, the veterans' paramilitary organization, in stark terms. He stated that Armenia had, in his words, "completely cleansed" both Armenia and Nagorno-Karabakh of Azerbaijanis, presenting this as the resolution of what he described as a centuries-old problem. He also praised the military "victories" achieved by Armenian forces, including the seizure of territories beyond the borders of the former Nagorno-Karabakh. The recording resurfaced publicly in early 2025, amid claims that its release was politically motivated, though it captured statements made at a pivotal stage of the war.

Consolidation of State Authority

As Azerbaijan continued to lose ground on the front lines, Heydar Aliyev moved quickly to consolidate power in Baku. Within weeks, he brought the state's core institutions under his authority, and parliament formally confirmed his leadership. On 3 October 1993, Aliyev was elected president, marking the beginning of a new phase in Azerbaijan's post-Soviet political order. His first months in office were shaped by parallel challenges: restoring central authority at home and securing legitimacy abroad. In the south, Aliakram Humbatov proclaimed the short-lived "Talysh-Mughan Republic." The attempt collapsed rapidly after Aliyev appealed directly to the local population, and Humbatov was arrested. Elsewhere, remnants of the Popular Front retained control over local administrations and segments of the armed forces, requiring sustained pressure to bring them under central authority.

On the diplomatic front, Aliyev acted decisively. He reopened relations with Moscow, traveling there in September to formalize Azerbaijan's entry into the Commonwealth of Independent States. At the same time, he engaged the OSCE Minsk Group, pressing for international recognition of Azerbaijan's territorial integrity. Contacts with Western energy companies were renewed, laying the groundwork for what would later become the "Contract of the Century."

Political consolidation in Baku unfolded amid accelerating military collapse. By the time Aliyev moved to reassert central authority, Armenian forces had already overrun multiple districts east and south of Karabakh. In several areas, local administrations still aligned with the former Popular Front leadership refused to cooperate with the new government, leaving frontline units fragmented and without coordination or support. The territorial losses deepened an already severe humanitarian crisis, driving the number of internally displaced persons beyond half a million and underscoring the scale of the state failure Aliyev was forced to confront.

The international response followed a familiar pattern. The UN Security Council adopted Resolution 853 in July and Resolution 874 in October, both calling for the withdrawal of Armenian forces. Like Resolution 822 earlier that year, these measures failed to alter the situation on the ground.

Armenian units consolidated their gains and continued advancing southward, triggering new fighting around Horadiz and Zangilan.

In November, Aliyev established the State Defense Council and assumed its chairmanship, concentrating authority over military decision-making in his own hands. In a national address, he called for full mobilization, prompting thousands of former Soviet officers and civilian volunteers to enlist in the military. These measures expanded manpower, but chronic equipment shortages, uneven training, and weak discipline limited their immediate impact on the battlefield. By the end of 1993, Azerbaijan had suffered profound losses. Nearly one-fifth of its territory was under occupation, the army was severely weakened, and hundreds of thousands had been displaced. At the same time, under Aliyev's leadership, the foundations of a more centralized and pragmatic state began to take shape, defined by tighter political control, institutional reconstruction, and a growing emphasis on restoring state authority and ensuring political stability.

From War to Ceasefire (1994)

Winter Offensive

In the opening days of 1994, Azerbaijan attempted to reverse a year of defeats with a coordinated winter counteroffensive on three axes. In the north, forces advanced toward Martakert and Kalbadjar. In the east, units pushed from Aghdam toward Martuni. In the south, Azerbaijani troops moved across the Araz plain toward Horadiz and Fuzuli. The plan was ambitious, aiming to stretch Armenian defenses while recovering lost territory.

Initial gains raised cautious hopes in Baku. On 6 January, Azerbaijani forces, supported by Afghan volunteer fighters, recaptured sections of the Fuzuli district, including the Horadiz railway junction near the Iranian border. The advance restored Azerbaijani access to the Araz River corridor, but the town of Fuzuli itself remained beyond reach. On 10 January, a northern offensive followed, targeting the Agdare enclave. Azerbaijani units achieved temporary advances in both north and southern Karabakh, yet these gains proved unstable. Armenia responded by deploying regular army formations and Internal Security troops to reinforce its lines, while Yerevan expanded conscription to men up to forty-five years of age.

Two weeks later, Azerbaijani brigades advancing from the Kalbadjar direction broke through Armenian positions, capturing more than a dozen villages and threatening the Martakert–Kalbadjar highway. For the first time in months, Azerbaijani forces regained visible ground, and morale briefly improved. The momentum, however, proved short-lived. Coordination between the three operational fronts deteriorated as field commanders acted independently, supply lines became overstretched, and communications faltered. Harsh winter conditions further strained logistics and mobility.

As the advance stalled, Azerbaijani commanders increasingly relied on hastily mobilized recruits to sustain pressure. Poorly trained units, including minors, were sent into frontal assaults with minimal preparation or support. Casualties rose sharply. The winter campaign cost Azerbaijan several thousand killed and wounded, while Armenian losses remained significantly lower. Aliyev's mobilization expanded manpower but failed to correct deeper deficiencies in training, logistics, and centralized command. By late January, Armenian forces stabilized the front, redeploying experienced units to threatened sectors.

By mid-February, the Azerbaijani offensive had collapsed. Units that had pushed toward Kalbadjar in January were forced into a disorderly withdrawal across snowbound mountain passes. The retreat over the Omar Pass became the deadliest episode of the war to that point. Contemporary estimates placed Azerbaijani losses at over 5,000 men, with Armenian fatalities approaching 2,000. Entire brigades ceased to function as organized formations. Long after the fighting subsided, reports continued to emerge of frozen bodies left scattered across the highlands.

By March 1994, the front had frozen once again, this time after months of exceptionally heavy losses. The winter campaign confirmed that neither side could achieve a decisive military victory. Despite intensified fighting, the involvement of irregular forces, and continued accusations of external interference, territorial changes remained limited. The war had settled into a prolonged contest of endurance, draining manpower and resources while leaving the strategic balance essentially unchanged. Armenia remained economically strained under blockade, while Azerbaijan faced deepening war fatigue and public disillusionment.

Spring Offensive

March opened with tragedy. On March 17, Armenian air defenses mistakenly shot down an Iranian C-130 Hercules transport aircraft near Stepanakert. The plane was carrying the families of Iranian diplomats from Moscow to Tehran. All thirty-two passengers and crew, most of them women and children, were killed. The incident highlighted the increasingly chaotic nature of the war, in which contested airspace, weak coordination, and heavy weaponry blurred the line between combatant and civilian.

In the south, Azerbaijan intensified its air operations. On March 25, Azerbaijani aircraft bombed Armenian positions near Horadiz, but poor targeting led to friendly-fire incidents that caused casualties among Azerbaijani troops. Air activity expanded further in April. On April 10, Armenian forces launched a major offensive near Tartar, committing roughly 1,500 soldiers and thirty armored vehicles, including seventeen tanks, supported by heavy artillery. Azerbaijani units under General Elbrus Orujev, who had earlier commanded the defense of Shusha, mounted a determined defense from prepared positions. That same day, an Azerbaijani Su-25 aircraft carried out retaliatory strikes on Stepanakert. Air raids continued throughout April, marking one of the war's most intense aerial phases.

Fighting in the air relied primarily on Soviet-era equipment. Both sides used Mi-8 and Mi-17 transport helicopters, while the Mi-24 attack helicopter remained the principal assault platform. Armenia's small air force possessed only two Su-25 aircraft, one of which was lost to friendly fire. Its air defense network, however, proved highly effective, shooting down multiple Azerbaijani aircraft and helicopters. Azerbaijan fielded approximately forty-five combat aircraft, many flown by Russian and Ukrainian mercenary pilots operating MiG-25s, Su-24s, and older MiG-21s. Despite this numerical advantage, Armenian surface-to-air systems sharply limited Azerbaijan's ability to operate freely over Karabakh.

On the ground, the Tartar front emerged as the bloodiest sector of the campaign. From mid-April through early May, Armenian forces, reinforced by the 5th Motor Rifle Brigade and elite assault units drawn from Karabakh's core formations, sustained pressure against Azerbaijani defenses. Resistance was fierce, but the

Azerbaijani lines gradually weakened. Armenian units captured several villages north of Aghdam and west of Tartar, along with twenty-eight armored vehicles. Casualties were severe. Between April 14 and 21, Azerbaijani losses were estimated at approximately 2,000, which included around 600 killed, with many others wounded or missing. Armenian casualties were also substantial. Despite these losses, the offensive successfully advanced the front line closer to Aghdam.

By late April, the limits of continued combat were evident. Fighting around Tartar, intensified air operations, and mounting losses on both sides made further offensives increasingly costly while yielding little strategic gain. The war had settled into a pattern of sustained pressure without decisive results. As exhaustion spread along the front, external actors stepped up efforts to press for a negotiated halt, setting the stage for the diplomatic initiatives that followed.

The Bishkek Protocol and the Ceasefire

By late spring 1994, the accumulated human and material losses had narrowed the space for continued fighting, allowing diplomacy to gain momentum. The first viable initiative emerged from an unexpected venue: Kyrgyzstan. Medetkhan Sheremkulov, Speaker of the Kyrgyz parliament, proposed Bishkek as a venue for renewed talks under the auspices of the CIS Interparliamentary Assembly, with Russia as the principal mediator. After years of sustained warfare, exhaustion pushed both Baku and Yerevan toward an arrangement aimed at suspending the violence, rather than ending the conflict.

On May 5, 1994, representatives of the Milli Majlis of Azerbaijan, the Supreme Council of Armenia, and the authorities of Nagorno-Karabakh convened in Bishkek. The talks were tense and frequently contentious. Azerbaijan's delegation objected strongly to the participation of representatives from the Karabakh Armenians, viewing their presence as an attempt to legitimize the separatist administration. Baku demanded that Nizami Bakhmanov, the displaced mayor of Shusha, be named in the protocol as the legitimate representative of Karabakh's Azerbaijani population. After prolonged debate, a compromise was reached. Russian envoy Vladimir

Kazimirov later recalled that President Heydar Aliyev, though reluctant, agreed to include Bakhmanov's name, fully aware that it could complicate already fragile negotiations. Bakhmanov himself, however, was unreachable and did not sign the document.

The Bishkek Protocol was a brief and narrowly framed document. It called for an immediate ceasefire to take effect at midnight on May 8–9, 1994. It was neither a peace treaty nor a comprehensive settlement. Instead, it reflected a battlefield stalemate and a shared desire to halt further bloodshed. Formal signatures followed in rapid succession. On May 9, Azerbaijani Defense Minister Mamedrafi Mamedov signed the ceasefire in Baku. On May 10, Armenian Defense Minister Serzh Sargsyan signed in Yerevan. On May 11, Samvel Babayan, commander of the Karabakh Armenian forces, signed in Stepanakert. At midnight on May 12, firing across Karabakh ceased. For the first time in years, large-scale combat came to an end.

The ceasefire contained no provisions for neutral monitoring forces or international peacekeepers. President Heydar Aliyev rejected Moscow's proposal to deploy Russian troops in the conflict zone, citing concerns over sovereignty and long-term dependence. As a result, the truce relied entirely on self-enforcement by the same military forces that had just concluded the war. For Azerbaijan, the ceasefire froze an unfavorable reality. Nearly one-fifth of its internationally recognized territory remained under Armenian control, and more than half a million people were displaced. For Armenia and the ethnic Armenian authorities in Nagorno-Karabakh, the agreement secured territorial gains but came at the cost of diplomatic isolation, economic dependence on Yerevan, and the absence of recognized political status.

The Bishkek Protocol ended active hostilities without resolving any of the core political disputes. It marked a transition from open warfare to a prolonged ceasefire lacking a negotiated settlement, a condition later described as a frozen conflict. In practice, this meant enduring displacement, fragile diplomacy mediated by the OSCE Minsk Group, and a truce whose durability remained uncertain.

Aftermath and Uncertain Peace

The First Karabakh War fundamentally reshaped the political geography of the South Caucasus. The ceasefire froze front lines into de facto borders without legal recognition, replacing open warfare with an uneasy silence. Armenian forces in Karabakh, backed by Yerevan, now controlled most of the former Nagorno-Karabakh Autonomous Oblast as well as a broad belt of surrounding Azerbaijani districts. Kalbadjar, Lachin, Gubadli, Jabrail, and Zangilan lay entirely under Armenian control, along with large portions of Aghdam and Fuzuli. Nearly one-fifth of Azerbaijan's internationally recognized territory was lost. In parallel, Armenia relinquished its own enclaves within Azerbaijan, most notably Artsvashen, while securing several Azerbaijani exclaves along its borders.

The human cost was immense. Conservative estimates place the death toll at more than 20,000, with higher figures suggested by some sources. Tens of thousands were wounded, and nearly 4,000 Azerbaijani soldiers remain missing, many without known burial sites. Between roughly 700,000 and one million Azerbaijanis were displaced, fundamentally reshaping the country's demography and social fabric. Families fled through mountain passes or crossed the Araz River into Iran, often to find limited capacity and few resources on the other side.

For Armenia and the Armenian population of Karabakh, military success carried heavy consequences. Territorial gains ensured survival, but at the price of prolonged isolation and economic collapse. Landlocked and blockaded by Azerbaijan and Turkey, Armenia faced acute shortages of fuel and food. In Yerevan, electricity was rationed to a few hours a day, and winters brought severe hardship. In Karabakh, recovery remained fragile. Schools reopened in basements, churches were restored, and daily life resumed amid ruins that testified to the scale of destruction.

For Azerbaijan, the war ended in defeat and displacement. However, amid the collapse, Heydar Aliyev consolidated power and reasserted state authority. Shifting focus from the battlefield to diplomacy and economic recovery, he turned to oil as the foundation of Azerbaijan's survival and reemergence. Western energy companies, led by BP and Amoco, entered Baku even as refugee camps spread across the countryside. The resulting agreements, later known collectively as the "Contract of the Century," anchored Azerbaijan within Western strategic and economic networks and laid the groundwork for future diplomatic engagement.

The United Nations Security Council adopted four resolutions demanding the withdrawal of occupying forces, but none were enforced. Russia positioned itself as the principal broker, maintaining leverage through diplomacy, pressure, and selective support to both sides. The OSCE Minsk Group emerged as the formal framework for negotiations, but its efforts produced little beyond interim arrangements and unresolved texts.

The war had ended, but the conflict endured. The ceasefire hardened into a frozen confrontation, marked by trenches, minefields, and armed conscripts facing off across unresolved lines. Displaced families waited for a return that never came, while those holding the territory lived under the constant expectation of renewed fighting. The First Karabakh War ended without resolution, leaving the region in a state of prolonged uncertainty.

Territorial Control Following the First Karabakh War, 1994
———— Line of contact (1994)   ---------- International border

Post-War Order (1994–2020)

The Rise of the Karabakh Clan

The 1994 ceasefire produced a postwar order in the South Caucasus defined by military victory without political resolution. In Armenia, this outcome profoundly reshaped the political landscape. President Levon Ter-Petrosyan struggled to reconcile battlefield success with the requirements of long-term state survival. He cautiously argued for compromise, maintaining that a partial settlement was preferable to an indefinite conflict. This pragmatic position placed him at odds with hardliners within the Karabakh leadership and segments of Armenia's political and military elite.

By 1998, amid mounting pressure within his government and the armed forces, Ter-Petrosyan was forced to resign. His departure cleared the path for Robert Kocharyan, a native of Stepanakert and former leader of the self-proclaimed Nagorno-Karabakh Republic, to assume the presidency. Kocharyan's rise marked the consolidation of what became known as the "Karabakh clan," a network of former field commanders and political allies whose influence would dominate Armenia's political, military, and economic life for nearly two decades.

The authority of this group rested on its role as the guardian of wartime gains. In the years following the ceasefire, military and political elites increasingly merged into a single system in which loyalty to the Karabakh cause functioned as both moral justification and political protection. The occupied territories were framed as sacred achievements, tangible proof of national sacrifice. Questioning their status was often treated as disloyalty. Although large-scale fighting had ceased, Armenian politics remained shaped by a siege mentality in which mobilization continued in ideological form.

The fragility of this order was exposed dramatically on October 27, 1999, when five gunmen led by Nairi Hunanyan stormed the Armenian National Assembly in Yerevan. Eight senior officials were killed, including Prime Minister Vazgen Sargsyan and Parliament Speaker Karen Demirchyan, two figures who had recently formed an alliance that threatened entrenched interests. The attack, later known as the October 27 massacre, traumatized Armenian society and extinguished hopes for political renewal. While the perpetrators claimed patriotic motives, many Armenians suspected deeper political forces at work. President Kocharyan, who personally managed the crisis, was accused by critics of benefiting from the elimination of his most powerful rivals. The aftermath reinforced the dominance of the Karabakh elite and accelerated Armenia's drift toward centralized and opaque governance.

For Kocharyan and later Serzh Sargsyan, Karabakh functioned as a central pillar of political legitimacy. In a country burdened by poverty and limited economic growth, the memory of wartime victory remained the most potent source of authority. Diplomatic initiatives, including proposals advanced by the OSCE Minsk Group, the Key West talks in 2001, and the Madrid Principles of 2007, encountered the same constraint: negotiation was permissible, but meaningful concession was politically untenable. This produced a politics of stasis, in which defending the status quo became an end in itself.

Over time, this system fostered corruption, patronage, and impunity. Veterans of the Karabakh war and their associates entrenched themselves across government institutions, the security services, and key sectors of the economy. Power became increasingly concentrated in the hands of a narrow elite, while inequality widened and emigration accelerated. Large segments of the economy fell under oligarchic control tied to the presidency, discouraging foreign investment and limiting reform. Armenia grew more dependent on remittances and deepened its strategic reliance on Russia, including for military procurement. While Azerbaijan used rising energy revenues to modernize its armed forces and expand diplomatic influence, Armenia relied primarily on Russian-supplied weaponry, much of it inherited or refurbished Soviet-era equipment. Confidence from earlier battlefield success gradually gave way to complacency.

By the mid-2010s, the contradictions of Karabakh-centered governance had become difficult to ignore. The system that emerged from wartime triumph increasingly appeared stagnant, exclusionary, and detached from social realities. Public frustration grew as economic opportunity narrowed and political dissent was constrained through control of security institutions. The victory in the First Karabakh War, which was once a unifying achievement, has been compromised by ineffective governance. That cycle was finally disrupted in 2018, when mass protests propelled Nikol Pashinyan, a journalist and political outsider, into power, bringing an end to the long dominance of the Karabakh elite and opening a new chapter in Armenia's postwar history.

The Rise of a New Azerbaijan

In Baku, Heydar Aliyev emerged from the war years as the architect of a fragile but functioning state. After the political collapse and military defeats of the early 1990s, his leadership restored centralized authority and imposed order on a fractured system. Azerbaijan pursued a pragmatic foreign policy, balancing relations with Russia while deepening strategic ties with Turkey. The partnership with Ankara became a pillar of Azerbaijan's security and cultural diplomacy, reinforcing shared linguistic, historical, and geopolitical interests.

Aliyev's most consequential achievement, however, lay in converting Azerbaijan's energy resources into international leverage. The Contract of the Century, signed in 1994 with a Western-led consortium headed by BP and Amoco, marked Azerbaijan's return to the global economy. It anchored a network of strategic pipelines, including the Baku–Tbilisi–Ceyhan oil pipeline and the Baku–Tbilisi–Erzurum gas line, linking the Caspian basin to European and Mediterranean markets. Through these projects, Azerbaijan positioned itself as a key energy corridor while preserving room for maneuver among regional powers in the volatile post-Soviet landscape.

Aliyev's consolidation of power rested on firm institutional foundations. The New Azerbaijan Party, which he had established earlier in Nakhichevan and expanded nationwide after 1993, became the central mechanism of political control. It ensured policy continuity and disciplined governance within a tightly managed political system, reducing the volatility that had characterized the postwar years.

As Heydar Aliyev's health declined in the early 2000s, attention shifted toward his son, Ilham Aliyev. Educated at the Moscow State Institute of International Relations, where he earned a doctorate in history, Ilham built a career that combined academic credentials with steady advancement within the ruling elite. He entered public service in the 1990s and rose through the leadership of the New Azerbaijan Party, becoming first deputy chairman by 2001.

A constitutional referendum in 2002 designated the prime minister as next in line for the presidency, a change widely understood as preparing a managed transition. In August 2003, Ilham Aliyev was appointed prime minister, a move boycotted by opposition parties who denounced it as dynastic succession. Following Heydar Aliyev's death later that year, Ilham Aliyev won the presidential election. Despite protests and allegations of irregularities, the transfer of power was completed without institutional disruption, reinforcing continuity over political pluralism.

Under Ilham Aliyev, Azerbaijan entered a new phase characterized by energy-driven growth, state-led modernization, and an increasingly centralized political order. The government invested heavily in military reform, infrastructure, and urban development while restricting opposition activity and tightening control over political life. Many observers described the system as a form of managed or authoritarian democracy, combining electoral procedures with strong executive dominance.

Modernization was most visible in Baku itself. The capital was transformed through large-scale redevelopment projects that reshaped its skyline with glass towers, marble boulevards, and redesigned waterfronts along the Caspian. Landmark projects such as the Flame Towers, the Heydar Aliyev Center, and the redevelopment of Baku Boulevard became symbols of state ambition. Infrastructure expansion and architectural renewal were projecting stability, confidence, and international relevance. Azerbaijan positioned itself as a host for global events, including the Eurovision Song Contest, the European Games, and significant energy and diplomatic forums, reinforcing its image as a modern state at the crossroads of Europe and Asia.

However, modernization unfolded alongside an unresolved conflict. The loss of Karabakh remained deeply ingrained in Azerbaijan's political consciousness, experienced simultaneously as collective trauma and an unresolved national question. Economic recovery, military reform, and diplomatic activism were not ends in themselves but components of a longer strategic horizon. As construction cranes transformed Baku and foreign investment poured into the capital, the occupied districts of western Azerbaijan remained empty and in ruins. Their destruction and continued depopulation served as a persistent reminder that the postwar order was provisional, built on a ceasefire rather than a settlement, and anchored in an unresolved territorial dispute.

Life in the Occupied Lands

While refugee camps inside Azerbaijan came to symbolize loss and displacement, the occupied territories along the former front line told a parallel story of abandonment and enforced transformation. When Armenian forces consolidated control over the buffer districts in 1993–1994, nearly the entire Azerbaijani population fled. Cities such as Aghdam, once home to tens of thousands, were left hollowed out. Buildings deteriorated, roofs collapsed, and whole neighborhoods were stripped of usable materials. Over time, satellite imagery documented the systematic destruction of urban infrastructure, revealing districts reduced to skeletal remains. For many Azerbaijanis, Aghdam became a symbol of irreversible loss and deliberate erasure.

The territories did not remain entirely dormant. Particular attention was given to securing the land corridor between Armenia and Karabakh. Limited resettlement began in Lachin and Kalbadjar, where small numbers of people returned under challenging conditions. These settlements remained modest in scale but carried political significance. They signaled an intention to retain territorial control rather than facilitate eventual return. Along newly built or improved roads, residential structures appeared, including homes for permanent residents and seasonal villas associated with wealthier Armenians and members of the diaspora. In Baku, these developments were interpreted as an effort to normalize occupation and entrench permanence.

Economic activity further altered the landscape. Gold and copper extraction, particularly around the Sotk deposit along the Kalbadjar frontier, attracted Armenian firms and foreign partners operating in territory legally disputed by Azerbaijan. Timber harvesting and agricultural use expanded through a combination of state-backed initiatives and informal networks, some of which were linked to diaspora organizations. Within Karabakh, small-scale tourism emerged, centered on monasteries, mountain routes, and rural landscapes presented as sites of endurance and revival. To Azerbaijanis, such activity represented the monetization of displacement and the transformation of exile into opportunity.

Militarization completed the transformation. The occupied districts evolved into a layered defensive zone, reinforced with trenches, bunkers, minefields, and permanent outposts. Armenian regular forces rotated through these areas, converting them into a buffer designed to delay or deter any Azerbaijani advance. Over time, this system became known as the Ohanyan Line, after Seyran Ohanyan, a Karabakh-born commander who oversaw its development and later served as Armenia's defense minister. Stretching across the length of the Line of Contact, the fortifications institutionalized a low-intensity conflict marked by sniper fire, periodic shelling, and reconnaissance incursions.

As years passed, the occupied territories remained suspended in decay and fortification. Ruined towns stood unchanged, while beyond the Line of Contact, Azerbaijan pursued reconstruction and economic growth. In refugee settlements, a generation came of age shaped by displacement and unresolved grievance. The contrast between immobilized spaces of loss and a society moving forward underscored the fragility of the postwar order. The division hardened into a condition that neither side accepted as permanent, yet neither could dismantle without renewed war.

Oil Wealth and the Rebuilding of a State

When the guns fell silent, Azerbaijan's oil sector began its revival. Aging Soviet-era infrastructure, long neglected, became the foundation of a new phase of state reconstruction. A consortium of Western and regional energy companies led by BP secured development rights to the Azeri–Chirag–Gunashli fields. In 1997, oil was first extracted, marking Azerbaijan's reentry into global energy markets.

Pipeline diplomacy followed. The Baku–Supsa pipeline to the Black Sea opened in 1999, providing an initial export route independent of Russia. It was soon eclipsed by the Baku–Tbilisi–Ceyhan pipeline, which began operations in 2006 and linked the Caspian directly to the Mediterranean. In parallel, the development of the Shah Deniz gas field introduced natural gas as a second strategic asset. The South Caucasus Pipeline connected Azerbaijan to Turkey and onward to European markets, further diversifying export options and reducing reliance on Moscow. Energy transformed Azerbaijan's foreign policy leverage and reinforced domestic stability.

In 1999, the government established the State Oil Fund of Azerbaijan (SOFAZ) to manage rising revenues and insulate the economy from volatility. Oil income financed large-scale infrastructure projects, including highways, ports, and urban redevelopment in Baku. By the mid-2000s, poverty rates declined sharply. New settlements were built to house displaced families, and long-delayed investments in education, utilities, and public services resumed.

The strategic lessons of the First Karabakh War were not forgotten. The collapse of the early 1990s had shown that an underfunded and fragmented state could not defend its territory. That conclusion shaped development priorities. Infrastructure projects, energy diversification, and fiscal reserves were not only instruments of growth but also components of national security planning. Oil revenues underwrote reconstruction while quietly financing military modernization.

By the late 2000s, Azerbaijan's economy had expanded several times over, and the state possessed financial buffers capable of absorbing fluctuations in global energy prices. Economic recovery was no longer the primary objective; the focus shifted to capacity building. With core institutions stabilized and revenues secured, the groundwork was laid for a gradual reassertion of state power. Azerbaijan's postwar revival marked the opening phase of a longer journey that transitioned from economic reconstruction toward the rebuilding of military capability and strategic leverage.

The Military Revival: From Petrodollars to Firepower

The Azerbaijani forces that entered the First Karabakh War were not an army in the modern sense of the term. They consisted of a patchwork of inherited Soviet matériel, ad hoc volunteer brigades, and hastily mobilized recruits with uneven training. Equipment existed in quantity, aging tanks, armored vehicles, and artillery, but without effective coordination, logistics, or operational doctrine. Communications routinely failed in mountainous terrain, artillery fire was often imprecise or misdirected, and air defense capabilities were minimal. What Armenia faced in the early 1990s was not a coherent military institution but a collection of units fighting without integration, command depth, or sustained support. The result was a pattern of battlefield reversals, eroding morale, and a weak negotiating position rather than an inevitable defeat. By the 2000s, Baku resolved that such a failure would never be repeated. Over the following years, Azerbaijan deliberately moved beyond its Soviet inheritance, constructing a hybrid military that combined Turkish training, Israeli electronics, Russian heavy systems, and a growing domestic defense industry into something fundamentally different.

The first step was institutional. In 2005, Azerbaijan entered into formal cooperation with NATO, granting its officers access to staff colleges, interoperability exercises, and Western operational curricula. NATO standards gradually filtered into military academies, reshaping the professional culture of the officer corps. In 2007, a National Security Concept articulated the state's central objective with unusual clarity: the restoration of territorial integrity. This was reinforced by a new Military Doctrine adopted in 2010, which embedded that goal as the organizing principle of force development. These were not abstract policy documents; they were frameworks for long-term war preparation.

The second step was industrial. In 2005, Baku established the Ministry of Defense Industry to address a core vulnerability inherited from the Soviet system: total dependence on foreign maintenance and repair. Initial efforts focused on small arms and ammunition, but the program soon expanded to armored vehicles, communications equipment, and joint ventures with partners in Turkey, Ukraine, and Belarus. The goal was not self-sufficiency but sustainability: ensuring that imported weapons could be serviced, upgraded, and maintained in operational condition within Azerbaijan.

The third step was procurement, and here the contrast with the 1990s was stark. Where the earlier force relied on massed manpower and static artillery, the modernized army was designed to fight through sensors, precision, and maneuver. Warfare would be driven by awareness and reach rather than attrition alone.

In pursuit of advanced capabilities, Azerbaijan turned to Israel, a state defined by its emphasis on precision warfare. Baku soon became one of Israel's key defense clients, acquiring reconnaissance drones and loitering munitions such as the Harop, systems capable of locating and destroying radar and air-defense assets without risking pilots. Significant acquisitions, including the $1.6 billion arms package signed in 2012, were tailored to counter Armenia's reliance on fixed positions and layered defenses.

Modernization extended across all branches of the armed forces. To prevent a recurrence of the 1990s, when enemy aircraft operated with relative freedom, Azerbaijan acquired modern surface-to-air systems, including the Russian-made S-300 PMU-2, establishing credible long-range coverage over Baku and key infrastructure. Firepower was expanded through heavy multiple-launch rocket systems such as the Smerch, now integrated with drone reconnaissance to enable coordinated strikes rather than indiscriminate bombardment. Mobility and command were overhauled with modern vehicles, digital communications, and networked control systems, many sourced from Turkey and Israel.

Yet hardware alone could not produce victory. Transforming technology into combat power required doctrine, discipline, and training. For that final element, Azerbaijan turned to Turkey.

Forging a Modern Army

If oil revenues supplied the material foundation, Turkey provided the institutional model. From the first years of independence, Baku confronted a strategic choice: preserve the inherited Soviet military system or restructure its armed forces along Western lines. The former entailed outdated doctrine, an abusive barracks culture, and institutional stagnation. The latter required professionalization, modern operational thinking, and sustained external guidance. That role fell to Ankara.

The relationship was not new. In 1918, Ottoman forces entered Baku to defend the short-lived Azerbaijan Democratic Republic, establishing an early precedent for military cooperation. After the collapse of the Soviet Union, the phrase "two states, one nation" captured the revival of those historical ties. By 1992, Azerbaijan had signed its first formal military training agreement with Turkey. Azerbaijani cadets and junior officers began studying at the Turkish Military Academy, the War College, and the Gulhane Military Medical Academy, while non-commissioned officers trained in Turkish NCO schools. There, they encountered a military culture grounded in discipline, leadership, and accountability, all largely absent from the conscript-heavy Soviet system Azerbaijan had inherited.

What made this partnership transformative was its practical focus on the conditions of the Karabakh battlefield. Turkish officers trained Azerbaijani units in mountain warfare, winter operations, river crossings, and urban combat, precisely the environments that had exposed Azerbaijan's weaknesses in the 1990s. Exercises emphasized mobility over the massing of forces, coordination over improvisation, and initiative at the small-unit level. Troops practiced moving light armor across rugged terrain, bridging under simulated fire, and integrating artillery, air support, and unmanned systems against dispersed defenses. Night operations, rapid clearance drills, and decentralized decision-making became routine. These habits, both tactical and cultural, would later prove decisive.

The cooperation extended beyond field training. Turkish advisers helped reorganize Azerbaijan's military academies, revise doctrine, and professionalize command structures. Joint exercises expanded in scale and complexity, translating theory into practice. By the early 2000s, Azerbaijani units were deploying alongside Turkish forces in Kosovo, Iraq, and Afghanistan, operating under NATO command frameworks and returning home with practical experience in coalition warfare.

This process was formalized in the 2010 Agreement on Strategic Partnership and Mutual Support. Azerbaijani and Turkish units began conducting regular joint exercises, while Turkish officers rotated through Baku to assist with planning, logistics, and doctrinal development. The result was a force that blended Soviet hardware with Western operational standards and a distinctly Turkish approach to tactics and training.

By the mid-2010s, the effects were visible along the Line of Contact. Azerbaijani units equipped with modern communications and trained in maneuver warfare displayed greater flexibility than the rigid formations of the 1990s. Combined-arms coordination became routine, and initiative increasingly flowed downward rather than being confined to senior command. The army was beginning to function as a modern force.

What emerged bore little resemblance to the disorganized formations that had entered the First Karabakh War. Financial resources had been converted into sustained capability, doctrine had been reshaped, and training had instilled discipline and adaptability. Yet the Line of Contact remained unstable. Skirmishes and flare-ups hinted at a changing balance, while negotiations stagnated. As diplomacy failed to resolve the conflict, the contrast between Armenian inertia and Azerbaijan's growing military confidence became increasingly evident, exposing a widening gap between the formal peace process and realities on the ground.

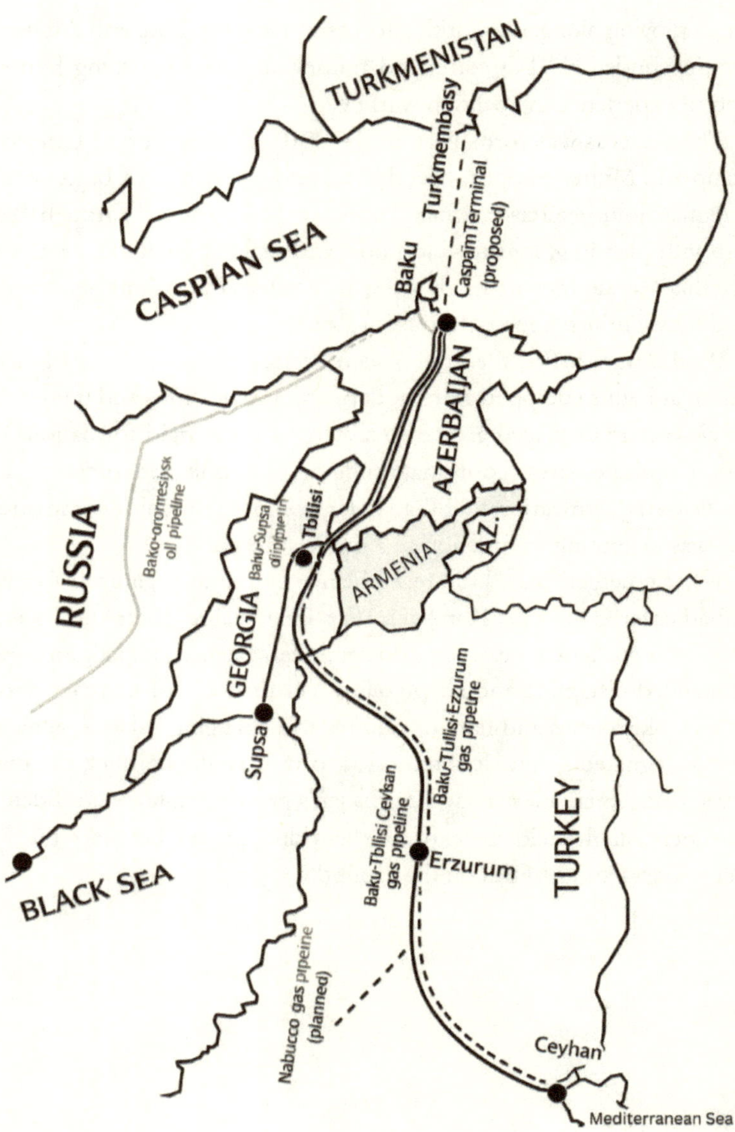

Major Energy Export Pipelines from Azerbaijan

Hardening Lines

The Peace Process: Cycles of Hope and Failure

After 1994, diplomacy played a role in addressing the conflict, but over time, it increasingly lost its effectiveness in resolving the issues at hand. The OSCE Minsk Group, co-chaired by Russia, France, and the United States, remained the formal framework for negotiations. Over time, however, the process became less a vehicle for settlement than a ritual of management. High-level meetings produced carefully worded statements and renewed optimism, yet none of the proposed formulas translated into change on the ground.

One of the most serious attempts came at the turn of the millennium. Between 1999 and 2001, U.S.-led mediation brought Armenian President Robert Kocharyan and Azerbaijani President Heydar Aliyev into sustained negotiations, culminating in the Key West talks. American diplomats advanced ambitious proposals involving territorial exchanges and status arrangements. For a brief moment, compromise appeared possible. It ultimately failed. Aliyev was unwilling to concede sovereignty, while Kocharyan remained constrained by the legacy of military victory and a domestic public opposed to territorial withdrawal. When the talks collapsed, so did confidence in a negotiated breakthrough.

A second phase followed in 2007 with the introduction of the Madrid Principles. These outlined a phased return of occupied Azerbaijani territories, an interim status for Karabakh, the eventual determination of its final status through a referendum, and the return of displaced populations. On paper, the framework aimed to balance territorial integrity and self-determination, but in practice, it reinforced the stalemate. Baku saw the proposed referendum as an indefinite postponement of sovereignty, while Yerevan treated the ambiguity as justification for retaining control over the occupied districts.

The years that followed were marked by recurring summits and symbolic gestures. Presidents met in Paris, Moscow, Saint Petersburg, and Kazan, exchanging handshakes and declarations before returning home to societies unwilling to accept compromise. The Minsk Group came to symbolize a process that preserved stability without producing resolution. Its role narrowed to crisis management rather than conflict settlement.

With hindsight, the effects of this prolonged diplomatic inertia are apparent. For Armenia and the de facto authorities in Karabakh, delay functioned as a strategy. Time was expected to solidify territorial control, normalize the status quo, and weaken Azerbaijan's determination, but in Baku it produced the opposite effect. Negotiations no longer softened positions, and instead, they hardened them. Azerbaijan's official stance became clear: territory would be restored through diplomacy, if possible, but by force if necessary. By the 2010s, confidence in the negotiating process had eroded. Talks ceased to influence outcomes and instead primarily served to postpone an inevitable confrontation.

At the same time, a generational divide deepened the conflict. In Armenia and Karabakh, a cohort came of age immersed in narratives of wartime survival and victory, shaped by mythologized resistance and enduring hostility toward Turks and Azerbaijanis. In Azerbaijan, a generation raised in refugee families absorbed memories of displacement, loss, and violence, along with a lasting sense of grievance toward Armenians. On both sides, lived experience of coexistence receded, replaced by inherited trauma and politicized memory. Within such conditions, peace became not only politically elusive but psychologically remote for an entire generation.

Major Ceasefire Breaches and Escalations

The ceasefire established in 1994 was never truly stable. It eroded through recurrent episodes of localized violence that underscored how narrow the distance between war and peace had become. The first serious breach occurred in March 2008, days after Armenia's disputed presidential election, when clashes near Mardakert left at least sixteen soldiers dead, the heaviest losses since the ceasefire. The timing made clear that political instability in Yerevan could translate directly into violence along the Karabakh front. Two years later, in June 2010, another exchange of fire claimed additional lives in a single night. By that point, a new generation of conscripts manned the trenches, inheriting a ceasefire that functioned less as a peace mechanism than as a suspended battlefield, one increasingly shaped by expectation of renewed war rather than its avoidance.

Tensions escalated again in August 2014, when several days of fighting left at least fifteen Azerbaijani soldiers and several Armenian troops dead. In Baku, the clashes were presented as proof of Azerbaijan's readiness to defend its positions and respond decisively to provocations. In Yerevan, the same events were framed as deliberate Azerbaijani escalation intended to erode the ceasefire. Both sides buried their dead with military honors, and the episode further entrenched mutual distrust.

The most consequential breakdown came in the early hours of April 2, 2016, when fighting erupted along the Karabakh front. Each side accused the other of initiating hostilities, but Azerbaijan launched a limited offensive against entrenched Armenian positions in the northeast and southeast sectors. What began as localized exchanges quickly escalated into the most intense fighting since 1994. Over four days, both sides employed tanks, heavy artillery, multiple rocket launchers, and limited air power. Azerbaijani forces captured several tactically significant positions, including the village of Talish and the heights near Leletepe. Dozens of soldiers were killed on both sides, along with several civilians. Alongside the battlefield fighting, an information war unfolded, with each government inflating enemy losses and publicizing alleged atrocities. Baku justified its actions as retaliation for Armenian shelling of civilian areas, but the operation also served a broader purpose: it tested Armenian defensive lines and demonstrated that Azerbaijan's years of military modernization had altered the balance on the ground.

By April 5, the fighting ended as abruptly as it had begun. The ceasefire was brokered through Russian channels, with parallel statements issued by the Karabakh authorities, Armenia, and Azerbaijan. President Vladimir Putin spoke separately with Serzh Sargsyan and Ilham Aliyev, underscoring Moscow's central role. International reactions from Washington and Brussels were limited to routine calls for restraint, while Turkey publicly declared its support for Azerbaijan. Despite its limited territorial scope, the April fighting carried disproportionate political weight. For Azerbaijan, the gains broke the psychological paralysis that had followed its defeat in the 1990s. In Armenia, the clashes briefly galvanized public support but also punctured the long-standing belief in the invulnerability of its defensive lines. Instead of encouraging restraint, these episodes hardened attitudes on both sides.

Beyond the ceasefire, the war left a psychological legacy that extended well beyond the front lines. In 2004, Ramil Safarov, an Azerbaijani army officer who had grown up amid displacement from the occupied district of Jabrail, killed Armenian lieutenant Gurgen Margaryan during a NATO-sponsored training program in Budapest. The attack carried out while Margaryan slept, shocked both governments and international observers. Hungarian courts classified the act as premeditated murder and sentenced Safarov to life imprisonment. The case did not end there. In 2012, Safarov was extradited to Azerbaijan under a prisoner transfer agreement and immediately pardoned, promoted, and publicly honored. The decision provoked widespread international condemnation and led Armenia to sever diplomatic relations with Hungary. The episode illustrated how unresolved wartime trauma continued to shape political behavior, distorting legal norms and extending the conflict's moral and psychological reach far beyond Karabakh itself.

The Tovuz Clashes and the Death of a General

In July 2020, the conflict escalated unexpectedly far from Karabakh, along the Armenia–Azerbaijan state border near Tovuz. The fighting unfolded near critical infrastructure, including oil and gas pipelines, railways, and highways that carry Caspian energy to Europe. This was not a routine exchange of fire but a confrontation near Azerbaijan's strategic lifelines. Artillery duels lasted several days, killing at least seventeen soldiers and one civilian. Neither side gained lasting ground, but the clash carried significant political and symbolic weight. Among the dead were Major General Polad Hashimov and Colonel Ilgar Mirzayev.

Hashimov's death marked a profound break in Azerbaijan's modern military history. No serving general had previously been killed in combat. Widely respected as a frontline commander, he was known for operating alongside his troops in forward positions rather than directing operations from rear headquarters, a reputation reinforced by wounds he had sustained during the fighting in 2016. His death in Tovuz transformed him almost immediately into a national symbol, bringing the human cost of the prolonged stalemate into sharp and unavoidable focus.

The confrontation also played out in the media and in the diplomatic arena. Armenian officials and diaspora voices framed the events as an Azerbaijani provocation, warning of regional escalation and highlighting Turkey's support for Baku. In Azerbaijan, coverage emphasized the loss of senior officers and what was widely perceived as an imbalance in international reporting, seen as echoing Armenian narratives. By this stage, confidence in negotiations had largely collapsed, and the Minsk process was increasingly regarded in Baku as an empty ritual rather than meaningful diplomacy. Hashimov's funeral, attended by large crowds chanting "Karabakh" from Sumgait to Baku, gave public expression to that disillusionment and underscored a growing conviction that the existing status quo could not endure.

Aftermath: Protests, Politics, and a Nation on Edge

General Hashimov's death catalyzed an outpouring of public anger. On July 14, tens of thousands poured into the streets of Baku and Sumgait, demanding war and declaring their readiness to fight. Pandemic restrictions briefly collapsed under the weight of public emotion. The country appeared to reach a political and psychological breaking point. The unrest peaked in the early hours of July 15, when demonstrators forced their way into the parliament building. Windows were smashed, police vehicles overturned, and chants of "Karabakh" echoed through the capital alongside calls for retribution. Rumors that Hashimov's battlefield coordinates had been leaked intensified suspicions of internal betrayal, further eroding trust in the state's institutions.

Aliyev's government responded with a dual strategy. The president publicly acknowledged the depth of popular anger and promised decisive action, while simultaneously moving to suppress dissent at home. Opposition figures were blamed for the unrest and labeled a "fifth column," and dozens of activists and journalists were detained. The message was clear: public fury would be redirected outward, while political control would be reinforced domestically. Nevertheless, the signal from the streets remained unmistakable, the demand was no longer patience, but action.

Turkey moved swiftly to reinforce its support. Within weeks, large-scale joint military exercises brought Turkish drones and combat aircraft into Azerbaijani airspace, signaling that Baku would not face any future confrontation alone. In retrospect, July 2020 marked a decisive turning point. The logic of deterrence gave way to active preparation, and preparation, in turn, to a determination to resolve the conflict by force.

Domestic Shifts in Armenia: The Rise of Pashinyan

As Azerbaijan grew more assertive, Armenia entered a period of mounting political strain. For nearly two decades, power in Yerevan had been concentrated in the hands of the so-called Karabakh clan, a ruling network that framed corruption, economic stagnation, and international isolation as unavoidable costs of security. Within this system, compromise in negotiations or even the open discussion of Karabakh's status was politically impermissible. Any suggestion of concession was recast as disloyalty, and dissent was treated as a threat to the state itself.

That era ended abruptly in 2018. Public frustration over corruption and Serzh Sargsyan's attempt to extend his rule ignited mass demonstrations across Armenia. Led by journalist-turned-politician Nikol Pashinyan, the protests, later called the Velvet Revolution, forced Sargsyan's resignation within weeks. Pashinyan's rise from opposition figure to prime minister promised reform, accountability, and a break from the Karabakh clan's monopoly on power.

From Baku's perspective, Armenia's new leadership offered no indication of a shift toward compromise. Seeking to consolidate his nationalist credentials, Nikol Pashinyan anchored his legitimacy firmly to the Karabakh issue. At a rally in Stepanakert, he declared, "Karabakh is Armenia, period." The symbolism deepened in 2019 when he visited Shusha and participated in public celebrations alongside veterans of the first war. To Azerbaijani leaders, these gestures marked the effective end of diplomacy.

Pashinyan's stance also deepened divisions within Armenian society. Veterans of the former Karabakh elite regarded him as an outsider and distrusted his populist style, while his supporters embraced his defiance as evidence of strength and national resolve. By binding his political authority so closely to the Karabakh issue, however, Pashinyan effectively eliminated any remaining room for compromise.

In Baku, President Ilham Aliyev framed Armenia's new leadership as reckless, arguing that rhetorical maximalism had supplanted negotiation. If Yerevan insisted that Karabakh was irrevocably Armenian, Aliyev maintained, the dispute would be resolved by force rather than diplomacy. Speaking at the Valdai Conference (Russia), he openly mocked Pashinyan's declaration, responding, "Karabakh is Azerbaijan, exclamation mark." The Velvet Revolution, rather than easing tensions, had replaced one governing elite with another, leaving the conflict more rigid and less negotiable than before.

The Final Drift Toward War

By 2020, the initial momentum of the Velvet Revolution in Yerevan had dissipated. Pashinyan's government, once celebrated as a rupture with the postwar order, increasingly reproduced the same assumptions that had shaped Armenia's approach to Karabakh since 1994. Official rhetoric hardened, portraying Karabakh as inseparable from Armenia and elevating past victories, particularly in Shusha. Policy itself showed little evolution, remaining anchored in confidence drawn from earlier military success and the belief that the ceasefire was permanent. These assumptions extended beyond the state and permeated society. In interviews and public discourse, many Armenians expressed the conviction that renewed fighting would be brief and end decisively in Armenia's favor, with some even asserting that Azerbaijani cities could be taken with ease. The prevailing belief was that Azerbaijan lacked both the capacity and the resolve to overturn the status quo.

In Baku, Ilham Aliyev had spent nearly two decades preparing for the opposite outcome. Fluent in the language of international diplomacy, he invested heavily in lobbying efforts in Washington and Brussels, framing Azerbaijan's position through international law and linking it to Europe's dependence on Caspian energy. At home, his rhetoric grew steadily firmer, emphasizing patience but warning that it was not unlimited. Abroad, Azerbaijan was presented as a restrained actor denied justice through diplomacy, while domestically, the message was one of readiness and inevitability.

The clashes of July 2020 exposed how fragile the balance had become. The death of General Polad Hashimov and the mass protests that followed aligned public sentiment with the long-standing direction of state policy. The pandemic sharpened the contrast between the two societies. Armenia grappled with mounting internal pressures and political strain, while Azerbaijan projected order, discipline, and readiness. By late summer, the framework of "no war, no peace" had effectively collapsed. Negotiations had lost credibility, compromise had vanished from political discourse, and positions on both sides had hardened. Armenia increasingly relied on historical claims and the memory of past victories. Azerbaijan placed its confidence in international law, diplomacy, and the capabilities built through years of military modernization. Neither side showed any willingness to yield. The forty-four days of war that followed in the autumn were therefore not an abrupt rupture. They were the outcome of prolonged drift, shaped by political choices, intensified by regional and global pressures, and ultimately triggered by Baku's conclusion that the moment for decisive action had arrived.

The 44-Day War

By the autumn of 2020, Azerbaijan had spent more than a decade preparing for a war it no longer intended to postpone. Between 2010 and 2020, Baku invested an estimated US$24–42 billion in its armed forces, producing not incremental improvement but transformation. Soviet-era armor and artillery were now integrated with Israeli loitering munitions, Turkish Bayraktar TB2 drones, layered air-defense systems, and cyber and information warfare capabilities. Training shifted toward mobility and precision, with special forces prepared for complex operations in fortified and mountainous terrain. Turkish officers were embedded as advisers, and joint exercises in the summer of 2020 demonstrated that the alliance had moved beyond symbolism. The force that emerged bore little resemblance to the army that had collapsed in the 1990s. It was organized, equipped, and trained for a rapid, decisive campaign.

Across the frontline, Armenia prepared differently. Funding from Yerevan and diaspora donations was used to fortify the Bagramyan and Ohanyan lines, deep defensive belts of trenches, bunkers, and artillery positions dug into commanding mountain slopes. These defenses, impressive in scale, reflected an assumption: that any future war would resemble the First Karabakh War: slow, attritional, and decided on the high ground. Over time, that confidence encouraged complacency and, in certain circles, a degree of overconfidence. In the final days before hostilities, Armenian officials continued to express confidence in the deterrent value of static defenses, underestimating the extent to which the character of warfare had shifted.

The border clashes near Tovuz in July 2020 provided a clear indication of what was to come. These confrontations showcased Azerbaijan's evolving military tactics, particularly the use of drones for real-time surveillance and strikes. This marked the onset of a new type of warfare that combined advanced technology with information warfare. Armenia should have recognized this as a glimpse into the future, but the conflict was dismissed as just another fleeting skirmish. In Azerbaijan, civilian pickup trucks were quietly repurposed for military use, and logistical movements across the country increased. These actions fueled speculation about an impending war. However, after decades of ceasefire, few believed that large-scale fighting would actually resume.

The global context added another layer to the unfolding crisis. The COVID-19 pandemic had closed borders, disrupted diplomatic routines, and absorbed the attention of major powers. Armenia faced severe public-health pressures and political strain, while Azerbaijan, though also affected, emphasized internal order and continuity. With international actors preoccupied by domestic emergencies, Baku assessed the likelihood of rapid external intervention as limited. In early September, Operation *Iron Fist* entered its final preparatory phase. When fighting began later that month, the strategic conditions were already in place: Azerbaijan had completed years of military preparation, Armenia misjudged both the timing and scale of the challenge, and the international system was distracted by a global health crisis.

Week One

At dawn on September 27, 2020, the relative calm along the Nagorno-Karabakh front collapsed. From Talish in the north to Martuni in the southeast, Azerbaijani artillery struck villages, defensive positions, and rear support areas along the roughly 200-kilometer Line of Contact. Armenian units, many caught before fully manning their trench lines, scrambled for cover under an opening barrage that combined rockets, heavy artillery, and unmanned strikes. The pattern and timing of the fire indicated a coordinated operation prepared in advance rather than a spontaneous escalation.

From the outset, Azerbaijan prioritized the suppression of Armenian air defenses. Radar sites and surface-to-air missile systems were activated across the front, precisely as Baku intended. Dozens of obsolete Soviet-era An-2 biplanes, cheaply acquired and converted into remotely piloted decoys, were deliberately sent into Armenian airspace. As Armenian crews engaged these slow-moving targets, their positions were exposed. Turkish-made Bayraktar TB2 drones and Israeli Harop loitering munitions, already on station, tracked the emissions and struck in quick succession. By the end of the first day, much of the Armenian frontline air-defense network had been disabled, opening the airspace to persistent drone operations that would define the campaign.

By the afternoon, Azerbaijani forces reported capturing several villages along the southern front. In the north, troops advanced into the Murovdag mountain range and secured Murov Peak, a commanding position overlooking the Vardenis–Agdare highway. Control of the heights placed this critical supply route under direct fire, threatening Armenia's ability to move reinforcements, fuel, and ammunition from its territory into central Karabakh.

The opening day exposed a stark contrast in military approaches. Armenian defenses were organized around trenches, bunkers, and fortified mountain positions shaped by assumptions of attritional warfare. Azerbaijan's offensive emphasized speed, deception, and technology. Drones rendered the battlefield visible in real time, artillery struck as soon as radar systems activated, and special forces exploited gaps created by air and electronic suppression.

Alongside the fighting, a struggle over narrative unfolded. Armenia accused Azerbaijan of striking Stepanakert and other civilian areas. Azerbaijan countered that Armenian artillery had shelled frontline villages, including Gapanly, Alkhanli, and Jojug Marjanli. By mid-morning, Baku announced that it had launched a counteroffensive "to suppress Armenian fire and protect civilians." Yerevan rejected this claim, calling the operation a declaration of war. Both states imposed martial law and initiated mobilization.

Before noon, President Ilham Aliyev addressed the nation, condemning Armenia for what he described as renewed aggression, praising the army's early successes, and reaffirming Azerbaijan's position: "We are fighting on our own land. Karabakh is Azerbaijan." In Yerevan, Prime Minister Nikol Pashinyan urged calm while insisting that Armenia was acting in self-defense. Turkey responded quickly. President Recep Tayyip Erdogan contacted Aliyev and publicly declared Ankara's full support for Azerbaijan. International reactions followed familiar lines. The OSCE Minsk Group co-chairs called for restraint, while Western capitals urged an immediate cease-fire. These appeals carried little weight. In both Baku and Yerevan, leaders had already committed to escalation, and diplomacy lagged behind events on the ground.

By the morning of September 28, the operational pattern became clearer. Azerbaijani units pressed northward near Madagis while armored formations in the south probed Armenian positions along the Araz Valley. The objective was to fix Armenian forces in the mountains and central sectors while driving deeper into the lowlands, where defenses were thinner and maneuvering easier.

That day, Armenia declared martial law and general mobilization, framing the war as a struggle for the survival of Artsakh, the Armenian designation for Nagorno-Karabakh. In Baku, reservists were called up, and volunteers gathered at recruitment centers across the country. Ankara emerged as the most outspoken external supporter. President Erdogan reiterated that Azerbaijan had been compelled to act after decades of failed negotiations. By evening, both sides issued competing claims. Azerbaijan reported further advances and the destruction of Armenian units near Madagis. Armenia alleged that a Turkish F-16 had shot down an Armenian Su-25, a claim denied by both Ankara and Baku. Overhead, drones continued to map, strike, and disrupt, further degrading Armenian air defenses.

In the days that followed, Azerbaijan's main effort shifted decisively south. Advances along the Araz River targeted lightly manned villages and rear-area defenses, opening a corridor that threatened Armenian logistics, command routes, and withdrawal paths linking southern Karabakh to its interior.

On September 30, European Council President Charles Michel spoke with Ilham Aliyev, urging a return to negotiations. Aliyev responded that Azerbaijan was acting in accordance with international law to restore its territorial integrity. At the same time, Azerbaijani media broadcast extensive drone footage of strikes and advances, reinforcing the government's assertion that battlefield momentum had shifted decisively in its favor.

Early October brought both tactical and symbolic developments. On October 3, Azerbaijani forces captured Madagis, and Aliyev announced the restoration of its historical name, Sugovushan. That evening, he announced the capture of additional villages across the Tartar, Jabrail, and Fuzuli districts, presenting each announcement as part of a broader effort to reclaim sovereignty.

Armenia responded by expanding the conflict beyond the immediate battlefield. On October 4, missiles struck Ganja, Azerbaijan's second-largest city, killing civilians and bringing the war deep into the country's interior. Further strikes targeted areas near Mingachevir, including infrastructure linked to the country's largest hydroelectric facility, though severe damage was avoided. Baku characterized the attacks as deliberate efforts to terrorize civilians and internationalize the conflict. Images of destroyed apartment buildings and rescue operations became central to Azerbaijan's diplomatic messaging.

That same day, Aliyev announced the capture of Jabrail, a district that had been abandoned since the 1990s but is strategically important as a gateway into southern Karabakh. In a nationally broadcast address, he framed the advance as irreversible, declaring that Azerbaijan had entered a decisive phase of the war.

By the end of the first week, Azerbaijan had seized both the battlefield initiative and the broader regional momentum. Armenian defenses were under sustained pressure, air-defense systems had been degraded, and the rear areas were growing increasingly vulnerable to precision strikes. The conflict unfolded simultaneously in two domains: physical combat and information warfare. Azerbaijani media circulated extensive drone footage showing destroyed armor and targeted strikes, reinforcing claims of operational superiority. Armenian and Karabakh outlets, by contrast, emphasized civilian suffering and appealed to their well-organized diaspora to shape Western political and media narratives. From the outset, the war demonstrated that control over perception would be contested as fiercely as control over territory.

Week Two: The Battle Shifts South

By the second week of the war, fighting was no longer confined to ridgelines and fortified trenches in Nagorno-Karabakh. The conflict had expanded into a campaign of maneuver in the south, long-range missile strikes against urban centers, and a diplomatic struggle unfolding in parallel with combat operations.

On October 5, Azerbaijani rockets struck Stepanakert with renewed intensity, while Armenian forces targeted the Azerbaijani towns of Beylagan, Barda, and Tartar. Civilian casualties mounted on both sides. Azerbaijani authorities reported ninety-three civilian deaths from Armenian shelling. In Karabakh, Armenian defensive positions around Hadrut showed visible strain as Azerbaijani commanders pressed their advantage.

By October 6, nearly half of Nagorno-Karabakh's civilian population, approximately 40,000 people, had fled. Prime Minister Nikol Pashinyan publicly blamed Turkey's support for Baku as a catalyst for the war, but diplomatic rhetoric had little effect on battlefield dynamics. Azerbaijani drones and artillery continued to shape operations through precision strikes, forcing Armenian units to withdraw toward higher ground. That same day, Moscow delivered a decisive clarification: Kremlin spokesman Dmitry Peskov confirmed that Russia's CSTO defense obligations did not apply to Nagorno-Karabakh, which was internationally recognized as part of Azerbaijan. The message was clear: Yerevan would not receive any military assistance based on a treaty.

The implications became clear on October 9, when Azerbaijani forces announced the capture of Hadrut and eight surrounding villages. Satellite imagery released by Baku reinforced the political significance of the advance. Hadrut was the first town with a predominantly Armenian population to fall during the war. Militarily, its capture disrupted access to the M-12 Highway, a critical supply route. Politically, it dealt a severe blow to Armenian morale.

On October 10, Armenian forces attempted a counterattack near the village of Tug on Hadrut's outskirts. The effort was poorly coordinated and quickly repelled, underscoring Armenia's diminishing capacity for maneuver operations. The Azerbaijani Ministry of Defense reported the destruction of multiple artillery systems and missile launchers, along with significant personnel losses. That evening, after ten hours of negotiations in Moscow, Russia announced a humanitarian ceasefire. Fighting resumed almost immediately, with both sides accusing the other of violating the truce.

Missile strikes soon complemented artillery fire. On October 11, Armenia launched its third attack on Ganja. A Soviet-era Scud missile struck a residential neighborhood, killing seven civilians. Images of destroyed apartment buildings circulated widely in Azerbaijani media, reinforcing Baku's claim that Armenian forces were deliberately targeting civilians. Azerbaijan responded with further air and drone strikes on Stepanakert, which had already endured sustained bombardment.

Meanwhile, Azerbaijan's campaign of deep strikes continued to degrade Armenian military capacity. Drones systematically targeted air defenses, artillery units, and armored vehicles, weakening Karabakh's ability to organize counterattacks. Supply routes grew increasingly vulnerable, and reinforcements struggled to reach forward positions. By sustaining pressure in the north while concentrating its main effort in the south, Azerbaijan forced Armenian forces into a largely reactive posture.

On the diplomatic front, President Ilham Aliyev maintained a constant presence in international media. In interviews with outlets ranging from Al Jazeera and Euronews to CNN-Turk and Sky News, he framed Azerbaijan's actions as an effort to restore territorial integrity under international law. In the information sphere, however, Baku faced persistent challenges. Armenian advocacy networks in Europe and the United States remained more established and effective in shaping Western public opinion. By the end of the second week, however, momentum on the battlefield had shifted decisively in Azerbaijan's favor.

Week Three: Escalation and Ceasefire Illusions

By the third week of fighting, control of the air had become increasingly one-sided. On October 12, the Artsakh Defense Army announced the downing of another Azerbaijani An-2 aircraft along the eastern sector. In practice, these obsolete biplanes had been deliberately repurposed as remotely piloted decoys. Their role was not combat but provocation: to trigger Armenian air-defense fire and reveal radar positions. By mid-October, Armenia's s once-layered air-defense system had been forced into a largely reactive posture, relying primarily on shoulder-fired Igla-S missiles that proved ineffective against sustained unmanned aerial operations.

The information war intensified alongside the fighting. In Yerevan, officials denied the loss of Hadrut, insisting that Azerbaijani special units had merely probed the outskirts. Local media echoed claims that the town remained under Armenian control. On the ground, however, Azerbaijani forces were consolidating their positions, securing access routes, and cutting remaining supply lines.

On October 14, Azerbaijan announced the capture of Bulutan, Malikjanli, Kamartuk, Taka, and Taghaser in the Khojavend district. Two days later, President Ilham Aliyev reported further gains, including Arish in Fuzuli, Dosulu in Jabrail, and additional villages in Khojavend. In an interview with France 24, Aliyev rejected allegations that Syrian mercenaries were fighting on Azerbaijan's behalf, describing them as unfounded. He did, however, openly acknowledge the decisive role played by Turkish-made drones, operated by Azerbaijani crews, which he described as a significant factor shaping the battlefield.

By October 16, confidence in Baku had increased. Aliyev claimed that Armenian military losses exceeded two billion dollars in equipment. Yet the narrative of a controlled campaign was complicated by a disturbing video that circulated online showing the execution of two Armenian captives near Hadrut. Independent investigators later verified the footage. Its spread drew international attention and underscored the brutality unfolding beyond official statements.

On October 17, France attempted to broker another ceasefire. That same day, Aliyev announced extensive Armenian losses, including large numbers of tanks, artillery systems, and air-defense assets. Despite the cease-fire declaration, artillery fire and drone strikes continued along multiple sectors, and the truce collapsed within hours. On October 18. Azerbaijan Later that evening, Aliyev announced the capture of thirteen additional villages in the Jabrail district and confirmed that Azerbaijani forces had raised the national flag over the Khudaferin Bridge, a medieval crossing over the Araz River that has long marked the region's strategic and historical significance.

By the third week, the war had settled into a grim pattern of sustained offensives, brief ceasefires, and parallel battles in the physical and digital domains. Azerbaijani gains were broadcast nightly through official statements and social media, framed as the restoration of long-denied justice. Armenian authorities responded with denials, diplomatic appeals, and the mobilization of diaspora networks, which resonated in Western capitals. On the battlefield, however, momentum increasingly favored Azerbaijan. The southern front gathered strength, setting the conditions for a breakthrough that would carry the conflict into its decisive phase.

Voices Beyond the Battlefield

As artillery rumbled across Karabakh, a parallel front opened thousands of miles away in legislatures, newsrooms, and media platforms across the West. The Armenian diaspora, long established and politically organized, mobilized rapidly and in coordination. Nowhere was this more visible than in Southern California, home to the largest Armenian population outside Armenia. In Los Angeles, mass demonstrations filled the streets, demanding that U.S. officials condemn Azerbaijan and Turkey and intervene diplomatically.

This pressure quickly translated into political action. California State Senator Anthony Portantino, whose district includes a dense Armenian-American constituency, publicly condemned Azerbaijan's campaign and urged federal accountability. State Senator Bob Archuleta and Assemblymember Adrin Nazarian joined press conferences and rallies, framing the war in moral and historical terms. At the federal level, Representative Adam Schiff, working with Representative Jackie Speier, introduced a House resolution condemning Azerbaijani and Turkish actions and calling for a ceasefire, while Representative Brad Sherman supported legislative efforts to restrict U.S. defense assistance to Azerbaijan. Local officials, including Los

Angeles City Council leaders, echoed these positions, reinforcing the perception of broad political alignment with Armenian claims.

Celebrity advocacy amplified the message further. Kim Kardashian West, whose social media following numbered in the hundreds of millions, called for recognition of Artsakh and humanitarian aid to Armenia. Singer Cher issued similar appeals. Together, elected officials, activists, and public figures helped shape Western media narratives, ensuring that Armenian perspectives dominated coverage in the United States during the war's early weeks.

The Azerbaijani diaspora, smaller and less embedded in Western political life, could not match this level of influence. Communities in Germany, the United States, and Turkey organized rallies, petitions, and online campaigns, but their reach remained limited. Their messaging emphasized international law, framing the War as an effort to restore sovereignty recognized by the United Nations rather than an expansionist campaign. In Baku, the state sought to offset this imbalance. President Ilham Aliyev maintained a steady presence in international media, granting frequent interviews in which he reiterated that Azerbaijan was conducting military operations on its own territory. Yet on the broader information battlefield, Azerbaijan struggled to penetrate narratives shaped over decades by Armenian diaspora activism.

***

Research conducted for my dissertation on the Azerbaijani community in the Upper Midwest of the United States illustrates how acutely this imbalance was felt at the grassroots level. The 44-Day War triggered an unprecedented surge of unity within a small and relatively young community. Fundraising efforts mobilized rapidly and, on a scale, previously unseen in the community, though they remained modest when compared to the institutionalized Armenian networks operating across the West. Armenian advocacy relied on narratives of survival and historical trauma. Azerbaijani organizers countered with images of destruction in Ganja and Barda, presenting the War as defensive and grounded in international law. Protests in U.S.

cities aimed not only to express solidarity with Azerbaijan but also to challenge media coverage widely perceived as one-sided.

The struggle extended into digital spaces. Telegram channels, Facebook groups, and messaging platforms became nightly arenas of engagement, as community members followed developments in real time, often at personal cost. Beneath expressions of pride and optimism ran a deeper current: accumulated frustration over decades of defeat, displacement, and marginalization. For many participants, the war was not solely about territory but about restoring dignity. The 44-Day War marked a psychological break, reinforcing the belief that Azerbaijan was no longer condemned to permanent loss.

This unity, however, also exposed fragility. When attention shifted from mobilization to fundraising, participants described a chaotic process marked by mistrust, weak coordination, and logistical barriers. Transferring aid to Azerbaijan required navigating multiple agencies, prolonged delays, and, in some cases, scrutiny from security services. Unlike the Armenian diaspora's institutionalized fundraising structures, Azerbaijani efforts relied on loosely organized, event-driven coordination rather than durable organizations. Even so, raising nearly two million dollars was unprecedented for the community and carried tangible meaning for those affected.

These experiences exposed structural weaknesses that had accumulated over the years. Despite strong individual commitment, the Azerbaijani community remained fragmented and dependent on a narrow circle of organizers. There was no central institution capable of coordinating sustained advocacy or maintaining momentum beyond moments of crisis. Many Azerbaijanis in the United States described their community as still formative, closer to a social network than a consolidated political presence. Compared to diasporas with established councils, lobbying arms, and professional fundraising mechanisms, Azerbaijani initiatives were vulnerable to exhaustion once urgency faded. These were not failures of intent but of institutional development. The War revealed limitations that could no longer be ignored. Without stronger organization, unified messaging, and durable leadership structures, the Azerbaijani diaspora's ability to shape narratives or influence policy remained constrained, even during moments of national emergency.

Diaspora mobilization during the war was not entirely spontaneous. It was also supported by the Azerbaijan State Committee on Work with

Diaspora, established in 2008 and, during the conflict, chaired by Fuad Muradov. The committee coordinated outreach between Baku and communities abroad, organizing information campaigns, cultural initiatives, and online advocacy. It provided guidance and verified materials to help volunteers counter misinformation and amplify humanitarian appeals. This state-supported model distinguished Azerbaijan's approach from Armenia's largely self-sustaining diaspora networks rooted in host-country institutions. In Azerbaijan's case, diaspora engagement functioned as an extension of state diplomacy rather than an independent political force.

During the 44-Day War, the Azerbaijani diaspora spoke with a degree of unity it had not previously achieved. Across continents and time zones, individuals acted with a shared purpose: to defend their country's image and assert its narrative in the international arena. For many, this marked the first moment when collective action replaced the long-standing sense of marginalization that followed the defeat of the 1990s.

Week Four: Toward the Lachin Corridor

The fourth week of the war opened with another ceasefire that collapsed almost immediately. Within hours of the truce's announcement, both sides accused each other of violations. Baku claimed that Armenian forces had fired rockets toward the Baku–Novorossiysk oil pipeline. Although the missiles were reportedly intercepted, the allegation carried profound implications. Any strike on energy infrastructure risked drawing the conflict into broader regional and European security concerns. Yerevan denied the accusation, dismissing it as an attempt to manufacture international sympathy. That same night, President Ilham Aliyev announced the capture of thirteen villages in the Jabrail district near the Iranian border, underscoring the continued momentum of Azerbaijan's southern advance.

By October 22, Azerbaijani forces had taken the town of Agbend, securing the final segment of the border with Iran. The gain was both strategic and symbolic. Agbend lies near the junction of Azerbaijan, Armenia, and Iran, and its capture further restricted Armenian logistical access to the south. On the same day, Armenian forces launched Russian-made tactical ballistic missiles deeper into Azerbaijani territory, striking near Gabala, well beyond the immediate combat zone. The contrast was increasingly apparent. Azerbaijan emphasized precision strikes supported by real-time surveillance, while Armenia relied more heavily on long-range missile fire that carried higher risks for civilian areas.

Media narratives mirrored this divergence. Turkish outlet TRT World aired interviews with Azerbaijani officials and analysts, including ADA University Vice Rector Fariz Ismailzade, who highlighted the army's discipline and the collapse of long-standing assumptions about Armenian military superiority. Azerbaijani commentators emphasized that the campaign was being conducted without foreign ground forces, relying instead on domestically operated systems supplied by Turkey and Israel. Meanwhile, drone footage circulated widely on social media, reinforcing the image of a methodical and technologically driven offensive.

Battlefield success, however, came at a cost. On October 23, Aliyev publicly announced the death of Colonel Shukur Hamidov, a National Hero of Azerbaijan, killed during fighting in the Gubadli district. His death underscored the risks even senior commanders face operating near the front. The advance nevertheless continued. On October 25, Azerbaijani authorities reported the capture of additional villages across Zangelan, Jabrail, and Gubadli, pushing closer to the Lachin corridor.

The regional consequences of the fighting were becoming increasingly visible. Iran, unsettled by clashes near its border and by heightened nationalist sentiment among its own Azerbaijani population, deployed armored units and Revolutionary Guard forces to areas near Julfa and Khodafarin. Tehran officially described the move as a border security measure, but it also reflected concerns over the increasing military alignment between Azerbaijan and Turkey along its northern border.

By late October, Azerbaijan controlled the entire southern border with Iran, had driven deep into Armenian defensive lines, and brought the Lachin corridor within artillery range. The campaign was entering a decisive phase.

Week Five: Toward Shusha

On October 26, a ceasefire brokered by the United States briefly raised expectations of de-escalation. Like in previous attempts, it collapsed within minutes. Armenian counterattacks near Lachin stalled Azerbaijani armored units short of their objective. Small-unit ambushes and concentrated artillery fire demonstrated that, despite Azerbaijan's operational momentum, Armenian defenses retained the capacity to impose significant losses.

Two days later, violence struck far from the front. On October 28, cluster munitions hit the center of Barda, killing more than twenty civilians and wounding over sixty. Images of the aftermath circulated rapidly, drawing international attention. Azerbaijani authorities condemned the strike as deliberate terror against civilians. Amnesty International later confirmed the use of cluster munitions, describing the attack as indiscriminate and unlawful.

By October 29, President Ilham Aliyev announced that Azerbaijani forces had advanced to within five kilometers of Shusha, the cultural and strategic center of Karabakh. The statement carried both military and psychological weight and was amplified across domestic and international media. That same day, Russian President Vladimir Putin remarked that "everyone has their own truth," a formulation that reflected Moscow's continued reluctance to intervene decisively. Aliyev also spoke with Turkish President Recep Tayyip Erdogan, reaffirming political coordination. On the battlefield, Turkish and Israeli systems had already reshaped the fight, and diplomatically, Ankara's support reinforced Azerbaijan's confidence.

The final days of October merged into November amid intensifying combat. On October 31 and November 1, Azerbaijani artillery targeted Shusha directly, while Armenian Prime Minister Nikol Pashinyan appealed publicly to Moscow for urgent assistance. By November 2, Armenian officials acknowledged that nearly 90,000 civilians, more than half of Karabakh's prewar population, had fled the region. In Azerbaijan, nightly announcements of newly captured settlements reinforced a growing belief that the campaign was approaching its decisive phase.

On November 4, Azerbaijani forces seized Dashalti, a small village situated below Shusha's cliffs. Dashalti controlled the primary approach to the city and overlooked sections of the Lachin Corridor. With this advance, the war narrowed to a single focal point. Control of Shusha would determine not only the outcome of the campaign but the political settlement that followed.

Phones, Songs, and Shadows

The First Karabakh War of the 1990s unfolded in an age of grainy footage, censored reports, and delayed announcements. News traveled slowly, filtered through state television, newspapers, and diaspora newsletters. The Second Karabakh War was different. In 2020, the conflict lived online, unfolding in real time. The front lines were no longer only trenches and ridgelines but also Telegram channels, smartphones, and helmet-mounted cameras.

Telegram, with fewer content restrictions than platforms such as Facebook or Twitter, became the war's raw feed. Videos often appeared there hours or days before official statements. In many cases, the Ministry of Defense confirmed victories only after shaky clips had already circulated: drone strikes, firefights in villages, soldiers resting in the mud, exchanging jokes between bursts of gunfire. These fragments cut through formal messaging. They showed soldiers sleeping on bare ground, rifles propped against rocks, humming familiar melodies. The strains of *Karabakh Shikastasi,* a traditional mugham music associated with the region, drifted through valleys, carrying echoes of Uzeyir Hajibeyov, Bulbul, and Karabakh's musical heritage. Even under fire, the region's soundscape endured. In one widely shared video, young men described villages they had fled as children, imagining a return to the streets and homes of their parents after decades of exile. Such moments, unpolished and intimate, carried a credibility no press release could replicate.

The same technology also exposed the war's darkest edges. Alongside laughter and songs, images of cruelty appeared. Videos surfaced showing Armenian prisoners forced to chant "Karabakh is Azerbaijan," their voices strained by fear and humiliation. Even more disturbing was footage from Hadrut, later examined by Human Rights Watch, that appeared to show the execution of two Armenian captives. Elsewhere, Armenian soldiers used phones taken from fallen Azerbaijani troops to call grieving families. One widely circulated video captured an Armenian voice mocking an Azerbaijani mother on the phone, taunting her with crude remarks about her dead son. Pro-Armenian Russian vloggers shared graphic footage of burned Azerbaijani soldiers trapped in an ambushed vehicle. Grief that once unfolded in private became a public spectacle, replayed across screens and comment threads faster than any official account could respond.

The humiliation of prisoners reveals the emotional scars of a conflict that has never been psychologically resolved. Deep-rooted grievances, intergenerational trauma, and the narratives of victimhood heightened the desire to degrade the enemy once power changed hands. Understanding these dynamics clarifies how such acts took place, but it does not justify them. According to the laws of war, humiliating and abusing prisoners are crimes, regardless of the motives or history behind them.

Not all recordings told the same story. In interviews released from Baku, captured Armenian soldiers described being trapped and wounded in a basement for days before their capture. They spoke of fear, exhaustion, and surprise when Azerbaijani troops spared their lives, provided food, and treated them humanely. Some noted that religious sites and personal belongings were left intact. These accounts did not negate the brutality of the war, but they revealed its moral complexity. Violence and restraint, vengeance and mercy, coexisted on the same battlefield.

As the conflict intensified, Azerbaijan's Ministry of Defense issued warnings to its own troops. Smartphones, officials cautioned, were liabilities. They could reveal positions, expose movements, or damage the country's international image, but the flow of footage proved impossible to contain. Fueled by momentum, emotion, and a sense that the war was personal, soldiers continued to record and share. The story of the war no longer belonged solely to states or historians. It was being told by anyone with a camera and a signal, from mountain trenches to living rooms across the world.

This marked the fundamental difference between the two wars. In the 1990s, memory slowly emerged from veterans' testimony and official archives. In 2020, it was etched instantly into pixels, unedited and irreversible. The drone footage provided clear images of destroyed armored vehicles and shattered fortifications. Smartphones revealed something else entirely:

exhaustion, hope, cruelty, and pain, captured in real time and impossible to erase.

Battle for Shusha

Shusha's strategic position made it central to the 2020 campaign. Overlooking Stepanakert and controlling the main mountain routes into the Karabakh interior, the city offered commanding high ground and logistical leverage. For Azerbaijan, it also carried profound historical weight, having been lost in 1992. Its recapture would represent not only a military turning point but a reversal of the war's most consequential defeat. By late October 2020, Azerbaijani commanders understood that time was running short. Russia, France, and the United States had already brokered three ceasefires, each of which collapsed within hours. Diplomatic pressure was intensifying, and another imposed truce risked freezing the front lines with Shusha still beyond reach. The southern axis was largely secured. What remained was a decisive move before external mediation hardened the battlefield. Shusha was both the objective and the risk.

The plan broke with conventional doctrine. Instead of advancing armor along the heavily defended Lachin road, Azerbaijani commanders chose an approach on foot. Nearly 400 Special Forces commandos departed the Hadrut area in late October, organized into small detachments tasked with converging on Shusha from the south, east, and west. For five days, they moved through forests, ravines, and steep ridgelines, slipping past Armenian positions under the cover of terrain and weather. Each soldier carried his rifle, ammunition, mortars or rocket launchers, and only minimal supplies.

Logistics became its own ordeal. Engineers carved a narrow, single-file track through the mountains so trucks could inch forward if reinforcement became necessary. Soldiers marched night after night under loads heavier than their own bodies. Packs were stripped to essentials. Ammunition, ropes, and weapons replaced food. Many survived on little more than a few candy bars carried in their pockets. One sergeant later recalled hauling 60 kilograms (approximately 130 pounds) through fog so dense that men tied ropes around each other's wrists to avoid losing contact. Rain fell almost constantly. Uniforms stayed soaked, and sleep came in brief intervals of less than an hour before the climb resumed. The same fog and rain that grounded drones also concealed the Special Forces' movements, turning the mountains into a shield.

Armenian intelligence dismissed the possibility of such an approach. The prevailing assumption was that any serious assault would rely on armored forces advancing along the Lachin corridor. The infiltration was therefore dismissed as a diversion. While Armenian commanders waited for columns that never arrived, Azerbaijani units were already closing in. Operational secrecy was rigidly enforced. Even among the troops, few knew the actual objective. Units were told they were moving to secure the Lachin road or to seize Dashalti. The name Shusha was never spoken. Only senior commanders understood the whole plan, and even they received orders incrementally. For most of the men advancing through the mountains, the mission was simple: reach the next point and keep moving.

Dashalti

Dashalti, the village guarding the southern approach to Shusha, had been the site of one of the most devastating episodes of the First Karabakh War. In 1992, an Azerbaijani detachment was ambushed there and suffered catastrophic losses. The name became etched in national memory as a symbol of defeat and unresolved reckoning. Nearly three decades later,

Azerbaijani Army units, reinforced by Special Forces brigades, returned to the same valley with a clear objective: to secure Dashalti as a foothold for the final advance on Shusha. Control of the village meant more than territorial gain. It would keep supply routes open, expose Armenian logistics, and dismantle defensive positions shielding the fortress above.

By late October, fighting had closed to within five kilometers of Shusha. Armenian forces held the high ground and directed artillery fire into the valleys below. At dawn on November 1, a column of 31 trucks carrying roughly 200 Azerbaijani soldiers under the command of Colonel Tehran Mansimov advanced into the forested gorge leading toward Dashalti. As the convoy entered the narrow passage, Armenian units opened fire from both flanks. The lead and rear vehicles were struck almost immediately, trapping the column inside what survivors later described as a killing zone.

Mortars and rockets followed, fired from positions near Lachin, Shushakend, and Stepanakert. The muddy, winding track offered no room to maneuver, making evacuation nearly impossible. Casualties mounted rapidly. Under constant fire, reconnaissance teams pushed forward to clear wreckage and pull the wounded to cover. Soldiers crawled through mud and smoke, dragging bodies aside and forcing damaged vehicles off the road by hand. Each attempt to reopen the route came at a high cost.

By November 3, Azerbaijani forces had reached the outskirts of Dashalti. The memory of 1992 loomed over the operation, but this assault followed a different logic. Units from several Special Forces brigades regrouped near Sygnakh and began ascending the ridgelines surrounding the village. Operational secrecy was strict. Only senior officers knew that the objective extended beyond Dashalti itself. For most soldiers, the mission was defined narrowly: seize the heights.

Before dawn on November 4, the assault began. Armenian defenders, entrenched along the ridges with machine guns and mortars, understood that losing Dashalti would expose Shusha itself. Fighting continued for hours in confined terrain swept by fire. Evacuation proved nearly impossible. Rain and fog grounded aerial reconnaissance but also concealed Azerbaijani movement, allowing assault groups to advance along covered routes. By nightfall, Azerbaijani troops had captured most of the key heights.

On November 5, a reconnaissance team entering Dashalti triggered mines and withdrew into the forest with its wounded. Expecting Azerbaijan to establish a command post in the village, Armenian artillery subjected Dashalti to heavy fire, including cluster munitions, Grad and Smerch rockets, and mortars. The village was leveled, but Azerbaijani units had already moved on.

Within hours, Armenian forces mounted counterattacks from Shusha, Stepanakert, and Lachin, committing nearly three thousand troops in an effort to overwhelm the smaller Azerbaijani detachments. Heavily outnumbered, the Special Forces held their positions for several hours before launching counter-maneuvers that broke through the encirclement. Exhausted, deprived of food and sleep, they pressed forward through rain and darkness. The knowledge that Shusha lay ahead sustained the advance.

Colonel Tehran Mansimov later described the road to Dashalti as a fight for every meter. The narrow gorge, steep slopes, and constant artillery fire turned each bend into a lethal choke point. Reconnaissance teams advanced under shelling, clearing wreckage by hand and extracting the wounded through smoke and mud. Small assault groups climbed the ridges to silence machine-gun positions while engineers widened the track to allow supplies to move forward. Combat often collapsed into close-range engagements, fought with grenades and rifles at arm's length. Losses were heavy, but the advance did not stop.

With the surrounding heights secured, Azerbaijani forces severed Armenian reinforcement routes, blocking the approaches from both Stepanakert and Lachin and isolating Shusha from immediate support. Through fog and smoke, the cliffs of the fortress city came into view. The battle was entering its decisive phase.

Shusha

In the early hours of November 5, Azerbaijani Special Forces began their ascent toward Shusha. The attack unfolded before dawn, under dense fog and intermittent rain. There were no armored columns and no tank convoys. Instead, small detachments, often fewer than a hundred men, advanced on foot, climbing cliffs and moving through gardens, stairwells, and narrow alleys. Some scaled the sheer eastern rock face, a thirty-meter ascent so steep that Armenian defenders had left it lightly guarded, assuming it was impassable. Other groups infiltrated from the south and west, using the fog to mask their movement.

Combat inside Shusha was close and unforgiving. Tanks maneuvered along narrow streets only to be struck at short range by handheld anti-armor weapons. Grenades detonated in stairwells. Fighting moved from room to room and house to house, often at distances measured in meters. A Russian correspondent on the scene later reported that control of individual streets changed hands several times within an hour.

The fog that concealed the assault also grounded aerial surveillance. For much of the first day, the battle unfolded face to face, without the drone dominance that had shaped earlier fighting. When the mist began to lift, Azerbaijani aerial reconnaissance returned. Reinforcements moving toward the city were detected and struck before they could reach the plateau. One Armenian commander reportedly requested artillery support, only to be told that ammunition stocks were exhausted. Isolated and undersupplied, the defenders were forced to fight without external support.

For three days, fighting raged across Shusha's terraces, courtyards, and steep streets. Armenian units repeatedly attempted to push reinforcements up from Stepanakert using armored vehicles, but each effort was halted on the exposed roads below the city. By November 7, Azerbaijani flags appeared at several commanding positions overlooking the town.

Among the advancing troops were soldiers whose families had been displaced from Karabakh in the 1990s, now standing in streets they had known only through memory and inherited story. These narratives of loss shaped identity and functioned as a powerful mobilizing force, reinforcing endurance, cohesion, and a willingness to accept risk in a campaign framed as the reversal of historical defeat. On November 8, after days of intense urban combat, Azerbaijani forces secured complete control of Shusha and raised the national flag over the city. With the fall of the fortress, the strategic balance of the war shifted decisively.

The Endgame

From the Armenian perspective, the battle for Shusha was framed as a final stand. On November 5, Armenia's Ministry of Defense announced that Azerbaijani assaults had been repelled, claiming that tanks and armored vehicles had been destroyed near the Lachin approach. Armenian media circulated footage of burning vehicles in forested areas, presented as evidence that access to the city remained blocked. Official statements insisted that Shusha was still under Armenian control.

Arayik Harutyunyan, the de facto leader of Nagorno-Karabakh, declared, "Whoever controls Shushi controls Artsakh," casting the fight as existential. Calls to reinforce the city followed, but they came too late. Azerbaijani units had already cut the primary routes linking Shusha to Stepanakert, depriving Armenian forces of effective reinforcement and resupply. Despite this, Russian war correspondent Semyon Pegov, whose reporting often reflected Armenian narratives, continued to suggest that the outcome remained uncertain. These assessments sustained the impression of resistance even as Azerbaijani forces consolidated their hold on the surrounding heights.

When President Ilham Aliyev announced Shusha's capture on November 8, Armenian officials maintained that fighting was still underway. On the ground, confusion was genuine. Isolated firefights persisted in pockets of the city, but organized Armenian control had already collapsed.

By then, Shusha's civilian population had long been evacuated. Panic instead gripped Stepanakert. Families fled in convoys stretching for kilometers, vehicles overloaded with mattresses, furniture, and household belongings. Headlights cut through fog and smoke as traffic crept through valleys still echoing with artillery fire. Images of the exodus flooded social media, capturing a population abandoning its homes with no certainty of return.

In Yerevan, Prime Minister Nikol Pashinyan confronted a rapidly deteriorating military reality. On November 9, after confirmation that Shusha had fallen and Stepanakert was close to encirclement, he announced Armenia's acceptance of a Russian-brokered ceasefire. The declaration shattered public confidence. Crowds stormed the National Assembly, vandalizing offices and demanding the resignations of officials.

In Baku, the reaction was the opposite. In a televised address, Aliyev hailed Shusha's liberation as the symbolic core of Azerbaijan's victory and the reversal of a decades-long loss. Celebration, however, did not obscure the military consequences. Control of Shusha fundamentally altered the battlefield. From its plateau, Azerbaijani forces gained commanding observation over Stepanakert. Supply convoys were disrupted, reinforcements failed to arrive, and Armenian commanders acknowledged that no operational reserves remained.

That same day, Armenian forces attempted a final counterattack, pushing tanks and infantry up the mountain road toward Shusha. The effort collapsed quickly. Drones detected the movement, artillery and rockets struck the columns, and ambushes fragmented the advance. Burning vehicles lined the route as survivors scattered into the hills. Azerbaijani forces now controlled the approaches from the south and east, while artillery fire rendered the Lachin corridor unusable. Stepanakert stood on the verge of encirclement.

On November 9, the conflict nearly expanded beyond Karabakh. A Russian Mi-24 helicopter was shot down near Nakhichevan, killing two crew members. For several hours, the risk of Russian intervention loomed. Azerbaijan issued an immediate apology, describing the incident as a tragic error under combat conditions. Moscow accepted the explanation, but the episode underscored how narrowly the war avoided regional escalation.

The Ceasefire

On the night of November 9–10, under Russian mediation in Moscow, a ceasefire agreement was reached in the early hours of the morning. The deal was concluded by video conference. Prime Minister Nikol Pashinyan did not appear on screen. Instead, he addressed the public from Yerevan in a brief and somber Facebook broadcast, his face pale in the glow of the screen. He acknowledged that Armenia had no alternative but to accept the terms. For many Armenians, the moment felt like a public reckoning, witnessed live by millions.

The ceasefire froze the new lines of control. Large swaths of territory were returned to Azerbaijan, while Russia entrenched its position as the region's decisive external power. On the plateau above Stepanakert, the Azerbaijani flag once again flew over Shusha. Battlefield victory did not bring peace, but it imposed a new reality. As Azerbaijani forces consolidated their gains, Russian peacekeepers deployed to the remaining Armenian-held areas of Karabakh, their convoys winding through the mountain roads. With their arrival, Moscow assumed the dual role of guarantor and gatekeeper of the postwar order.

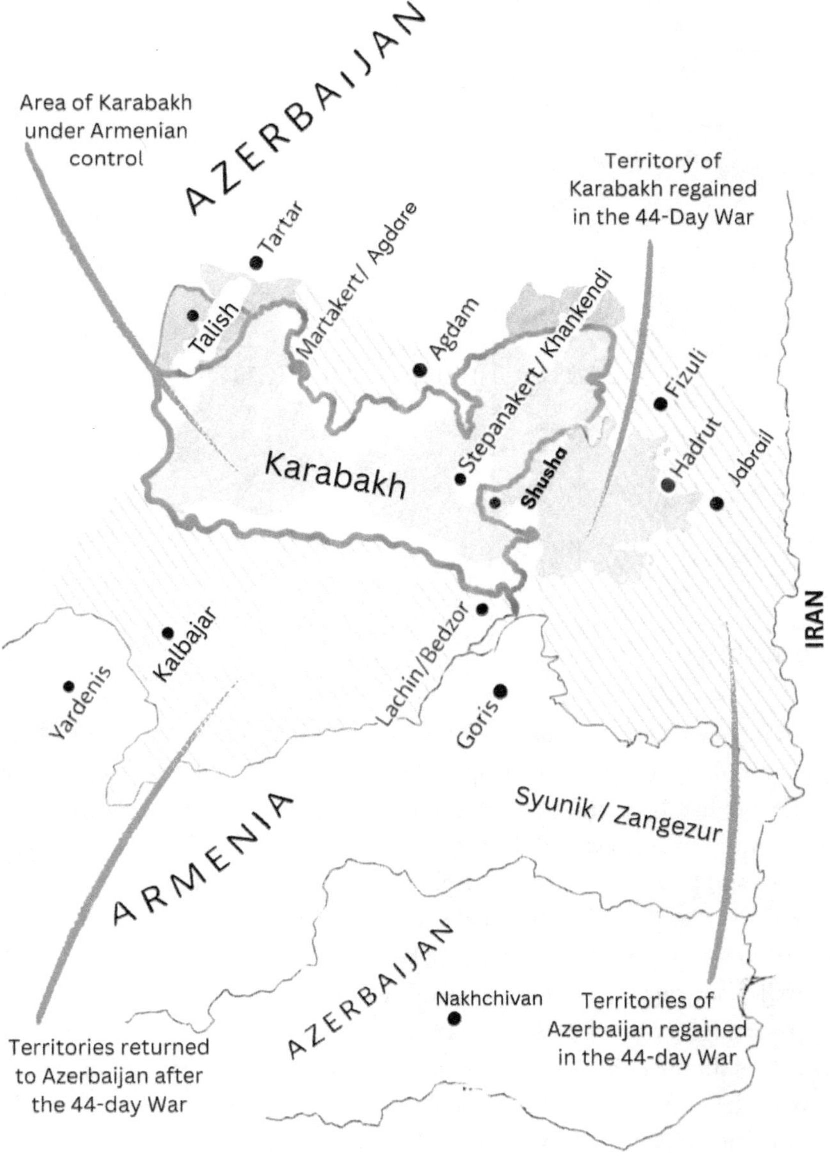

Territorial Control Following the First Karabakh War, 1994

Triumph and Vindication

November 10

The news of victory reached Baku before dawn on November 10, but the city did not sleep. As word spread that Shusha had been taken and that a ceasefire had been signed in Moscow, fireworks lit the sky above the Caspian, and car horns echoed through the streets. Crowds poured into public squares and boulevards, waving flags and chanting in celebration. President Ilham Aliyev appeared on national television before a large map of Azerbaijan, its newly regained districts highlighted in green. One by one, he named them: Jabrail, Fuzuli, Zangilan, Gubadli, Kalbadjar, Agdam, Lachin, Shusha. Each name was met with a roar from the streets outside. His address blended a military summary with a political declaration. "We have restored historical justice," he said, framing the outcome of the war as the reversal of the defeats of the 1990s. Shusha stood at the center of that narrative, presented not only as a battlefield success but as the symbolic culmination of the 44-Day War.

The celebration in Baku was deeply personal. For decades, hundreds of thousands of Azerbaijanis displaced from Karabakh and the surrounding districts had lived as refugees within their own country. Many had not survived to witness this moment; others had long abandoned the belief that return was possible. On the night the ceasefire was announced, that assumption shifted. What had existed only as a political promise or distant hope began to feel tangible. Families spoke not in slogans but in practical terms, about rebuilding homes, restoring cemeteries, and visiting villages and grave sites that had survived only in memory for years. Joy was intertwined with loss, and for 44 days, households across the country followed the war through constant updates, mourning the young soldiers killed at the front. When the flag was raised over Shusha, many felt that the sacrifice had found meaning, and chants of "Karabakh is Azerbaijan" filled the streets, turning a wartime slogan into a collective affirmation.

One detail stood out amid the celebrations. Alongside Azerbaijan's tricolor flew other flags: Turkey's red crescent, Pakistan's green and white, and Israel's blue and white marked with the Star of David. Each carried its own significance. Turkey's flag appeared almost as frequently as Azerbaijan's, reflecting Ankara's military, political, and symbolic support throughout the war. Pakistan's presence signaled longstanding diplomatic loyalty, rooted in its early recognition of Azerbaijan's independence and refusal to recognize Armenia. Israel's flag drew particular attention. Its drones and military technology had played a visible role on the battlefield, but the connection ran deeper. Azerbaijan has long been home to a Jewish community, and ties between Azerbaijani Jews and Israel remained strong. The flag honored both wartime cooperation and a broader relationship rooted in longstanding communal ties.

The banners symbolized a shift in alignment. The war for Karabakh, once treated as a localized post-Soviet conflict, had unfolded into a broader network of regional partnerships and external interests that reshaped the South Caucasus. Behind the celebrations stood the document that formalized the outcome. Signed in Moscow by Russia, Armenia, and Azerbaijan, the ten-point ceasefire agreement fixed new lines of control. Armenia committed to withdrawing from Agdam, Kalbadjar, and Lachin. Nearly two thousand Russian peacekeepers, supported by armored vehicles, were to deploy along the remaining Armenian-held areas of Karabakh and the Lachin corridor, with a mandate renewable after five years. The agreement promised the return of displaced persons under international supervision, the exchange of prisoners and remains, and the reopening of regional transport routes, including a transportation route linking mainland Azerbaijan to Nakhichevan under Russian border control. What had remained unresolved for decades was now bound to external guarantors and new enforcement mechanisms.

Even in victory, the contours of a new order were visible. Russian convoys moved into Karabakh under the guise of peacekeeping. Turkish officers are prepared to join a joint monitoring center near Aghdam. Azerbaijan had prevailed militarily, but the postwar landscape would be shaped by broader powers. That night, however, such considerations receded. Families who had carried displacement for nearly thirty years filled the streets, convinced that the road home had finally reopened.

The Aftermath in Yerevan

When Baku erupted in fireworks, Yerevan descended into shock. On the night of November 9–10, as President Ilham Aliyev announced victory, Prime Minister Nikol Pashinyan appeared briefly in a livestream from his office. He confirmed that Armenia had accepted a ceasefire agreement. Shusha was lost, significant territories had fallen out of Armenian control, and Russian forces would now secure what remained of Nagorno-Karabakh. Pashinyan described the decision as painful but unavoidable. To many Armenians, it sounded like capitulation.

The response was immediate. Within minutes, crowds gathered in Republic Square, the same space where Pashinyan had stood as the symbol of the 2018 Velvet Revolution. This time, the chants were accusatory. Protesters surged toward the National Assembly, breaking doors and windows, dragging Speaker Ararat Mirzoyan from the building, and beating him in the street. Government offices were ransacked, furniture overturned, and documents scattered. For many demonstrators, the loss of Karabakh was not only a military defeat but a defining blow to national identity.

In the days that followed, Yerevan remained tense and volatile. Police guarded government buildings, often ineffectively, as groups moved through ministries and corridors unchecked. The anger reflected the scale of the shock. For decades, Armenian society had internalized the belief that the army forged in the First Karabakh War was fundamentally superior. That belief collapsed in forty-four days.

Public rage quickly narrowed to Pashinyan, who was turned into a scapegoat for a collapse shaped by decades of military, political, and strategic miscalculations. Opposition parties accused him of incompetence and betrayal, demanding his resignation and the formation of a "national salvation" government. On November 11, protesters attacked media outlets perceived as sympathetic to the prime minister, vandalizing offices and harassing journalists. Western-linked organizations, including the Open Society Foundation, were also targeted. Political divisions that had once separated pro-Russian and pro-Western camps temporarily dissolved in a shared demand for Pashinyan's removal.

Pashinyan refused to step aside. He argued that the agreement had prevented further bloodshed and the complete collapse of Armenian defenses. His insistence only intensified the confrontation. By December, opposition forces coalesced into two major blocs: the pro-Russian Homeland Salvation Movement, centered around former prime minister Vazgen Manukyan, and the National Democratic Pole, a coalition of nationalist and pro-Western groups. Both called for an interim government. Even President Armen Sarkissian and senior figures in the Armenian Apostolic Church publicly urged Pashinyan to resign.

Through the winter, Yerevan became the scene of rolling protests. Vigils for fallen soldiers merged into political demonstrations. Freedom Square was filled repeatedly, sometimes with crowds numbering in the tens of thousands. In early December, opposition leaders issued ultimatums demanding Pashinyan's resignation. Demonstrations escalated into road blockades, sit-ins, and clashes with police. By late December, tents once again appeared in Republic Square, echoing the protests that had brought Pashinyan to power.

The unrest occasionally crossed into open calls for violence. In January 2021, opposition figure Vahan Badasyan publicly called for Pashinyan's physical elimination. He was arrested on charges of incitement. The crisis deepened in February when senior military officers issued a statement calling for the prime minister's resignation. Pashinyan denounced the move as an attempted coup. Competing rallies filled the capital as veterans, soldiers, and civilians mobilized on opposing sides. Armenia appeared briefly poised between political paralysis and institutional rupture.

When the immediate crisis subsided, Pashinyan announced early parliamentary elections for June 2021, effectively placing his leadership before the electorate. It was a gamble, as his approval ratings had collapsed, opposition forces were broad and ideologically fragmented, and the aftereffects of defeat remained acute. Despite the challenges he faced, he emerged victorious, gaining a renewed mandate. For many voters, the choice reflected less confidence than resignation. The former ruling elite, discredited by corruption and inertia, offered little alternative vision.

The damage, however, ran deeper. Across the Armenian diaspora, long central to advocacy and cultural identity abroad, reactions ranged from grief to fury. Vigils and protests spread from Los Angeles to Paris. Some blamed Azerbaijan and Turkey, others condemned Russia for failing to intervene, and many accused Pashinyan of betrayal. The sense of military invulnerability that had once unified diaspora discourse fractured into mutual recrimination.

Following the ceasefire, Armenia experienced political instability and underwent a profound national reckoning. Nearly four thousand soldiers were confirmed dead, with many more listed as missing. Families searched morgues and hospitals, waiting for identification. Funerals became daily events in towns and villages across the country. Mourning unfolded alongside political struggle, with no clear boundary between grief and blame.

For Armenians, the loss of Shusha carried particular weight. Although historically a predominantly Azerbaijani city, Shusha occupied a central place in Armenian cultural and political narratives through its association with Karabakh's Meliks and its symbolic elevation above Stepanakert. Many believed that without Shusha, the long-term viability of Armenian control in Karabakh was untenable, regardless of ceasefire lines or diplomatic assurances.

While Baku and Yerevan were overwhelmed by emotion, one by victory, the other by defeat, Stepanakert fell into silence. There were no demonstrations and no celebrations, only a heavy stillness in a city confronting an unresolved future suspended between survival and displacement.

Silence in Stepanakert

For weeks, the city had endured the relentless sounds of sirens and explosions. Now, with the guns silenced, the prevailing noises were the low thrum of helicopters and the rumble of tracked vehicles rolling over cracked asphalt. At dawn on November 10, columns appeared through the fog: Russian peacekeepers in green uniforms, convoy lights cutting across the city's outskirts. Armored personnel carriers rolled past abandoned and damaged military equipment and cratered intersections, turned through the central square, and continued toward checkpoints not yet established and boundaries not yet fixed. Their mission began the moment the ceasefire took effect.

The force, led by Lieutenant General Rustam Muradov and built around Russia's 15th Separate Motor Rifle Brigade, numbered 1,960 troops supported by armored vehicles and supply convoys that stretched through Karabakh's narrow valleys. A headquarters was established near Stepanakert, while observation posts were set up along the line of contact and in the Lachin corridor. Soldiers unrolled concertina wire, assembled prefabricated shelters, and mounted metal signs bearing a single word, written in Russian, that altered the city as decisively as artillery had weeks earlier: peacekeepers.

Their first tasks were practical and grim. The International Committee of the Red Cross coordinated the recovery and exchange of bodies from the hills around Shusha and nearby villages. Bulldozers cleared access routes to ravines where search teams worked methodically. Within days, demining crews began moving through fields and roadsides that appeared calm but concealed unexploded ordnance and decades of accumulated risk.

Peacekeepers

Russia was not alone in enforcing the new order. On November 11, Moscow and Ankara agreed to establish a joint monitoring center near the village of Marzili in Aghdam. The center became operational on January 30, 2021, staffed by sixty officers, evenly divided between Russia and Turkey. From a control room lined with wall-sized screens, they tracked ceasefire violations through drone feeds and surveillance data. Turkish sappers also arrived to assist Azerbaijani engineers with mine clearance and to train additional teams. In a war shaped by aerial observation, the peace that followed was monitored from above.

On the ground, maintaining calm proved less abstract. Russian patrols moved continuously along the Lachin corridor, five kilometers wide in the agreement, but far narrower where cliffs and switchbacks reduced traffic to a single lane. Convoys followed a set pattern: an armored vehicle in front, a medical truck, and a utility vehicle stacked with spare tires. Peacekeepers waved civilian cars through, halted others, and coordinated the passage of buses carrying returnees. By late November, approximately 25,000 displaced Armenians had returned to the region. By mid-December, Stepanakert's mayor estimated that 18,000 residents had come back to the city.

The single-page ceasefire agreement, which took effect at midnight on November 10, halted hostilities and outlined several key provisions. It mandated the phased transfer of districts, authorized a five-year deployment of Russian peacekeeping forces, subject to renewal. Additionally, it placed the Lachin corridor under Russian control, permitted the return of refugees under UN supervision, ordered the exchange of prisoners and remains, and reopened regional transport routes. This includes a future transportation road linking Azerbaijan to Nakhichevan, which will be overseen by Russian border guards. On the ground, each clause translates into delays, inspections, disputes, and stalled traffic. Diplomatic language became routine instructions: stop here, present documents, and wait for clearance.

Stepanakert adapted quickly to the procedures, but certainty returned slowly. Russian patrols circled the outskirts each evening, their lights visible from apartment windows. Their presence offered reassurance, but it also underscored a new reality: security now depended on external forces. In daily conversation, the term "corridor" entered routine use. Residents asked practical questions that reflected deeper uncertainty about safety and permanence: when buses to Goris would resume regular schedules, which roads were safe after dark, and how long the peacekeepers would remain.

Life in Stepanakert resumed in measured steps. Schools reopened, power lines were repaired, shops restocked, and neighborhoods refilled unevenly as families assessed whether return was temporary or permanent. The war's end produced three distinct realities: celebration in Baku, political rupture in Yerevan, and guarded silence in Stepanakert. Borders were fixed on paper, but authority and legitimacy remained unsettled. As the conflict hardened into a postwar order, it shifted from open warfare to international management, drawing in external actors whose presence would shape the region's uncertain future.

International Reaction

The ceasefire took effect at 1:00 a.m. Moscow time, but its consequences extended far beyond the Caucasus. Governments moved quickly to interpret the agreement through their own strategic lenses, greeting it as relief, reckoning, or opportunity. For the first time in decades, the Karabakh question was no longer suspended in diplomatic ambiguity. The map had changed, and international responses followed that reality rather than abstract formulas.

The OSCE Minsk Group, long tasked with managing the conflict, reiterated familiar language. Statements called for civilian protection, restraint, and a return to "substantive negotiations without preconditions." At the United Nations, Secretary-General Antonio Guterres and the Security Council urged an immediate halt to hostilities and the resumption of diplomacy. Brussels echoed similar appeals while avoiding direct confrontation with Ankara. NATO's position was deliberately cautious, emphasizing its partnerships with both Armenia and Azerbaijan and encouraging Turkey to support de-escalation. The words were well-worn, but events had already overtaken the process.

Russia emerged as the central broker. Moscow drafted the ceasefire terms, deployed peacekeepers, and framed the outcome as final under international law. Nagorno-Karabakh, Russian officials made clear, remained internationally recognized as part of Azerbaijan. Russia would manage the aftermath, not reverse the battlefield outcome. Turkey, for its part, claimed strategic vindication. Having backed Azerbaijan throughout the war and dismissed the Minsk framework as ineffective, Ankara now joined Moscow in a joint monitoring center near Aghdam. The postwar security order was shaped primarily by these two capitals.

The United States responded with calls for restraint and humanitarian access, constrained by an ongoing presidential election and political transition. Congress was divided along familiar lines. Some lawmakers urged sanctions against Azerbaijan and Turkey, while others emphasized Azerbaijan's territorial integrity and warned against external interference. In Europe, reactions became more overtly political. The French Senate adopted a nonbinding resolution urging recognition of Artsakh, a move welcomed in Yerevan and condemned in Baku. The French government quickly clarified that its official policy remained unchanged.

Elsewhere, positions hardened. Iran reaffirmed Azerbaijan's territorial integrity while warning against foreign fighters and instability along its borders. Pakistan voiced unequivocal support for Baku, citing United Nations resolutions. Ukraine echoed this stance, drawing parallels to its own territorial disputes. Israel expressed condolences to both sides while quietly maintaining its strategic partnership with Azerbaijan, prompting anger in Yerevan. Across much of the Turkic world, solidarity with Azerbaijan was widespread. In the Arab world, responses varied, shaped by regional rivalries and alignments.

Human rights organizations documented violations by both sides, including the use of cluster munitions and heavy weapons in populated areas, as well as abuse of prisoners and civilians. Each government highlighted the other's actions, ensuring that responsibility remained contested. Symbolic votes and declarations on Artsakh resurfaced in foreign legislatures, but they carried no legal force and provoked swift diplomatic backlash. By that point, political gestures lagged behind realities already determined on the battlefield.

Taken together, the international response revealed more than positions on Karabakh. It exposed Russia's dominance in regional security, Turkey's expanded influence, Europe's caution, Washington's distraction, and the enduring power of competing diasporas to shape narratives abroad. The ceasefire fixed the boundaries on the ground, and international assessments adjusted accordingly. What followed was an uneasy transition from war to aftermath. Prisoner exchanges, the recovery of the dead, and demining operations replaced active combat. Along the former front lines, a fragile postwar order began to emerge, shaped more by control and containment than by reconciliation. The 44-Day War had ended, but its consequences were only beginning to unfold.

Aftermath and Fragile Peace

Prisoners and the First Exchanges

In the weeks following the ceasefire of November 10, 2020, prisoner exchanges began under Russian mediation, led by Lieutenant General Rustam Muradov. Rather than taking place at border crossings, the transfers were conducted by military aircraft. On December 14 and 15, a Russian plane transported forty-four Armenian detainees to Yerevan and twelve Azerbaijani prisoners to Baku, according to statements from Muradov and both governments. Additional exchanges followed before the end of the year, including a swap on December 28 that returned four Armenians and two Azerbaijanis to their respective countries. The process unfolded before cameras and official statements, carefully presented as evidence of humanitarian cooperation. In practice, however, the atmosphere remained tense.

Baku maintained that many individuals captured in December were not prisoners of war but "saboteurs" who had entered Azerbaijani-controlled territory after the ceasefire. Criminal trials followed, with Armenian detainees charged under anti-terrorism statutes and some receiving lengthy prison sentences. Human Rights Watch and members of the European Parliament criticized the detentions as violations of the Geneva Conventions. In Armenia, families of the missing gathered outside government buildings, demanding information and action.

One of the most widely publicized cases was that of Maral Najaryan, a Lebanese Armenian who had resettled in Shusha shortly before the war's end. Her detention in late 2020 sparked protests across the Armenian diaspora, where her image appeared on posters in major Western cities. Armenian activists abroad have made her a symbol of civilian vulnerability and injustice. At the same time, Azerbaijani officials have maintained that her resettlement was illegal, asserting that she was detained during the collapse of Armenian control.

The exchanges revealed a central contradiction of the postwar moment: limited acts of cooperation were possible, yet they unfolded within a climate of deep mistrust and competing narratives. For families on both sides, the prisoner issue turned the ceasefire into a profoundly personal and unresolved ordeal.

The Kalbadjar–Lachin Withdrawal

As part of the ceasefire agreement, the districts of Kalbajar and Lachin were scheduled to return to Azerbaijani control. In the days that followed, the transfer unfolded amid hurried departures. Television footage showed long convoys of Armenian families, many from rural communities of modest means, moving through snowbound mountain passes, hauling stoves, furniture, and livestock. Villages emptied within days. Residents burned what they could not transport. Orchards were set ablaze, homes were reduced to ashes, and power lines were torn down. In some cases, families exhumed cemeteries and carried the remains of their dead across the border. Among those leaving, the destruction reflected an attempt to retain control in the final moments of displacement. In Azerbaijan, the same scenes were widely interpreted as deliberate vandalism.

In Charektar, in the Agdare district, smoke from burning houses was visible for miles, rolling through valleys as people loaded doors, mattresses, copper cookware, and household fixtures onto trucks. Images of families removing even toilets from their homes circulated widely online, becoming objects of ridicule in Azerbaijani media and popular culture. Beneath the mockery, however, lay a harsher reality: the desperation of people abandoning homes they believed they would never see again. Although the fighting had ended, competing narratives of ownership, loss, and belonging were only beginning to harden.

Azerbaijani officials condemned the destruction as "ecological terror," arguing that Armenian forces had chosen to devastate the land as they withdrew. In Yerevan, the same actions were framed as mourning rituals and acts of preservation, meant to prevent ancestral property from passing into enemy hands. At Armenia's request, Azerbaijan extended the evacuation deadline by ten days, a limited concession amid widespread upheaval. What Azerbaijan recovered was territory stripped of infrastructure and habitation, requiring reconstruction almost from the ground up.

Demining and Detainees

The immediate aftermath of the ceasefire was marked by friction rather than calm. Roadside encounters between Armenian and Azerbaijani soldiers, often involving disputes over flags, access routes, or detained personnel, were frequently filmed and circulated online. These incidents rarely escalated into violence, yet their symbolic weight was substantial. In Azerbaijan, such footage was presented as evidence that Armenian withdrawal had been reluctant and incomplete. In Armenia, the same images were interpreted as moments of humiliation, reinforcing narratives of defeat and loss.

Questions surrounding detainees quickly emerged as one of the most sensitive issues of the postwar transition. Russian forces assumed the role of intermediaries, overseeing ceasefire compliance and facilitating contacts related to prisoners and missing persons. Their presence highlighted a key characteristic of the new order, which relied on external supervision for stability. For the first time since the early 1990s, Russian troops were once again stationed on Azerbaijani territory. Although the war had been decided on the battlefield, the immediate aftermath, particularly concerning the fate of detainees, unfolded under Moscow's oversight.

While peacekeepers reduced the risk of renewed fighting, the landscape itself remained lethal. Nagorno-Karabakh and the surrounding districts ranked among the most heavily mined areas of the former Soviet Union.

Independent estimates suggested that hundreds of thousands—possibly more than a million—anti-personnel and anti-tank mines had been laid over decades, especially along the former line of contact in Aghdam, Fuzuli, and Jabrail, and years of entrenched warfare had turned farmland, roads, and forest paths into concealed hazard zones.

Casualties continued even after the ceasefire took effect. Russian peace-keepers were wounded when an armored vehicle struck an anti-tank mine. Azerbaijani soldiers engaged in clearance operations were killed or seriously injured. In June 2021, the issue gained national prominence when two Azer-baijani journalists died in Kalbadjar after their vehicle detonated a mine, in-tensifying public pressure for faster demining and greater international in-volvement. Unexploded ordnance soon became intertwined with unre-solved detainee cases. Armenia retained minefield records, while Azerbaijan continued to hold individuals captured after the ceasefire. These two issues increasingly shaped negotiations, linking humanitarian concerns with opera-tional and security imperatives.

A limited breakthrough came on June 12, 2021. With mediation from Georgia and support from the United States and the European Union, Azer-baijan released fifteen Armenian detainees in exchange for minefield maps covering approximately 97,000 explosives in the Aghdam district. Prime Minister Nikol Pashinyan confirmed the agreement, while President Ilham Aliyev described it as a humanitarian gesture. Azerbaijani officials, however, later reported that the materials were incomplete, estimating their accuracy at roughly one quarter.

Subsequent arrangements followed a similar pattern. Additional detain-ees were exchanged for maps related to Fuzuli and Zangilan, and further discussions continued in Brussels. Each agreement reduced immediate ten-sions but left broader grievances unresolved. Armenian families insisted that many captives remained in detention, while Azerbaijani authorities main-tained that the documentation provided did not meet operational require-ments.

By mid-2021, mine incidents had claimed the lives of seven Azerbaijani soldiers and twenty civilians. The state expanded its clearance capacity by acquiring specialized equipment, including British mine-flail vehicles, and by deploying Turkish technical teams. Even so, officials acknowledged that full clearance would require decades and substantial financial investment. Reconstruction and resettlement could proceed only where mines had been systematically removed.

In the postwar period, unexploded mines and unresolved detentions came to symbolize the conflict's aftermath. Each reflected a different dimension of its legacy: the persistent physical dangers embedded in the land and the human consequences entangled in legal and political disputes. Together, they demonstrated that the end of fighting did not bring closure. Instead, it marked a prolonged and contested transition from war to peace.

Road Through Eyvazli

The ceasefire also reshaped political dynamics in the south. Control of several short segments of the Goris–Kapan highway returned to Azerbaijan, giving Baku authority over a vital route connecting Armenia to Iran. For the first time in decades, Azerbaijani border guards and customs officers returned to this stretch of road, reasserting authority over territory internationally recognized as Azerbaijani.

Tensions surfaced quietly in the summer of 2021. On August 11, Iran's ambassador to Baku, Seyed Abbas Mousavi, was summoned to the Azerbaijani Ministry of Foreign Affairs and presented with a formal note of protest. Azerbaijani officials accused Iranian companies of transporting goods into Khankendi, an area under Russian peacekeeper control, without Baku's authorization, in violation of the November 10 ceasefire statement. The ministry stated that "our dissatisfaction with the constant entry of Iranian vehicles into the Karabakh region without the permission of official Baku was once again raised before the ambassador." According to Azerbaijani data, between August 11 and September 10, fifty-eight Iranian trucks entered the region, most carrying fuel and lubricants, and fifty-five later exited. Officials further alleged that some vehicles switched to Armenian license plates near the peacekeeper zone to obscure their origin, a claim Baku said was supported by photographic and surveillance evidence. Azerbaijan also announced the installation of video monitoring along the Lachin corridor to track traffic between Armenia and the Russian-controlled area.

On September 11, Azerbaijan's Interior Ministry confirmed the establishment of a checkpoint on the section of the Kapan–Goris highway passing through Azerbaijani territory. Iranian trucks were stopped near the village of Eyvazli and required to pay road taxes and customs duties under Azerbaijani law, typically ranging from $120 to $130 per trip for international transport permits. The State Customs Committee emphasized that these fees applied uniformly to all foreign vehicles entering or exiting Azerbaijan. Iranian drivers complained that they were charged twice, once traveling north and again on their return, and claimed that officers sometimes instructed them to turn off their phones to prevent filming.

The dispute quickly reverberated beyond Azerbaijan. In Yerevan, opposition deputy Vahe Hakobyan cautioned that developments near the Vorotan River, which borders Eyvazli, could have serious economic repercussions for Armenia, highlighting that over 40% of Armenia's trade with Iran relies on this corridor. Babken Tunyan, a lawmaker from the ruling Civil Contract party, described the inspections as "a serious problem" that introduced uncertainty and risk, while expressing hope for a negotiated resolution.

From Baku's viewpoint, the checkpoint was a clear assertion of sovereignty: the road was on Azerbaijani territory, and its use was governed by Azerbaijani law. In Tehran, however, the move was seen as part of a broader shift in regional power. Iranian officials feared erosion of secure access to Armenia, one of Iran's few remaining trade partners amid international sanctions. They accused Azerbaijan of facilitating Turkish and Israeli influence near Iran's northern border. In response, Iran conducted large-scale military exercises along the Araz River, deploying tanks, artillery, and drones in a visible demonstration of its military might.

President Ilham Aliyev questioned Tehran's timing, asking, "Why now? Why not when the Armenians occupied our lands?" Hardline Iranian media outlets escalated the rhetoric, accusing Azerbaijan of participating in an "anti-Iran alliance" with Turkey, Israel, and Western powers. Despite the sharp rhetoric, neither side allowed tensions to escalate into direct conflict. In the months that followed, relations gradually improved, settling into a more pragmatic and carefully managed framework. By the end of autumn, the Goris–Kapan highway had become a focal point where postwar sovereignty claims intersected with trade dependencies and regional rivalry. The ceasefire had altered not only control on the ground but also the strategic calculations of neighboring states, revealing how the new geography of Karabakh carried consequences well beyond the battlefield.

Between Ethnicity and Politics

While Azerbaijani police confronted Iranian truckers at the border, a quieter and revealing dynamic persisted inside Armenia itself. For decades, ethnic Azerbaijanis from Iran traveled freely to Yerevan, speaking Azerbaijani Turkish in markets, hotels, and public spaces. Archival videos from the 2000s and 2010s show them moving without harassment, treated as Iranian visitors rather than as ethnic Azerbaijanis or Turks, as they are often called in Iran. This contrast revealed an essential distinction. In Karabakh, speaking Azerbaijani marked one as an enemy. In Yerevan, the same language was tolerated because its speakers carried Iranian passports, not Azerbaijani ones. Their presence posed no challenge to territorial control and had no implication of return or political claim. They were perceived as Iranian first, Azerbaijani second.

The distinction underscores a central reality of the conflict: Karabakh was never solely about ethnicity. If it were, Iranian Azerbaijanis would have faced the same hostility as Azerbaijanis from Ganja or Baku. Instead, the conflict revolved around land, sovereignty, and political authority. Ethnic identity became combustible only when tied to territorial claims. This insight offers both caution and perspective. It suggests that coexistence is possible when questions of sovereignty are absent but also reveals how quickly tolerance erodes when territory is contested. For Azerbaijanis, the lesson was clear. Peace depends less on reconciling identities than on resolving borders. Where sovereignty remains unsettled, identity is easily politicized, and neighbors are transformed into adversaries.

Rebuilding Karabakh and the Victory Parade

If the acceptance of Iranian Azerbaijanis in Yerevan suggested that co-existence was possible beyond contested borders, the liberated districts of Karabakh revealed a harsher reality regarding the material legacy of war. Entire cities such as Aghdam and Fuzuli lay in ruins. Orchards had been cut down, mosques damaged or defaced, and cemeteries disturbed. Sovereignty had been restored both on paper and on the battlefield, but the human and cultural fabric of the land still had not returned.

President Ilham Aliyev cast reconstruction as the next stage of victory. The state's Great Return program promised large-scale resettlement through new roads, airports, and planned "smart villages." The Victory Road linking Fuzuli to Shusha opened within a year, followed by the construction of international airports in Fuzuli and Zangilan. The village of Aghali in Zangilan became the first pilot smart village, with newly built homes equipped with solar panels, digital infrastructure, and modern utilities.

Reconstruction progressed unevenly, constrained by the scale of destruction and the persistent danger of landmines. For displaced families, the hope of returning home lingered in a fragile balance between memories of the past and the harshness of their current reality. The gardens, courtyards, and houses they remembered could not be returned. Modern structures replaced the old, designed for safety, permanence, and daily life in the post-war era, signaling a new beginning. Beyond its practical aims, reconstruction became a political and symbolic project, transforming military gains into visible expressions of restored sovereignty.

That symbolism reached its height in Baku on December 10, 2020. The Victory Parade filled Azadliq Square with 3,000 soldiers, 150 armored vehicles, Bayraktar drones, and captured Armenian military equipment. A towering installation made from seized Armenian license plates bore the slogan "Karabakh is Azerbaijan," deliberately reversing imagery used after the First Karabakh War, when Armenian forces had displayed Azerbaijani plates as trophies. President Aliyev stood alongside Turkish President Recep Tayyip Erdogan, presenting the outcome as both a national triumph and a product of close alliance.

For Azerbaijanis, the parade affirmed that decades of loss and displacement had not been in vain. For the state, it marked the public celebration of sovereignty in the capital's central square. Internationally, it signaled a clear shift in the regional balance of power in the South Caucasus. Critics outside of Azerbaijan dismissed the event as triumphalist, while in Yerevan, it was criticized as humiliating. However, in Azerbaijan, the parade served as a moment of collective relief, encapsulating 30 years of dispossession into a single, powerful declaration that the war's outcome was definitive.

Politics After the 44-Day War

The victory parade in Baku affirmed Azerbaijan's restored military strength and underscored its success on the battlefield. Yet the ceasefire agreement of November 2020 did not resolve the conflict. Instead, confrontation shifted from trenches to negotiating tables. In the months and years that followed, President Ilham Aliyev and Prime Minister Nikol Pashinyan met repeatedly in Moscow, Sochi, and Brussels, sometimes under Russian mediation and at other times with European Union oversight. Each meeting was announced as a breakthrough, but none produced a durable political settlement. Beneath the handshakes and carefully scripted statements, the tensions that had driven the war remained unresolved.

Aliyev entered these talks with the confidence of a victor. His rhetoric was direct and uncompromising. "Karabakh is Azerbaijan" was no longer presented as a claim but as an established fact. His objective was not to argue legitimacy, but to secure implementation: reopening regional transport routes, formalizing borders, and pressing Armenia to explicitly recognize Azerbaijan's sovereignty. Negotiations, from Baku's perspective, were about consolidating gains already achieved on the battlefield.

Pashinyan, by contrast, negotiated from a position of weakness. His priority was political survival rather than leverage. In public statements, he oscillated between conciliatory language, including references to recognizing Azerbaijan's territorial integrity, and defensive appeals focused on the "rights and security" of Karabakh Armenians. These shifts reflected the bind he faced: restoring credibility abroad while managing a society still reeling from defeat.

Mistrust defined the process. Armenia accused Azerbaijan of unlawfully detaining soldiers captured after the ceasefire. Azerbaijan countered that Armenia was delaying border demarcation and allowing armed groups to operate under the cover of Russian peacekeepers. Brussels emphasized humanitarian measures and regional connectivity, while Moscow focused on preserving its peacekeeping mandate. Talks continued, but progress remained fragile, keeping leaders engaged even as publics on both sides grew increasingly skeptical.

This diplomatic stalemate unfolded alongside profound domestic upheaval in Armenia. After the war, Aliyev appeared triumphant, while Pashinyan stood on the brink of political collapse, confronting mass protests, mounting pressure, and the prospect of snap elections. In June 2021, his Civil Contract Party nevertheless secured a decisive electoral victory, surprising both domestic rivals and international observers. Despite the bitterness of defeat, many Armenians continued to place greater trust in Pashinyan than in the former ruling elites associated with corruption and patronage. The result exposed a political paradox: even in loss, Pashinyan retained democratic legitimacy.

That reelection reshaped Armenia's political narrative. Pashinyan spoke less about reversing the war's outcome and more about stabilizing the state. He introduced the phrase "an era of peaceful development," signaling a shift away from territorial ambition toward survival and long-term security. In practice, this meant exploring normalization with Turkey, expanding engagement with the European Union, and gradually acknowledging Azerbaijan's sovereignty over Karabakh. The transition was neither immediate nor uncontested, but by 2022 and 2023, Armenia's position had been fundamentally reframed. Karabakh was no longer the cornerstone of national identity; it had become a traumatic loss to be managed through diplomacy, humanitarian concerns, and international guarantees.

Aliyev capitalized on this contrast. Domestically, he reinforced his image as the leader who restored national dignity, expanded Azerbaijan's regional influence, and compelled Armenia to accept new realities. His position was strengthened by close strategic ties with Turkey and Israel, as well as by presenting Azerbaijan as a critical energy partner for Europe. The divergence was unmistakable. The divergence was unmistakable. Aliyev negotiated from the position of a victor, while Pashinyan confronted the limitations imposed by defeat. Azerbaijan entered the talks with clear military, political, and psychological leverage, reflecting the new strategic realities created by the war.

Cultural Revival of Karabakh

While diplomacy faltered, Azerbaijan pursued a different form of statecraft through culture. Victory was made visible, celebrated, and projected outward. Karabakh, once referred to as the "Black Garden," a phrase that had come to signify loss, grief, and the moral burden of a land transformed into a battlefield, was now being reimagined as the "Fertile Garden," reclaiming its original meaning. This new narrative emphasized renewal, presenting Karabakh as a space where life, culture, and state authority could once again take root.

In May 2021, the Khari Bulbul Music Festival returned to Shusha after nearly three decades. Azerbaijani folk ensembles, mugham singers, and dancers performed in the city's historic setting, marking the restoration of a long-lost cultural center. Broadcast nationwide, the festival conveyed a clear message: Karabakh was not only liberated but culturally revived. International recognition soon followed. Shusha was declared Azerbaijan's Cultural Capital and, in 2022, named the Cultural Capital of the Turkic World by TURKSOY. Delegations from Turkey, Qazakhstan, Uzbekistan, and Kyrgyzstan attended concerts, conferences, and exhibitions. For Baku, these gatherings reinforced cultural solidarity while also strengthening regional alliances.

The cultural revival extended to heritage preservation. Mosques in Aghdam and Zangilan were reconstructed, while churches were placed under state protection. Officials framed multiculturalism, long presented as a cornerstone of Azerbaijani identity, as central to Karabakh's future. Although critics abroad questioned these assurances, the government moved forward, announcing plans for museums, libraries, and academic forums in Shusha.

Concerts by internationally known performers, youth forums, and organized diaspora visits transformed cultural activity into political signaling. These events framed Karabakh as an integral part of Azerbaijan, emphasizing restoration, continuity, and state presence rather than contestation.

The Last Exodus

Shifting Global Context

When Russia launched its full-scale invasion of Ukraine in February 2022, global attention shifted decisively eastward. The South Caucasus, once a focal point of great-power maneuvering, slipped down the international priority list. The battles for Kyiv, Kherson, and Bakhmut eclipsed a conflict that had dominated diplomatic agendas only two years earlier. In both Baku and Yerevan, the repercussions of the war in Ukraine were immediate and consequential.

Moscow, which had cast itself as the principal guarantor of the November 2020 ceasefire, became increasingly absorbed by its own military campaign. Russian peacekeepers remained deployed in Karabakh, but their capacity to shape events or enforce arrangements weakened as attention and resources were redirected elsewhere. This shift did not remove external constraints on Azerbaijan, but it altered its balance, reducing the immediacy of Russian leverage. Armenia, for its part, deepened a reassessment already underway after the 44-day war, as Russia's ability and willingness to function as a security patron came into question.

By 2022, the image of Russian authority in Karabakh had visibly weakened. Only two years earlier, armored patrols along the Lachin Corridor and a constant presence in Stepanakert had projected control and reassurance.

Now, repeated drone incursions, gas disruptions, and mounting territorial pressure drew little visible response. To many Armenians, particularly those who had long viewed Moscow as the ultimate guarantor of security, the peacekeepers' silence felt less like neutrality and more like disengagement.

As Russia's role weakened, Europe moved to fill the diplomatic space. Brussels hosted a series of meetings between President Ilham Aliyev and Prime Minister Nikol Pashinyan, with European Council President Charles Michel acting as mediator, a role previously dominated by the Kremlin. The European Union advanced proposals focused on border recognition, regional connectivity, and diplomatic normalization. Notably, these frameworks contained no discussion of special status for Nagorno-Karabakh. This omission reflected a broader shift: internationally, the conflict was no longer framed as a question of self-determination but as one of Azerbaijani territorial sovereignty.

At the same time, Azerbaijan's strategic value increased. Although Aliyev had signed a new alliance declaration with Moscow shortly before the invasion of Ukraine, Baku quickly positioned itself as an essential energy partner for Europe. Gas exports from the Caspian Sea gained new importance as European states sought alternatives to Russian supply. The Ukraine war, which exposed Moscow's vulnerabilities, simultaneously enhanced Azerbaijan's relevance. Baku emerged as a geopolitical hinge, supplying energy to Europe, maintaining channels with Russia, and balancing relations with Iran.

Armenia moved along a more uncertain path. Pashinyan's government struggled to navigate between continued reliance on Russia for security and a growing effort to diversify diplomatic and political engagement with Western partners. This balancing approach satisfied neither side. Domestically, critics accused Yerevan of remaining tied to a weakening security patron. Externally, Western engagement offered political dialogue, monitoring missions, and economic cooperation, but stopped short of providing binding security guarantees. For Armenians living in Karabakh, the implications were sobering. Confidence that Yerevan could ensure its security weakened, while the post-2020 order increasingly appeared provisional rather than durable.

The Lachin Blockade

The ceasefire agreement granted Armenians in Karabakh safe passage through the Lachin Corridor, a narrow mountain road that, as in previous decades, served as their sole link to Armenia. For a time, that guarantee held, but in 2022, Baku rerouted the corridor, constructing a new highway that bypassed the town of Lachin and several nearby villages. The move followed Clause 6 of the November 2020 ceasefire agreement, which stipulated that within three years a new route would be built connecting Armenia to Karabakh, after which control of Lachin, and adjacent settlements would revert to Azerbaijan. By August 2022, the new 32-kilometer road was completed. Residents of Lachin, Sus, and Zabukh (Aghavno) were given roughly three weeks to evacuate. On August 26, Azerbaijani forces entered the area and raised the national flag.

Baku framed the handover as the implementation of the ceasefire and the restoration of sovereignty over internationally recognized territory. For Armenians remaining in Karabakh, however, the transfer marked a more immediate shift: everyday life would now unfold under expanding Azerbaijani administrative authority. That shift became unmistakable in December. Groups of Azerbaijani demonstrators appeared along the corridor, waving flags and identifying themselves as environmental activists protesting what they described as illegal mining in the region. They pitched tents at the road's narrowest point near Shusha, effectively transforming the corridor into a barrier. Cameras broadcast the scene worldwide: chanting protesters, banners, and Russian peacekeepers standing nearby without intervening.

Scrutiny quickly followed. Few participants had prior records of environmental activism, and reporting linked many to state-affiliated companies, ruling-party organizations, or student groups that offered stipends for participation. Protesters were transported by bus and housed in hotels in Shusha. President Ilham Aliyev praised them as "the face of Azerbaijani youth," while critics abroad described the action as weaponized environmentalism, civic language used to legitimize state pressure. Traffic slowed, then stopped altogether. What started as a protest transformed into clear political demands for customs checks, police oversight, and complete control of the corridor by Azerbaijan. In Baku, the movement was portrayed as spontaneous activism; in Stepanakert, it was widely perceived as a siege.

By mid-winter, the protest had hardened into a blockade. Movement along the Lachin Corridor nearly ceased. Trucks carrying food, fuel, and medicine were turned away, and Russian peacekeepers struggled to secure consistent access for humanitarian deliveries. Gas supplies from Armenia were repeatedly cut, triggering electricity outages that plunged towns into darkness. Shops emptied within days. A rationing system emerged, distributing limited amounts of flour, sugar, and oil that barely sustained households for a week. Fuel shortages paralyzed transport and agriculture, while schools and hospitals operated on shrinking reserves. Entire villages were left isolated. Even when convoys from the International Committee of the Red Cross were permitted to pass, the supplies delivered were insufficient for a population of roughly 120,000.

International concern mounted. European institutions passed resolutions condemning the blockade, and the International Court of Justice ordered Azerbaijan to restore unimpeded passage. Human rights organizations warned that deprivation was being used as a coercive tool. Russia, formally responsible for security under the ceasefire agreement, remained largely passive.

By April 2023, Azerbaijan installed a permanent checkpoint on the corridor, effectively ending the principle of free passage. By September, after nine months of isolation, Karabakh was exhausted, malnourished, and cut off from the outside world. The conditions that followed no longer suggested crisis management, but the closing phase of a strategy whose outcome was increasingly unavoidable.

The 23-Hour Operation

The November 2020 ceasefire did not signify true peace. Azerbaijani intelligence reports and drone footage showed that Armenian forces had not withdrawn as required by the agreement. Instead, new fortifications appeared across the mountainous terrain of Karabakh: trenches, dugouts, and bunkers extending for nearly 480 kilometers. Minefields spread across valleys and hillsides, supplied with ordnance traced to Armenian factories. Heavy equipment and air-defense systems that had been declared dismantled were quietly repositioned through the Lachin Corridor.

By mid-2022, Azerbaijani forces began conducting limited "retaliatory operations" following skirmishes and alleged provocations. Each incident reinforced Baku's assessment that the Karabakh Armenian military structure remained operational and well-organized. Azerbaijani officials pointed to evidence of more than 500 fortified positions and roughly 350 rebuilt artillery sites constructed after the 2020 war. Surveillance systems, weapons depots, and trench networks transformed the enclave into a heavily militarized zone. Russian peacekeepers, tasked with enforcing the ceasefire, proved increasingly ineffective. Their observation posts frequently coincided with Armenian troop rotations and munitions movements. However, when Azerbaijani forces executed targeted strikes, the same peacekeepers called for restraint.

The decisive moment came on September 19, 2023. That morning, a convoy traveling along the Fuzuli–Shusha Road struck landmines, killing two Azerbaijani civilians and four police officers. Azerbaijani officials described the incident as the culmination of sustained sabotage and infiltration. Within hours, the Ministry of Defense announced the launch of "local anti-terrorist measures" to disarm illegal armed formations and restore full sovereignty. At 13:10, Azerbaijani artillery and drones struck Armenian positions across Agdare, Askeran, Khojaly, and Martuni. Command posts, air-defense systems, and trench networks were targeted. At the same time, text messages and leaflets were distributed in populated areas, directing civilians toward designated humanitarian corridors. Although framed as a limited operation, the impact was swift and decisive. Azerbaijani special units advanced along multiple axes, seizing ninety fortified positions, destroying dozens of vehicles, and capturing settlements including Charektar, Drmbon, and Harav. Minefields slowed movement, but engineering units cleared routes, and by evening Stepanakert was plunged into darkness amid sustained fire.

On September 20, the offensive continued. Azerbaijani forces secured the Kashen mine, a key economic asset, as the separatist military structure collapsed. Samvel Shahramanyan, president of the self-declared Artsakh, called for negotiations, but Baku insisted on complete disarmament and the dissolution of the separatist administration. By 13:00, less than twenty-four hours after the operation began, Artsakh authorities agreed to a ceasefire mediated by Russian peacekeepers. The conditions amounted to unconditional surrender. Weapons were to be handed over under Russian supervision, armed units were to be disbanded, and preparations were to be made for reintegration into Azerbaijan. Lists of commanders and officials were also requested for legal proceedings.

That evening, President Ilham Aliyev addressed the nation, declaring, "Karabakh is Azerbaijan. The iron fist has shattered separatism forever." In Stepanakert, the announcement coincided with the formal termination of political structures. On September 28, Shahramanyan signed a decree dissolving the Republic of Artsakh, effective January 1, 2024. A separatist project that had endured for more than three decades reached its decisive end through a brief but consequential military operation, followed by rapid political dissolution. In Baku, the 23-hour campaign was framed as a counterterrorism and law-enforcement action. In Armenia and its diaspora, it was understood as the extinguishing of a long-held national aspiration. For the South Caucasus, this moment closed a long chapter of armed confrontation, while leaving the terms of peace unsettled.

Exodus from Karabakh

President Ilham Aliyev presented integration as the official framework for the postwar order: Armenians could remain in Karabakh as citizens of Azerbaijan or depart. In practice, this offer generated sharply divergent interpretations. Some international observers characterized the situation as involving coercive pressure rather than formal compulsion, noting that although no explicit orders to leave were issued, restrictions on movement, energy supplies, and access to goods severely constrained civilian life. Former International Criminal Court prosecutor Luis Moreno Ocampo described these conditions as constituting what he termed "genocide by attrition," pointing to prolonged isolation and repeated disruptions of essential services. Azerbaijani authorities rejected this characterization, insisting that residents were free to remain under Azerbaijani jurisdiction with full civil rights. Regardless of legal interpretations, the outcome was evident, and within weeks, the Armenian civilian population almost entirely departed, ending the continuous presence of Armenian life in Karabakh.

On September 24, the first convoy of 1,050 people crossed into Armenia. The following day, thousands gathered at fuel stations to receive the first free gasoline they had seen in ten months. That night, catastrophe struck. A fuel depot near Berkadzor exploded as families and vehicles crowded around it, killing at least 170 people and injuring more than 300. Subsequent investigations pointed to chaotic handling, unsafe storage, and extreme overcrowding born of desperation. Symbolically, it became the darkest moment of the exodus: death at the threshold of departure.

Between September 25 and 27, the road from Stepanakert to Kornidzor turned into a corridor of flight. What usually took two hours stretched into a thirty-hour ordeal. Families loaded their most valuable belongings into cars and buses; those without vehicles waited for transportation, while others slept in their cars during long delays. By the end of the week, virtually the entire Armenian population of Karabakh, more than 100,000 people, had left.

At the border, Azerbaijani journalists interviewed those departing. Their responses reflected a range of emotions: resignation among the elderly, exhaustion among working-age adults, and quiet uncertainty among young families. Some people spoke in Azerbaijani, reminiscing about past decades of friendship and coexistence, and wondering if such relations might ever be restored. Others emphasized that the crossing itself was orderly and that no physical force had been used. Yet the pauses, hesitations, and silences suggested fears that could not be openly articulated. After spending long hours on the road, feelings of nostalgia, doubt, and fatigue began to blend together.

Hours of footage from Kornidzor captured the atmosphere more vividly than official statements ever could. Volunteers worked with quiet efficiency, their faces drawn and movements deliberate. The departure unfolded as a gradual, intentional withdrawal, driven more by exhaustion than by panic. Those leaving carried a subdued awareness that the possibility of return had already faded.

In the days that followed, the self-proclaimed president of Artsakh, Samvel Shahramanyan, signed a decree dissolving the Republic of Nagorno-Karabakh effective January 1, 2024. It was more than a legal formality. It marked the end of a political project that had existed for over three decades. By October 1, Armenian officials confirmed that more than 100,000 Armenians, nearly the entire pre-war population, had left. When a United Nations mission visited shortly thereafter, only a few hundred civilians remained. The departure was sudden, comprehensive, and irreversible.

The population's flight did not halt the arrests of former officials, commanders, and prominent figures associated with the separatist authorities. Among the most visible was Ruben Vardanyan, a Russian-Armenian businessman and former state minister of the self-proclaimed republic, who was detained on September 27 while attempting to cross into Armenia with civilians. Other arrests followed. Former presidents Arkadi Ghukasyan, Bako Sahakyan, and Arayik Harutyunyan, together with senior military and parliamentary officials, were detained during the exodus and subsequently transferred into Azerbaijani custody. Prosecutors announced charges ranging from terrorism and financing illegal armed groups to war crimes dating back to the 1990s. Domestically, the trials were framed as long-delayed accountability for decades of occupation and violence.

Images of former Karabakh leaders escorted into custody carried a powerful symbolic charge for Armenians. Diaspora organizations denounced the proceedings as political prosecutions aimed at erasing the legacy of Artsakh's self-rule, while human rights groups raised concerns about due process and the prospects for fair hearings in Azerbaijani courts. The implications were clear. With the civilian population gone and the former political elite detained, Nagorno-Karabakh ceased to function as a separate political entity. The arrests signaled the formal termination of the separatist project itself. For Azerbaijan, this moment affirmed the restoration of sovereignty over territory that had long been beyond its control. For Armenians, it marked the end of effective political and military authority in Karabakh, even as historical claims and narratives of loss endured.

International reactions mirrored the divisions that had characterized the conflict throughout. Armenian officials described the events as ethnic cleansing, while diaspora organizations increasingly invoked the language of genocide. The European Parliament issued condemnations, and Freedom House linked the episode to broader patterns of democratic backsliding. The United States and the European Union, however, focused their response on humanitarian assistance, prioritizing refugee relief over political intervention. By late 2023, the two had together committed tens of millions of dollars in emergency aid for displaced Armenians from Karabakh, supporting food, shelter, medical care, and psychosocial services for approximately 120,000 refugees in Armenia. The scale of assistance acknowledged the human cost of the exodus, but it did not alter the political or territorial realities established on the ground. Other governments avoided legal classifications altogether, framing the situation as a humanitarian emergency rather than a matter of accountability.

Turkey welcomed the consolidation of Azerbaijani control, with President Recep Tayyip Erdogan publicly praising Ilham Aliyev in the days that followed. Russia, exposed by its inability to prevent the collapse of the post-2020 order and the erosion of its peacekeeping authority, confined its response to formal statements. With global attention fixed on Ukraine, Karabakh quickly receded from international headlines.

By the end of September 2023, the Armenian population had departed, the separatist leadership had been dismantled, and the three-decade project of self-rule had come to an end. Azerbaijan reasserted sovereignty over the territory, while Armenia absorbed the political and psychological consequences of defeat. The gradual withdrawal of Russian peacekeepers, along with the arrival of international delegations and renewed diplomatic engagement, marked the beginning of a new phase. This phase was defined by the persistent challenge of turning military victory into lasting peace.

Victory on Display

On November 8, 2023, Khankendi was no longer a contested capital. It served instead as the setting for Azerbaijan's most consequential public display since the end of the Karabakh conflict. That morning, under clear skies, President Ilham Aliyev arrived in the city as Supreme Commander-in-Chief to preside over a military parade marking Victory Day.

The choice of location was deliberate. Just three years earlier, Khankendi had functioned as the administrative center of the self-proclaimed Republic of Artsakh. Now, Azerbaijani troops marched through its streets in formal formation, led by Colonel General Kerim Valiyev, Chief of the General Staff, and overseen by Defense Minister Zakir Hasanov. Units that had taken part in both the 44-Day War of 2020 and the September 2023 operation passed in review before the official stands.

Captured military equipment occupied a central place in the procession. Tanks, artillery pieces, and armored vehicles, stripped of their original insignia, were displayed as trophies. One truck carried the same towering installation of license plates taken from seized Armenian military vehicles that had previously been shown in Baku, a stark visual statement of defeat and control. Aliyev declared that Azerbaijan had demonstrated its strength and resolve before the international community.

Beyond ceremony, the parade functioned as an assertion of political finality. Holding it in Khankendi signaled the consolidation of Azerbaijani sovereignty over the former administrative core of the separatist enclave. Armenian self-rule in Karabakh had ended, replaced by the Azerbaijani state's institutional presence. The city itself, largely emptied of its Armenian population, reflected the broader transformation underway as Karabakh entered a new post-conflict phase under Baku's authority.

Trials of the Separatist Leaders

The victory parade in Khankendi did not close the chapter of the Karabakh conflict. In the final days of September 2023, while ordinary civilians were permitted to pass through the Kornidzor checkpoint into Armenia, those who had governed or commanded the former separatist entity were subjected to a different process. Azerbaijani security services detained figures who had embodied the political and military leadership of the separatist project. Those detained during the September 2023 operation, now central defendants in the proceedings, included former "state minister" Ruben Vardanyan; former presidents Arkadi Ghukasyan, Bako Sahakyan, and Arayik Harutyunyan; former foreign minister David Babayan; parliamentary speaker Davit Ishkhanyan; former "defense minister" Levon Mnatsakanyan; and several senior military officials.

In Azerbaijan, these arrests were framed as long-delayed accountability. Prosecutors announced extensive charges ranging from terrorism and war crimes to crimes against peace and humanity, the establishment and financing of illegal armed formations, and violations of the laws and customs of war. Nearly 1,400 criminal cases were consolidated, covering alleged acts committed between 1987 and 2023. These included missile strikes on civilian centers such as Ganja and Barda, hostage-taking, forced displacement, and killings during the First Karabakh War. State media broadcast images of the detainees under escort. This presenting the proceedings as the legal culmination of decades of conflict and the restoration of full sovereignty.

The trials formally opened in January 2025 after more than a year of pretrial detention. Azerbaijani authorities justified the delay by citing the scale and complexity of the indictments, which they said comprised thousands of pages of testimony, forensic evidence, archival material, and seized documents. Vardanyan was tried separately on more than forty counts, while fifteen other defendants, including former presidents and ministers, were tried jointly before the Baku Military Court. Although hearings were officially declared open, access was limited mainly to state media, with independent observers and most foreign journalists excluded.

By late 2025, proceedings were ongoing. In its closing arguments, the prosecution framed the case within both domestic criminal law and international legal instruments. Prosecutors cited UN Security Council Resolutions 822, 853, 874, and 884, arguing that they confirmed Armenia's occupation of Azerbaijani territory and established the context for the crimes under review. Particular emphasis was placed on Additional Protocol I to the Geneva Conventions, which prohibits the transfer of an occupying power's civilian population into occupied territory. Evidence presented included Armenian-source records and online materials documenting settlement activity in districts such as Lachin.

Testimony during the hearings included notable admissions. Davit Ishkhanyan acknowledged that the strategic objective of the early-1990s campaign had been the annexation of Karabakh to Armenia. Arayik Harutyunyan admitted to ordering missile strikes during the 2020 war, including the bombardment of Ganja, a city located far from active combat zones. Azerbaijani prosecutors cited these statements as evidence of intent and command responsibility.

The Prosecutor General's Office sought life imprisonment for Ruben Vardanyan and several other defendants, including Arayik Harutiunian, Levon Mnatsakanian, Davit Babayan, Davit Ishkhanian, and Davit Manukyan, citing their alleged roles in planning and directing military operations, mass displacement, and acts characterized as systematic violence. For defendants above the age threshold specified under Azerbaijani law, including Arkadi Ghukasian and Bako Sahakian, prosecutors requested fixed-term sentences of up to twenty years. All sentences were to be calculated from the dates of detention in September–October 2023. In February 2026, a military court in Baku concluded the yearlong proceedings. Five defendants received life sentences, while Sahakian and Ghukasian were sentenced to twenty years' imprisonment. Additional defendants were given shorter terms. The convictions were based on charges including war crimes and other offenses connected to the decades-long conflict, all of which the defendants denied.

Ruben Vardanyan's case became one of the most closely watched proceedings. Prosecutors sought life imprisonment on charges that included war crimes, terrorism, and related offenses. In February 2026, however, the Baku Military Court sentenced him to twenty years in prison. During the final stage of the trial, Vardanyan declined to mount a conventional defense and delivered his closing remarks personally, reiterating his claim that the process was politically driven and did not meet the standards of a fair trial. His family and legal advocates appealed to Western governments, religious institutions, and human rights organizations, highlighting concerns about due process and transparency. Amnesty International, members of the European Parliament, and several advocacy groups echoed these concerns. Azerbaijani officials rejected the criticism, maintaining that the proceedings were conducted in accordance with domestic law and international norms and were necessary to address crimes linked to the conflict and to discourage future separatist movements.

Beyond their legal dimension, the proceedings carried substantial symbolic weight. For many in Azerbaijan, the appearance of former separatist leaders in a Baku courtroom represented closure and vindication, reinforcing the view that a political project which had displaced hundreds of thousands of Azerbaijanis in the 1990s had been defeated not only militarily but judicially. For Armenians, the trials deepened the sense of loss that followed territorial defeat and mass displacement, reinforcing perceptions of humiliation and the criminalization of leaders who had once claimed to act as protectors of their community.

International responses remained cautious. Western governments expressed concern over procedural safeguards but stopped short of formal condemnation. Armenian diaspora organizations denounced the trials as politically driven, framing them as collective punishment. In Baku, analysts argued that the proceedings served a broader purpose: to document the separatist period as a criminal enterprise and to establish a legal precedent intended to prevent its reemergence.

Diaspora Outcry and the "Ethnic Cleansing" Narrative

The near-total departure of Armenians from Karabakh in September 2023 immediately reverberated beyond the region, activating long-standing diaspora networks across Europe and North America. Within days, Armenian organizations mobilized demonstrations, petitions, and coordinated media campaigns that sought to define the meaning of the events as much as to protest them. From Los Angeles to Paris, public messaging framed Azerbaijan's operation as ethnic cleansing and called for international intervention to reverse or punish the outcome. Diaspora advocacy quickly entered formal political arenas. Members of the European Parliament adopted resolutions condemning Azerbaijan, while prominent human rights organizations warned of serious violations. These characterizations became central reference points in diaspora discourse, shaping how the episode was presented to Western publics and policymakers.

Governments, however, responded on a different register. Washington and Brussels avoided adopting legal classifications, emphasizing humanitarian relief and diplomatic restraint rather than accountability mechanisms. U.S. Agency for International Development Administrator Samantha Power announced assistance for displaced civilians, but neither the United States nor the European Union endorsed claims of genocide or ethnic cleansing. This gap between diaspora rhetoric and official policy underscored a familiar constraint: while diaspora activism could elevate visibility and moral urgency, it could not compel legal or strategic commitments that governments were unwilling to enforce.

Within Armenia itself, the consequences of the exodus were felt immediately. The influx of refugees strained housing, education, and social services, and public spaces were converted into temporary shelters. Uncertainty over legal status, employment, and property claims weighed heavily on displaced families. Many hesitated to formalize resettlement, fearing that integration would weaken claims to homes and land left behind. International assistance alleviated acute shortages, but it could not resolve the deeper tension between displacement as a humanitarian issue and loss as a political reality.

The diaspora response thus revealed both reach and limitation. Armenian advocacy succeeded in shaping narratives, mobilizing sympathy, and sustaining international attention in the short term. Yet it could not alter the territorial outcome or reverse the dissolution of Armenian political authority in Karabakh. The episode reinforced a recurring pattern in the conflict's history: global outrage and symbolic condemnation, coupled with practical restraint and acceptance of facts established on the ground. For Prime Minister Nikol Pashinyan's government, the challenge was not only logistical but political: managing a humanitarian crisis while continuing to argue that normalization with Azerbaijan remained the only viable path forward.

Diaspora's framing of the exodus as ethnic cleansing complicated this effort. For Armenian communities abroad, existential language reinforced mobilization and sustained a politics of grievance. Inside Armenia, however, priorities shifted toward more immediate concerns: securing assistance, stabilizing displaced families, and preventing renewed violence. A gap emerged between diaspora maximalism and Yerevan's cautious recalibration. Accusations of genocide hardened public opinion, reinforced existing hostility toward Azerbaijan, and strengthened domestic opposition to any peace initiative, further narrowing Pashinyan's already limited political space. Across the border, the same rhetoric resonated very differently. In Baku, officials and commentators pointed to the displacement of nearly 700,000 Azerbaijanis during the First Karabakh War in the early 1990s, many of whom spent decades in camps or temporary housing with limited international attention. Viewed through this lens, the 2023 Armenian departure was not interpreted as a singular injustice but as the reversal of an outcome produced by earlier expulsions. For Azerbaijan's leadership, the restoration of sovereignty over Karabakh was framed as historical redress rather than an act of ethnic targeting.

These parallel narratives reveal the central obstacle to reconciliation. Both societies carry unresolved traumas of forced migration, each convinced that its own suffering has been minimized or ignored. Diaspora discourse that emphasizes Armenian victimhood while overlooking earlier Azerbaijani displacement reinforces selective memory and mutual resentment. Without acknowledgment that both peoples endured displacement and that peace requires recognition of loss on all sides, the foundations of a durable settlement remain fragile.

Politics and Diplomacy After Karabakh

The fighting had ended, but debates over the region's future were only beginning. The contest shifted from the battlefield to the arena of diplomacy, where questions of sovereignty, recognition, and the future order of the South Caucasus moved to the foreground. From late 2023 onward, diplomacy became the primary terrain on which these issues were contested.

A tangible shift followed in 2024 with the gradual withdrawal of Russian peacekeepers. Once the most visible embodiment of the November 2020 ceasefire, their departure closed Moscow's operational role in Karabakh without formal rupture or confrontation. Convoys leaving Stepanakert marked the end of a security arrangement that had long been assumed to be open-ended. In Azerbaijan, the withdrawal was treated as procedural rather than consequential, consistent with Baku's position that external oversight was temporary and sovereignty indivisible. In Armenia, the moment carried different implications. The quiet exit of Russian forces confirmed that the security guarantees once taken for granted no longer functioned in practice, accelerating an overdue reassessment of Armenia's strategic posture.

Into this space stepped European and Western actors. Brussels hosted a series of talks throughout 2023 and 2024, while the European Union deployed monitoring missions along Armenia's border. France deepened military cooperation with Yerevan, and the United States signaled engagement through high-level visits, including those by USAID Administrator Samantha Power, emphasizing humanitarian and political support. Together, these moves reflected a broader shift: the South Caucasus was no longer an exclusive Russian sphere of influence.

Regional normalization efforts followed in parallel. In October 2023, at a summit in Granada, Prime Minister Nikol Pashinyan and Turkish President Recep Tayyip Erdogan shook hands publicly for the first time in years, signaling renewed dialogue. Subsequent talks advanced through envoys meeting at the long-closed Margara–Alican border crossing in July 2024, where steps toward reopening the frontier and easing visa regimes were discussed. In September 2024, on the sidelines of the UN General Assembly, Pashinyan promoted Armenia's "Crossroads of Peace" initiative, envisioning the country as a regional transit hub. Ankara, however, tied normalization firmly to progress between Yerevan and Baku, making clear that Turkish Armenian rapprochement depended on a comprehensive peace agreement with Azerbaijan.

Bilateral negotiations between Armenia and Azerbaijan advanced alongside these efforts. In April 2024, Armenia returned four border villages, an act presented as part of the restoration of internationally recognized boundaries. By October, at the BRICS summit in Kazan, Aliyev and Pashinyan announced that roughly ninety percent of a draft peace treaty had been finalized. The remaining issues were substantive: constitutional references in Armenia that Azerbaijan interpreted as implicit territorial claims, and unresolved questions surrounding border demarcation.

Diplomatic momentum accelerated in 2025. The leaders met in Tirana in May, Abu Dhabi in July, and Washington in August, where they initialed a seventeen-point "Agreement on the Establishment of Peace and Interstate Relations." The document formally declared the end of hostilities, acknowledged the conclusion of the OSCE Minsk Group's role, and introduced an American-backed initiative, the "Trump Route for International Peace and Prosperity," aimed at linking Azerbaijan with Nakhichevan through Armenian territory. In September, at the Shanghai Cooperation Organization summit, both leaders reaffirmed their commitments to the peace process. For the first time in three decades, Armenia and Azerbaijan publicly stated that peace had been achieved.

Yet the signatures did not resolve all tensions. Azerbaijan continued to press Armenia to amend its constitution to remove references linked to Karabakh. Pashinyan acknowledged the issue but deferred action until a national referendum planned for 2026, cautioning against changes made under external pressure. Proposed transport routes raised sovereignty concerns within Armenia, while both Iran and Russia viewed the expanding American role in the region with suspicion.

By the end of 2025, the South Caucasus stood at a transitional moment. The war had ended, and while peace remained a process rather than a settled condition, dialogue had gained structure and direction. For Baku, diplomacy became a means of consolidating battlefield gains. For Yerevan, it offered a path toward reform and diversified partnerships. Handshakes were cautious, but they reflected a growing recognition on both sides that lasting stability would depend on sustained engagement.

As leaders continued their summits and declarations, a quieter transformation unfolded on the ground. With Karabakh entering a phase of reconstruction, Azerbaijan turned to the long-delayed return of its internally displaced population. Families displaced for decades began moving into newly built housing complexes, supported by state programs and private investment. Roads, schools, and utilities were restored, and towns that had been long abandoned began to re-emerge. Diplomacy set the framework, but resettlement became the next defining test, translating political outcomes into lived realities.

After the War: Reconstruction and Realignment

Return of Azerbaijani IDPs and Resettlement

In the 1990s, nearly 700,000 Azerbaijanis were displaced from Karabakh and the surrounding districts. Many spent years in tent camps, public buildings, and improvised shelters. Only after the oil boom of the early 2000s did the state acquire the resources to dismantle most tent settlements and replace them with apartment blocks and planned communities. By 2011, more than 100,000 internally displaced persons had been rehoused, yet hundreds of thousands continued to live in temporary accommodations and relied on state assistance. For decades, the promise of return echoed through political speeches, school curricula, and family conversations, but it remained unrealized until the military victory of 2020.

The Great Return initiative, launched that same year, provided a framework for the organized and voluntary resettlement of displaced citizens to the liberated territories. After the 2023 operation brought all of Karabakh under Azerbaijani control, the long-deferred pledge began to take concrete shape. The government prioritized housing, infrastructure, and public services as the foundation of resettlement. Reconstruction moved beyond pilot projects toward comprehensive rebuilding, restoring utilities, transport links, and municipal administration. For Baku, the program was both a humanitarian obligation and a strategy to translate military success into durable stability and sovereign control.

The Great Return State Program for 2022–2026 channeled billions of dollars from the State Oil Fund and the national budget into reconstruction. Turkish firms, many of which had supported Azerbaijan during the war, received major contracts to rebuild roads, railways, and urban centers. Flagship projects such as the "smart village" of Aghali in Zangilan showcased the government's vision, incorporating renewable energy, digital infrastructure, and environmentally efficient housing. Alongside these innovations, more conventional institutions returned: schools, hospitals, public transport, and ASAN service centers, designed to anchor everyday life.

By early 2025, roughly 10,000 people had been resettled in towns including Fuzuli, Lachin, Jabrail, Shusha, Khojaly, Zangilan, and Tartar. Fuzuli led with more than 3,000 returnees, while Lachin and Shusha became visible symbols of renewal. Rail and bus connections were restored, reintegrating the region into national networks. Even so, the scale of the task remained immense. Of approximately 658,000 registered internally displaced persons, only a small fraction had returned, and meeting government targets for 2026 required a substantial acceleration of resettlement efforts.

The obstacles were formidable. Landmines and unexploded ordnance continued to claim lives, with hundreds of casualties recorded since 2020. Entire districts, including Aghdam, once home to some 150,000 residents, remained primarily in ruins. Social divisions also emerged. Older displaced residents often expressed a strong desire to return to ancestral villages, while younger families, integrated into Baku's urban economy, hesitated to uproot established lives. Officials framed participation in the return as a civic responsibility, but critics warned that housing alone was insufficient. Sustainable resettlement required employment, local enterprise, and long-term economic opportunity.

International assessments reflected both progress and vulnerability. The World Bank reported that internally displaced households continued to earn less than the national average and remained heavily dependent on state support. Analysts cautioned that without agricultural cooperatives, small businesses, and vocational training, the return risked remaining symbolic rather than permanent.

The issue also drew attention beyond Azerbaijan's borders. After the Washington summit in August 2025, Armenian Prime Minister Nikol Pashinyan described refugee return as a "dangerous factor," warning that reopening the issue could destabilize an already fragile peace process. His remarks reflected differing postwar priorities: Armenian officials focused on the humanitarian consequences of recent displacement, while Azerbaijani authorities emphasized the return of their internally displaced population as a matter of sovereignty and postwar normalization.

The Great Return functioned as both a state policy and a practical response to prolonged displacement. For Azerbaijan, it marked the transition from temporary accommodation to permanent resettlement and reconstruction. Beyond its political significance, the program committed the state to rebuilding infrastructure, restoring population presence, and establishing the social and economic conditions required for long-term stability.

Economics & Regional Integration After Karabakh

If the Great Return formed the core of Baku's postwar agenda, economic reconstruction supplied its momentum. By 2025, Azerbaijan had turned Karabakh into a nationwide reconstruction zone, combining large-scale infrastructure projects with industrial planning and investment incentives. Housing, roads, and substations rose alongside industrial parks, logistics facilities, and energy installations. The scale was substantial. For 2025 alone, the state allocated approximately $2.35 billion for reconstruction, part of a broader $8.6 billion program scheduled through 2028. Airports in Fuzuli and Zangilan became key entry points for cargo and officials. Highways and rail links extended toward Aghdam and Lachin, while power lines, water systems, and fiber-optic networks reconnected Karabakh to Azerbaijan's national grid. ASAN community service centers followed, signaling that governance and public administration would accompany physical rebuilding.

Economic policy advanced in parallel. Industrial parks in Aghdam and the Araz Valley Economic Zone in Jabrail offered tax exemptions, customs incentives, and prepared land for investors. Agriculture, historically central to the region, was targeted for revival through mechanization and cooperative models, though challenges remained in land distribution and irrigation. Tourism was promoted as an additional pillar, with projects such as the Shusha Hotel and Conference Center and new urban hotels in Aghdam intended to support both leisure and business travel.

Energy strategy provided a defining framework. Karabakh and East Zangezur were designated "green energy zones," with solar and hydropower projects developed in cooperation with BP and domestic firms. Plans to export clean electricity westward by the mid-2020s carried both economic and political significance, presenting the region as a contributor to diversification rather than a recipient of subsidies.

Regional integration extended beyond Azerbaijan's borders. In July 2025, Khankendi hosted a summit of the Economic Cooperation Organization, which endorsed a long-term strategy on trade, transport, and green growth through 2035. Baku positioned Karabakh as a node within the Middle Corridor linking Asia and Europe, while continuing to press for transit routes through Armenia to Nakhichevan.

Despite rapid construction, governance questions lagged behind physical progress. Uncertainty persisted over municipal administration, service provision, and the long-term management of rebuilt towns. International observers raised concerns regarding Armenian cultural heritage sites and the limited presence of external monitors. In response, Azerbaijani authorities organized investor forums, publicized restoration efforts, and highlighted the opening of schools, clinics, and markets, framing these measures as evidence of both stability and administrative capacity.

By late 2025, Azerbaijan's objective was explicit: to position Karabakh as a center of non-oil growth, renewable energy, and regional connectivity, while enabling displaced citizens to exchange temporary accommodation for permanent housing and employment. Whether that ambition would prove durable depended on unresolved constraints beneath and beyond the surface: the pace of demining, the depth of economic opportunity, and the political negotiations that would determine whether transport corridors became engines of trade or instruments of leverage.

Cultural Revival, Diplomacy, and Image-Building

Reconstruction was not limited to infrastructure. From the outset, Baku understood that reclaiming Karabakh also required reviving its cultural life and projecting that renewal beyond the region. Military success established control, but cultural programming, diplomatic summits, and high-profile visits were intended to affirm legitimacy and permanence.

By 2024, Shusha emerged as the focal point of this effort. Long known as the "conservatory of the Caucasus," the city hosted the seventh Khari Bulbul International Music Festival in May, expanded that year to include Lachin. The event coincided with ICESCO's designation of Shusha as the Cultural Capital of the Islamic World. In July, the Organization of Turkic States convened an informal summit in the city, reinforcing Shusha's role as both a cultural symbol and a political venue. Exhibitions such as Urbicide in Karabakh documented wartime destruction and framed reconstruction as resilience rather than loss.

In 2025, cultural diplomacy intensified. The Karabakh Revival Fund organized "Night of Karabakh" charity concerts to support monument restoration, including work at the Imaret Complex in Aghdam. Shusha hosted children's art festivals, while Khankendi's newly constructed Congress Center hosted the Economic Cooperation Organization summit in July. Visits by Kyrgyz President Sadyr Japarov and former Turkmen leader Gurbanguly Berdimuhamedow, conducted alongside President Ilham Aliyev, were carefully choreographed to underscore restored authority and regional reintegration.

These official initiatives were reinforced by softer forms of outreach. Bloggers, journalists, and social media figures were escorted through newly built towns and "smart villages," where solar infrastructure, new schools, and public facilities featured prominently in online coverage. Exhibitions such as *From Tragedy to Triumph* recast wartime devastation as a narrative of recovery and renewal.

Interpretations of these efforts diverged sharply. For Azerbaijan, festivals, summits, and guided tours signaled vindication and continuity, evidence that Karabakh was not only reclaimed but functioning again. Armenian diaspora organizations, by contrast, accused Baku of erasing Armenian cultural presence and warned of cultural cleansing. Azerbaijani officials rejected these claims, asserting that restoration projects preserved authentic heritage while correcting what they described as historical distortions. Between these competing narratives, culture became a contested space where music, monuments, and ceremony carried political weight.

Culture and diplomacy thus converged into a deliberate strategy of image-building. Authority was asserted not only through administration and security, but through performances, exhibitions, and international visibility. By saturating Karabakh with cultural events and diplomatic gatherings, Azerbaijan sought to anchor the region in the global imagination as a site of revival rather than dispute, embraced by some, contested by others, but no longer peripheral.

Armenia's Internal Struggle After Karabakh

The influx of refugees from Karabakh in the autumn of 2023 placed an immediate strain on Armenia's social and economic systems. By mid-2025, thousands of displaced families still lacked permanent housing or stable employment. Yerevan's budget deficit climbed above 5% as subsidies, rent assistance, and food aid strained state resources. For many families, the promise of safety inside Armenia was tempered by overcrowding, bureaucratic delays, and persistent economic insecurity.

These pressures soon translated into political unrest. The most sustained mobilization emerged in 2024, under the banner of the Tavush for the Homeland movement, led by Archbishop Bagrat Galstanyan. At its core was opposition to territorial concessions, particularly the return of four border villages in the Tavush region to Azerbaijan as part of border delimitation. Tens of thousands rallied in Yerevan, calling for the resignation of Prime Minister Nikol Pashinyan. Despite the scale of protest, the opposition failed to coalesce into a governing alternative. The ruling Civil Contract Party, holding a parliamentary supermajority, retained control and kept Pashinyan in office.

The church's role deepened these divisions. The Armenian Apostolic Church, long embedded in national identity, entered direct confrontation with the state. In 2025, tensions escalated with a security operation at the Mother See of Holy Etchmiadzin and the arrest of Archbishop Galstanyan. The episode intensified protests and reinforced perceptions that Pashinyan's administration was prepared to confront even the country's most revered institutions to preserve political authority.

Foreign policy reflected similar instability. Anger over Russia's inaction during the September 2023 offensive prompted Yerevan to freeze its participation in the Collective Security Treaty Organization and demand the withdrawal of Russian border guards from Zvartnots Airport. Confidence in Moscow as Armenia's security guarantor had eroded sharply. In response, Pashinyan accelerated engagement with Western partners. The European Union has expanded its monitoring mission along Armenia's borders, while its cooperation with Washington has deepened. However, this shift has been limited by economic realities. Russia remains Armenia's largest trading partner, its leading energy supplier, and an essential source of remittances from migrant labor. Political realignment collided with structural dependence, leaving Armenia positioned uneasily between competing blocs.

The peace process itself became another source of domestic fracture. Azerbaijan pressed for constitutional amendments, urging Armenia to remove references to Nagorno-Karabakh from its foundational documents. Pashinyan agreed to pursue constitutional reform through a referendum ahead of the 2026 elections. Critics interpreted the move as capitulation under pressure, while supporters argued it was necessary to normalize relations and prevent renewed conflict. Although the U.S.-hosted agreement of August 2025 promised mutual recognition of borders, public skepticism remained high. Many Armenians feared that concessions would only generate further demands.

Legal arenas mirrored these tensions. Armenia filed cases at the International Court of Justice accusing Azerbaijan of ethnic cleansing, while denouncing the trials of former Karabakh leaders in Baku as politically motivated. Each proceeding became another battleground for competing narratives, ensuring that the conflict's legacy continued to shape diplomatic and domestic discourse.

Before the 2026 parliamentary elections, Armenia's internal landscape remained marked by cumulative strain. Protests challenged but did not dislodge the government; the arrival of tens of thousands of refugees tested social cohesion and public finances; relations between the state and the Armenian Apostolic Church grew increasingly contentious; and a gradual shift away from Moscow unfolded under the constraints of economic dependence. Armenia moved forward without a settled consensus on its future direction. One course pointed toward difficult compromise in pursuit of stability, while the other remained shaped by loss, displacement, and unresolved claims. In contrast to Azerbaijan's narrative of victory and restoration, Armenia's post-Karabakh period became a prolonged reckoning, an effort to redefine sovereignty, security, and national purpose after defeat.

The debate over Armenia's future did not disappear, but the 2026 parliamentary elections provided a clearer indication of the direction favored by a majority of voters. Prime Minister Nikol Pashinyan and his Civil Contract party secured a parliamentary majority, enabling his government to continue pursuing normalization with both Azerbaijan and Turkey. In his post-election remarks, Pashinyan described the result as a public mandate for peace and regional cooperation, emphasizing that Armenia's priorities remained a peace agreement with Azerbaijan and the establishment of diplomatic relations with Turkey. While political divisions persisted and difficult issues remained unresolved, the election suggested that a significant portion of Armenian voters viewed regional cooperation, open borders, and negotiated settlements as the most realistic path toward long-term stability and a lasting peace in the South Caucasus.

Peace

On August 8, 2025, in the East Room of the White House, Armenia and Azerbaijan signed a U.S.-brokered declaration, presented by both governments and mediators, that was hailed as a turning point. The document committed the parties to the non-use of force, outlined steps toward border delimitation, and created a framework for reopening regional transport links. More than a ceremonial gesture, it was the most explicit public acknowledgment that the Karabakh war had ended, and that relations would shift, however cautiously, from armed confrontation to managed coexistence.

The ceremony did not resolve Armenia's internal debate; instead, it made it clearer. For displaced families and veterans, the loss of Karabakh remained a profound shock, and the ceasefire felt like capitulation after military defeat. Yet this reaction did not define Armenian society as a whole. In Yerevan and other urban centers, a growing share of the public had become exhausted by decades of conflict, militarization, and isolation tied to the Karabakh conflict. For them, the end of the war, however costly, opened the possibility of redirecting national priorities toward economic recovery, governance reform, and external integration rather than permanent mobilization. Continued electoral support for Nikol Pashinyan signaled that shift:

not indifference to loss, but rejection of a political order in which Karabakh monopolized national life and foreclosed alternative futures.

In Azerbaijan, the experience was less catharsis than closure. For families who lost relatives in the 1990s and again in 2020, grief remained. But it was now contained within a framework that offered finality and purpose: the state's long campaign had achieved its central objective. Loss was no longer framed as unresolved tragedy; it was incorporated into a narrative of completion that reinforced sovereignty and stabilized public consent around the postwar order. That framing narrowed the space for questioning the war's costs. It made the postwar settlement easier to accept as a settled outcome rather than a temporary pause.

In practical terms, peace now meant implementation. Armenia began the slow work of aligning state language, policy, and institutions with recognized borders and altered security realities. Azerbaijan accelerated the Great Return, expanding housing, utilities, and public services in Fuzuli, Lachin, Jabrail, Shusha, and nearby districts, while confronting the challenges posed by landmines, uneven employment prospects, and the immense cost of rebuilding. Armenia bore the social and political burden of defeat, while Azerbaijan faced the challenging task of transforming victory into lasting stability rather than ongoing mobilization.

The declaration also reshaped regional expectations. Turkey and Georgia framed reopened transport routes as an economic opportunity and a stabilizing corridor. Iran and Russia recalibrated to preserve influence under altered conditions. For Washington and Brussels, a formal peace between neighbors represented a diplomatic milestone. For residents of places like Zangezur, Aghdam, and Lachin, diplomacy mattered less on paper than in whether daily life began to feel normal again.

Narrative in Transition

For decades, the Karabakh conflict was not just a military struggle, but also a contest over historical interpretation. Competing narratives influenced political legitimacy, identity, and public support in both societies, contributing to the ongoing nature of the conflict even after the fighting on the battlefield had ceased. In Armenia, political discourse focused on miatsum as a means to rectify historical injustices and as a strategic principle of state policy. In Azerbaijan, historical interpretation followed a different trajectory, drawing on the legacy of the Karabakh and Irevan khanates, the loss of Zangezur, and the mass displacement and cultural erasure experienced during and after the First Karabakh War. Reinforced by war and selective memory, these frameworks organized grievance and identity on both sides, but they also narrowed political imagination, leaving little room for compromise or coexistence.

Between 2023 and 2025, those narrative structures fractured under the weight of events. The departure of Karabakh's Armenian population and the consolidation of Azerbaijani control rendered miatsum politically obsolete. Armenia's leadership responded by redefining statehood in practical terms: internationally recognized borders, economic access, and institutional reform. Pashinyan's Real Armenia concept and the promise of a new constitution by 2026 signaled an attempt to move from territorial symbolism toward civic viability and social stability within Armenia's existing borders.

In Azerbaijan, victory validated long-standing state narratives centered on sovereignty and continuity. Yet it also imposed constraints. The central task shifted from asserting ownership to administering consequences: reconstruction, resettlement, and the normalization of state presence. The change in perspective did not erase the long-held views of Armenia as an adversary. However, Azerbaijani rhetoric has increasingly focused on coexistence, connectivity, and economic integration as strategic goals. These goals are presented as pathways to stability and growth, offering alternatives to the isolation that has limited Armenia's financial opportunities.

Grief remained a significant undercurrent in both societies, though it took different forms. In Armenia, loss was bound to the collapse of a political project and the dislocation of a community whose fate had long been tied to national meaning. In Azerbaijan, trauma was rooted in forcible displacement, battlefield deaths, violence against civilians, and decades of absence from lost homes. A stable postwar narrative in either country could not ignore these realities, but it also could not treat them as permanent engines of mobilization.

Diaspora communities further complicated the transition. Armenian diasporas in France, the United States, and Russia had elevated Karabakh into a symbolic core of identity and advocacy, often detached from the constraints faced by the Armenian state. For many, postwar diplomacy looked like abandonment rather than adaptation. The Azerbaijani diaspora, although less influential in institutions, interpreted the outcome as a form of vindication and closure. Distance amplified rhetoric on both sides and reduced incentives to recalibrate. The question confronting diasporas was whether influence would remain anchored in symbolic struggle or shift toward investment, cultural engagement, and long-term stabilization.

Over time, the official language on both sides began to change. In Yerevan, talk of ancestral entitlement gave way to discussions of border talks, transport routes, and economic stability. In Baku, reconstruction and resettlement were presented less as triumph and more as the routine work of rebuilding. This shift did not erase mistrust, but it did signal a move away from symbolic claims and toward the practical language of governing.

Dissenting Voices: Peace Activism and the Cost of Narrative Departure

While official narratives in Armenia and Azerbaijan were shaped primarily by state interests, war outcomes, and historical claims, a small number of individuals sought to challenge the moral and psychological foundations of the conflict itself. Their efforts did not aim to resolve territorial disputes or negotiate treaties. Instead, they questioned the cultural habits, emotional reflexes, and narrative structures that sustained enmity long after violence had become normalized. These voices remained marginal, often stigmatized, yet their experiences illuminate the social limits placed on peace-oriented thinking in a polarized environment.

One such figure was Georgi Vanyan (1963–2021), an Armenian peace activist and founder of the Caucasus Center of Peace-Making Initiatives. Vanyan's work was rooted in direct engagement with the region and its societies. From the mid-2000s onward, he sought to create spaces for Armenian–Azerbaijani cultural contact when political dialogue was frozen. His initiatives included organizing Days of Azerbaijan in Yerevan schools, attempting to host Azerbaijani film festivals in Gyumri, and establishing a peace center in the Georgian village of Tekalo, near the Armenian and Azerbaijani borders. Each effort encountered resistance. Events were disrupted, venues blocked, and Vanyan himself was repeatedly labeled a traitor by nationalist groups. The hostility directed at Vanyan foreshadowed a broader pattern in Armenian political life, in which engagement with Azerbaijan was often equated with betrayal. Years later, Prime Minister Nikol Pashinyan would confront similar accusations from nationalist and diaspora circles as he pursued negotiations and acknowledged postwar realities. While the scale and stakes differed significantly, both cases reflected the enduring difficulty of reconciling compromise with collective memory shaped by loss and displacement.

The reaction intensified during the 2020 war. In November of that year, Vanyan was fined by Armenian authorities for a social media post calling for dialogue with Azerbaijan and criticizing the rhetoric of victory. His language rejected the idea that triumph over a neighbor could constitute success and argued instead for sustained conversation as the only viable alternative to destruction. The penalty was minor in legal terms but significant symbolically. It signaled that even nonviolent appeals for dialogue could be treated as transgressive at a moment of heightened national mobilization. Vanyan's experience showed that peace advocacy, when it contradicts dominant wartime narratives, can be viewed as disloyalty, rather than dissent.

A different, more indirect challenge to prevailing narratives emerged through the work of Kardash Onnig, a Lebanese-born Armenian artist and writer whose engagement with the South Caucasus unfolded primarily through cultural and artistic practice rather than organized activism. In the early 2000s, during the ceasefire period, Onnig spent time in Shusha as an artist-in-residence. His project was not political in the conventional sense. He taught art, documented the city's physical destruction, and recorded conversations with residents. Yet his observations cut against simplified moral binaries.

Onnig wrote about encountering memories of prewar coexistence alongside open expressions of hostility and violence. He noted how stories of friendship between Armenians and Azerbaijanis coexisted with accounts in which violence against civilians was recounted without remorse. Rather than presenting Armenians solely as victims or heroes, his work exposed the psychological processes through which war reshapes moral perception, how suffering can coexist with cruelty, and how identity can be reinforced through the normalization of harm inflicted on the other. This refusal to sanitize violence, even when committed by one's own side, provoked discomfort. Onnig was criticized by compatriots and accused of betrayal for documenting experiences that did not conform to an exclusively redemptive national narrative.

Vanyan and Onnig were not isolated anomalies, but they were among the few willing to bear the social cost of dissent, revealing how narrow the space for peace-oriented thought remained within a conflict-shaped political culture. Taken together, Vanyan and Onnig represent two distinct but complementary forms of dissent. Vanyan operated within the language of civic engagement and reconciliation, directly confronting the political costs of dialogue in a society shaped by unresolved conflict. Onnig approached the same problem through culture and memory, revealing how narratives of enmity are sustained by everyday storytelling, selective silence, and emotional inheritance. Both paid a price for departing from dominant frameworks. Neither sought to deny Armenian suffering or historical trauma. Instead, they questioned whether suffering must remain the organizing principle of identity.

Their marginalization underscores a broader pattern. In conflict-affected societies, peace advocacy is often tolerated only when it aligns with national consensus or external mediation. When it challenges internal moral hierarchies or exposes uncomfortable truths about one's own community, it is more likely to be rejected. Yet the existence of such figures complicates the assumption that Armenian society speaks with a single voice on questions of war and peace. Even at moments of heightened polarization, alternative ethical positions persisted, fragile but present.

These dissenting voices did not determine policy, nor did they halt violence. Their significance lies elsewhere: in demonstrating that the boundaries of political imagination were never absolute. They illustrate that, in addition to significant narratives of grievance and survival, there were limited and often disputed efforts to envision a different future, one based on the challenging work of recognition rather than on victory or victimhood.

Neighboring States and the Postwar Mentality

Peace in the South Caucasus has never been confined to national borders. The choices of Turkey, Georgia, Iran, and Russia have long shaped the space in which Yerevan and Baku define both conflict and coexistence. Between 2023 and 2025, each influenced how Armenians and Azerbaijanis assessed the costs, risks, and possibilities of peace through diplomacy and infrastructure, as well as through the lived reality of cross-communal coexistence beyond the battlefield.

Turkey entered the postwar period as Azerbaijan's closest ally and the most assertive regional actor. Its support had been central to Baku's battlefield success, and it moved quickly into joint infrastructure planning, including proposed transit routes linking Azerbaijan with Nakhichivan. Turkish officials framed these projects as economic integration within the broader Turkic world. For Armenians, particularly within diaspora communities shaped by the memory of 1915, Turkey's expanded role carried heavy emotional and symbolic weight. Yet Ankara also adjusted its diplomatic posture. Direct engagements between President Recep Tayyip Erdogan and Prime Minister Nikol Pashinyan in 2023 and 2024 signaled cautious openness to normalization, including the prospect of reopening the border and selective diplomatic reengagement. Pashinyan's working visit to Turkey in June 2025 further underscored this tentative shift, marking a continuation of dialogue at the highest level. Progress, however, remained conditional, linked to broader Armenian–Azerbaijani negotiations and to Turkey's dual role as both regional stakeholder and Azerbaijan's principal strategic partner.

Georgia's role was quieter but structurally indispensable. Major pipelines, rail corridors, and the Middle Corridor linking Central Asia to Europe pass through Georgian territory. Renewed confrontation would threaten these lifelines, so Tbilisi consistently favored de-escalation, positioning itself as a neutral facilitator and emphasizing shared economic dividends. Georgia also offered a living demonstration of coexistence: Armenian and

Azerbaijani communities in regions such as Marneuli, Bolnisi, and Gardabani maintained commercial ties, transport businesses, and everyday social relations largely insulated from interstate conflict. Markets operated effectively, diverse neighborhoods thrived, and collaboration continued even during tensions, illustrating that closeness does not necessarily lead to animosity.

Iran's response evolved from caution to pragmatic adaptation. Rather than openly contesting the post-2020 order, Tehran sought to avoid marginalization by remaining engaged economically and diplomatically. High-level visits and symbolic gestures reinforced this shift, including President Masoud Pezeshkian's visit to Karabakh and his use of Azerbaijani in public settings, emphasizing cultural familiarity alongside political pragmatism. Iran also sustained commercial ties with both Armenia and Azerbaijan. For decades, Iranian territory served as the principal overland route connecting mainland Azerbaijan to Nakhchivan. As postwar connectivity discussions accelerated, Iran signaled openness to expanded transit arrangements through its own territory, aiming to preserve its strategic relevance. For Armenia, Iran remained a crucial partner amid uncertainty in relations with Turkey and Azerbaijan; for Tehran, the goal was influence through commerce, infrastructure, and diplomacy rather than coercion.

Russia's role became more complicated. Politically, Moscow's authority as a security guarantor eroded after 2020 and even more so after 2022. Yet, socially and economically, Russia remained the largest shared space for everyday coexistence between Armenians and Azerbaijanis. In cities such as Moscow, St. Petersburg, Krasnodar, and Yekaterinburg, communities continued to live and work side by side in trade, construction, and services, with daily interaction operating largely outside the logic of national mobilization. Taken together, these regional dynamics shaped the prospects for peace in the South Caucasus.

Diaspora Narratives and Adaptation

Diasporas have long shaped how the Karabakh conflict was narrated beyond the South Caucasus. For decades, Armenian and Azerbaijani communities abroad carried the dispute into foreign legislatures, advocacy networks, media outlets, and cultural institutions. Physical distance often amplified symbolic language, allowing the conflict to be framed less as a political dispute and more as a question of historical destiny. After the wars of 2020 and 2023, and especially after the 2025 declaration, those narratives did not automatically adjust. Instead, diasporas faced a growing tension between inherited frameworks and rapidly changing political reality on the ground.

Within Armenian diaspora communities, Karabakh was frequently embedded in a broader historical imagination shaped by the memory of loss and dispossession. Yerevan's post-2023 turn toward negotiated settlement produced division rather than consensus abroad. Meetings between Prime Minister Nikol Pashinyan and President Ilham Aliyev, along with steps toward a formal peace treaty, were met with sharp criticism in some diaspora circles. In public discourse, Pashinyan was at times labeled a "traitor," reflecting the difficulty of reconciling territorial compromise with long-standing nationalist expectations. Similar reactions accompanied the trials of former Nagorno-Karabakh officials in Baku, which many diaspora organizations characterized as politically motivated. For older cohorts in particular, concessions and legal proceedings were interpreted through a lens of vulnerability and existential risk. Among younger Armenians in the diaspora, views were more varied: attachment to identity and memory remained strong, but there was greater openness to pragmatic considerations such as economic sustainability, mobility, and regional integration, even when that openness did not translate into endorsement of specific policies.

Azerbaijani diaspora dynamics followed a different trajectory. Throughout much of the post-Soviet period, Azerbaijani communities abroad mobilized primarily in response to Armenian advocacy, emphasizing displacement, civilian casualties such as Khojaly, and the legal principle of territorial integrity. Their political reach was more limited and frequently reinforced through state diplomacy rather than sustained grassroots networks. After the military outcomes of 2020 and 2023, the urgency of defensive advocacy diminished. Diaspora engagement increasingly shifted toward reconstruction narratives, investment initiatives, and forms of cultural diplomacy aligned with Azerbaijan's postwar priorities.

Findings from post–44-Day War qualitative research complicate assumptions of permanent hostility. When asked about future relations, a majority of Azerbaijani respondents, including members of the diaspora, expressed openness to renewed contact with Armenians. Many cited shared cultural practices, comparable social norms, and everyday similarities, suggesting that space for coexistence can persist even when official political narratives remain cautious or rigid.

Diaspora will continue to shape external perceptions of the conflict. The central question is whether their influence remains anchored in symbolic absolutes or adapts to the political and social realities now emerging in Yerevan, Baku, and the wider region.

Economic Normalization in Practice

After August 2025, normalization began to extend beyond formal diplomacy into practical forms of interaction, limited and cautious, but increasingly measurable. One visible sign came in October 2025, when an Azerbaijan Airlines aircraft landed in Yerevan for the first time in roughly three decades, carrying a delegation of Azerbaijani civil society representatives for bilateral discussions. Meetings on October 21–22 focused on confidence-building, the prospects for sustained societal dialogue, and opportunities for economic cooperation. Participants emphasized that the encounter took place without international mediation, signaling an effort to restore direct channels of engagement. Reciprocal exchanges followed in November, when Armenian civil society representatives traveled to Baku as part of the same initiative. These contacts unfolded alongside governmental dialogue and the gradual easing of transit restrictions, suggesting that normalization was beginning to operate simultaneously at diplomatic, economic, and societal levels.

The process continued in February 2026, when Azerbaijani and Armenian civil society representatives convened in Yerevan for another roundtable under the "Bridge of Peace" initiative. The Azerbaijani delegation crossed the border by land through the newly delimited Tavush–Qazakh sector, marking a notable practical confidence-building step.

Discussions addressed implementation of the Washington peace agenda, regional security arrangements, economic cooperation, and the role of civic actors in rebuilding trust. Participants also met with Armenian officials, indicating a growing overlap between unofficial dialogue and formal policy frameworks. The meeting, the third such exchange within six months, illustrated how normalization was gradually shifting from isolated gestures toward a more structured pattern of engagement.

Economic cooperation also took concrete form. In December 2025, Azerbaijan initiated fuel deliveries to Armenia for the first time in roughly three decades, shipping 1,220 metric tons of gasoline by rail via Georgia. The flow continued into early 2026: on January 9, a total of 2,698 tons of petroleum products were dispatched from Bilajari station, followed on January 11 by an additional shipment of 979 tons of Aİ-92 gasoline, again via Georgian transit routes.

These deliveries did not constitute a formal energy partnership, and they did not signal political reconciliation. Their significance lay in precedent: cooperation in a strategically sensitive sector requiring customs coordination, regulatory clearance, reliable transit, and sustained communication. The shipments followed deputy prime minister–level contacts and reflected the decision to permit regular cargo flows after decades of disruption. Modest in scale, they still suggested a shift from symbolism to functional logistics. The fuel deliveries also built on earlier confidence-building measures, including the transit of Qazakh and Russian grain through Azerbaijani territory and the gradual reopening of overland trade routes that had been closed for decades. Pashinyan publicly welcomed the shipments, linking them to the political conditions created by the post–August 2025 framework. The practical point was simple: the restoration of economic links was beginning to have a tangible effect on supply chains and planning, not just diplomatic rhetoric.

Whether these steps evolve into sustained normalization will depend heavily on domestic politics in both countries, including Armenia's 2026 elections and the outcome of negotiations on constitutional reform and border delimitation.

The Road Ahead

The Washington declaration mattered less for what it promised than for what it made necessary. It marked a transition from conflict as a default condition to peace as an obligation that must be managed. The test is no longer whether leaders can sign documents, but whether the region can sustain the habits necessary for durable peace.

Armenia now faces the task of internal consolidation after the loss. This includes supporting displaced families, restoring economic confidence, and affirming sovereignty within recognized borders. It also requires a deeper mental shift: moving away from a political culture defined by permanent emergency, grievance, and existential rhetoric toward one that allows ordinary life to take precedence. For peace to hold, public discourse must gradually make room for pragmatism, restraint, and the re-normalization of relations with neighbors, grounded less in historical fear and more in lived co-existence.

Azerbaijan confronts a different but equally demanding transition. Military victory must now be converted into administrative capacity, economic sustainability, and viable civilian life. Resettlement and reconstruction will matter not as symbols of triumph, but as lived conditions - whether towns function, work is available, and institutions are trusted. This process also demands a recalibration of mentality and language: moving from wartime narratives toward a civic posture that emphasizes stability, predictability, and the revival of regional customs of neighborliness and hospitality that once governed daily interaction in the South Caucasus. The durability of peace will depend not only on what is built, but on how relationships are imagined and sustained.

External actors still matter, but none can indefinitely impose outcomes or freeze the region in conflict. If peace collapses, it is more likely to fail from within than to be blocked from outside. The real test lies in society itself: whether rebuilt towns keep their residents, whether displaced families find stable work and homes, whether borders support trade instead of fear, and whether younger generations grow up with everyday normalcy rather than inherited hatred.

The future of the South Caucasus will be shaped less by declarations than by the habits that emerge after conflict. If institutions shift from mobilization to governance, if borders function as routes for trade and movement rather than symbols of division, and if daily life becomes predictable, safe, and economically viable across lines once defined by violence, peace will acquire substance. That transition also requires a gradual release from cycles of blame and judgment, from identities anchored in loss, and from narratives of grievance or imagined glory that no longer correspond to lived reality. Such a future will not erase memory or suffering, but it can prevent them from dictating daily life and political choice.

History will not judge the road to peace by the moment it was announced, but by whether it was taken. The path ahead is narrow and demanding, but it exists, and for the first time in decades, it leads forward.

Timeline

Before the 4th century CE

The region historically known as Karabakh lay within the broader cultural and political space of the South Caucasus. In antiquity, it formed part of Caucasian Albania, a polity distinct from both ancient Armenia and neighboring imperial formations. Its population was ethnically and linguistically diverse, reflecting the region's position at the intersection of multiple political spheres.

4th–7th centuries

The South Caucasus underwent a major religious transformation. Zoroastrian traditions associated with Persian rule gradually gave way to Christianity. In Karabakh, ecclesiastical institutions developed primarily within the Albanian Christian tradition, later intersecting with Armenian religious administration. These overlapping legacies would become central to later historical interpretations.

Early medieval period (7th–10th centuries)

Successive Arab and Persian administrations incorporated Karabakh into broader imperial systems. The region functioned as a peripheral frontier, governed locally but shaped by shifting centers of power and regional trade networks.

11th–15th centuries

Turkic migrations and political formations reshaped the demographic and linguistic landscape of the South Caucasus. Karabakh increasingly formed part of a Turkic-speaking cultural zone. At the same time, Christian communities persisted alongside Muslim populations under varying systems of local governance.

16th–18th centuries

Under Safavid and later Qajar Persian rule, Karabakh functioned as a semi-autonomous frontier region. Armenian melikdoms exercised limited hereditary authority in mountainous areas, while broader administration remained under Persian oversight. In the mid-18th century, the Karabakh Khanate emerged as a recognized political entity governed by a local Muslim dynasty.

Early 19th century

Following the Russo-Persian wars, Karabakh was incorporated into the Russian Empire. Imperial administration altered governance structures, introduced new settlement patterns, and laid the foundations for demographic and political changes that would shape the modern period.

1917–1920

The collapse of the Russian Empire opened a brief but violent period of competing territorial claims in the South Caucasus. The newly established Armenian and Azerbaijani republics asserted authority over overlapping territories, including Karabakh. Armed clashes, shifting control, and diplomatic failures marked this phase.

1920–1921

The Sovietization of Armenia and Azerbaijan ended their independence. Soviet authority reasserted centralized control, prioritizing political stability and regional integration over national aspirations.

1921–1923

The Soviet leadership established the Nagorno-Karabakh Autonomous Oblast within the Azerbaijan SSR. The arrangement granted limited cultural autonomy while fixing administrative borders that institutionalized competing interpretations of sovereignty and self-rule.

1920s–1980s

During most of the Soviet period, Karabakh remained relatively stable under centralized governance. Ethnic expression was constrained, and political disputes were suppressed rather than resolved. Beneath the surface, unresolved grievances accumulated and persisted into the late Soviet era.

Late Soviet period (1980s)

Economic stagnation, political rigidity, and declining legitimacy characterized the final decade of Soviet rule. Policies of perestroika and glasnost introduced limited openness, allowing long-suppressed grievances to surface. In Karabakh, debates over autonomy and administrative status re-emerged in public discourse, reflecting tensions that had accumulated under centralized governance.

1988–1991

Mass demonstrations began in Armenia and Nagorno-Karabakh, calling for changes to the region's status, while countermobilization emerged in Azerbaijan. Intercommunal violence, population displacement, and the erosion of Soviet authority escalated the crisis. As the USSR weakened, local disputes increasingly transformed into armed confrontation.

1991–1994: The First Karabakh War

Following the collapse of the Soviet Union, Armenia and Azerbaijan became independent states amid open warfare. Armenian forces gained control over Nagorno-Karabakh and the surrounding districts. Large-scale displacement affected both Armenian and Azerbaijani populations, and civilian casualties were widespread. The conflict ended with a Russian-brokered ceasefire in May 1994.

1994–2020: Frozen war, fragile peace

For more than two decades, the conflict remained unresolved. Nagorno-Karabakh functioned as a de facto Armenian-administered entity without international recognition, while surrounding territories remained under Armenian control. Negotiations mediated by the OSCE Minsk Group produced no final settlement. Periodic clashes and ceasefire violations underscored the instability of the status quo.

2020: The 44-Day War

In September–November 2020, large-scale fighting resumed. Azerbaijan regained control over significant portions of the territories lost in the 1990s, including key districts and the city of Shusha. A trilateral ceasefire agreement brokered by Russia ended the fighting and introduced Russian peacekeepers to parts of the region.

2020–2023

Negotiations, sporadic violence, and disputes over access, security, and governance marked the post-war period. Tensions persisted around transport routes and the status of Armenian residents in Karabakh. Russian peacekeepers remained deployed, though their role and effectiveness were increasingly questioned.

September 2023

Azerbaijan reasserted complete control over Karabakh following a brief military operation. The Armenian population of the region departed in large numbers within weeks. De facto Armenian governing structures dissolved, bringing the post-Soviet phase of the Karabakh conflict to a close.

2023–2025

Attention shifted from territorial control to diplomacy, reconstruction, and regional stability. Armenia and Azerbaijan engaged in bilateral negotiations, supported by international actors, focusing on border delimitation, transport links, and mutual recognition. The conflict transitioned from a military confrontation to a political and societal challenge.

August 2025

Armenia and Azerbaijan signed a U.S.-brokered declaration in Washington, committing to non-use of force and the normalization of interstate relations. While implementation continued, the agreement marked the most comprehensive peace framework since the end of the Soviet Union.

This timeline is intended as a thematic and chronological guide, aligned with the book's structure. It is selective rather than exhaustive, emphasizing historical turning points rather than comprehensive detail.

Bibliography

Abdullaev, Mehman. History of Azerbaijan. Baku: Tehsil Publishing House, 2018. ISBN 978-9952-504-10-1.

Aliyev, Hikmet, and Emin Mammadov. "The Role of Great Powers in Resolving the Nagorno-Karabakh Conflict: Analyzing the 2020 War." Caucasus Survey 9, no. 2 (2021): 173–189. https://doi.org/10.1080/23761199.2021.1926357.

Almammadov, Anar. "The Impact of the 2020 Nagorno-Karabakh War on Azerbaijan's Foreign Policy." Turkish Journal of Politics 12, no. 1 (2021): 41–60. https://doi.org/10.32388/turkp.823848.

Andreev, Evgeny. "The Second Karabakh War in the Context of Russian-Turkish Relations." Journal of Central Asian and Caucasian Studies 21, no. 1 (2021): 63–72. https://doi.org/10.52297/jcas.v21i1.574.

Angelov, Georgi. "Military Implications of the Nagorno-Karabakh Conflict: Tactics and Technologies." Information & Security 51, no. 1 (2022): 49–55. https://doi.org/10.11610/isij.5104.

Arkhipova, Elena V. "The USA's Impact in Solving Border Disputes in the Transcaucasia, 1919–1920." Science Journal of Volgograd State University: History, Area Studies, International Relations 27, no. 2 (2022): 45–57.

Bacon, Kevin H., and Marc Lynch. "Lost in Purgatory: The Plight of Displaced Persons in the Caucasus." World Policy Journal 19, no. 4 (2002): 66–71.

Balayan, Gagik, and Hovhannes Mirzoyan. "The Second Karabakh War: Background and Prospects for Conflict Resolution." Journal of Contemporary Eastern Asia 20, no. 2 (2021): 207–223. https://doi.org/10.17477/jcea.2021.20.2.207.

Baser, Bahar, and Ashok Swain. "Diasporas as Peacemakers: Third-Party Mediation in Homeland Conflicts." International Journal on World Peace 25, no. 3 (2008): 7–28.

Bournoutian, George A. A Concise History of the Armenian People. Costa Mesa, CA: Mazda Publishers, 2003.

Chernobrov, Dmitry. "Diasporas as Cyberwarriors: Infopolitics, Participatory Warfare, and the 2020 Karabakh War." International Affairs 98, no.2 (2022):631–651. https://doi.org/10.1093/ia/iiac015.

De Waal, Thomas. Black Garden: Armenia and Azerbaijan through Peace and War. New York: New York University Press, 2013.

Goltz, Thomas. Azerbaijan Diary: A Rogue Reporter's Adventures in an Oil-Rich, War-Torn, Post-Soviet Republic. Armonk, NY: M. E. Sharpe, 1999.

Grebennikov, Maksim. "The Puzzle of a Loyal Minority: Why Do Azeris Support the Iranian State?" Middle East Journal 67, no. 1 (2013): 64–76. https://doi.org/10.3751/67.1.14.

Guliyev, Anar. "First-Generation Azerbaijani Immigrants in the United States: Socio-Cultural Characteristics and Identity Issues." Khazar Journal of Humanities and Social Sciences 18, no. 2 (2015): 70–91. https://doi.org/10.5782/2223-2621.2014.18.2.70.

Iskandarov, Khayal, and Piotr Gawliczek. "Characteristic Features of the Second Karabakh War." Social Development & Security11, no.3 (2021):30–40.

https://doi.org/10.33445/sds.2021.11.3.3.

Iskandaryan, Alexander. "Armenia: A Stealthy Thermidor?" Demokrati-
    zatsiya 30, no. 4 (2022): 493–499.

Ismayilov, Rasim. "The Strategic Significance of the 2020 Nagorno-
    Karabakh War for the South Caucasus." Journal of Contemporary
    Eastern Asia 20, no. 2 (2021): 175–190.
    https://doi.org/10.17477/jcea.2021.20.2.175.

Kotanjian, Haik. "Armenian Security and U.S. Foreign Policy in the South
    Caucasus." Connections 3, no. 2 (2004): 15–32.

Köse, Gamze, and Koji Wakizaka. "The Historical Dynamics of the Sec-
    ond Karabakh War and the Shift in Turkey's Policy." Journal of Black
    Sea Studies 74 (2022): 311–327.

Kustra, Tomasz. "Sanctioning the Homeland: Diaspora Influence on
    American Economic Sanctions Policy." Journal of Conflict Resolu-
    tion 66, no. 3 (2022): 443–472.
    https://doi.org/10.1177/00220027211042681.

Loda, Cristina. "Azerbaijan, Foreign Policy, and Public Diplomacy." Irish
    Studies in International Affairs 27 (2016): 39–55.
    https://doi.org/10.3318/isia.2016.27.7.

Machowska, Magdalena. "Armenian Diaspora Main Lobbying Agendas in
    the United States in the 21st Century." Ukrainian Policymaker 6
    (2020): 52–62.
    https://doi.org/10.29202/up/6/6.

Melkonian, Markar. My Brother's Road: An American's Fateful Journey to
    Armenia. London: I. B. Tauris, 2007.

Najafizadeh, Mehrangiz. "Ethnic Conflict and Forced Displacement: Nar-
    ratives of Azeri IDP and Refugee Women from the Nagorno-
    Karabakh War." Journal of International Women's Studies 14, no. 1
    (2013): 161–183.

Postma, Jan. "Drones over Nagorno-Karabakh: A Glimpse at the Future
    of War?" Atlantisch Perspectief 45, no. 2 (2021): 15–20.

Swietochowski, Tadeusz. Russia and Azerbaijan: A Borderland in Transi-
    tion. New York: Columbia University Press, 1995.

Swietochowski, Tadeusz. Russian Azerbaijan, 1905–1920: The Shaping of National Identity in a Muslim Community. Cambridge: Cambridge University Press, 1985.

Van Hear, Nicholas, and Robin Cohen. "Diasporas and Conflict: Distance, Contiguity, and Spheres of Engagement." Oxford Development Studies 45, no. 2 (2017): 171–184.
https://doi.org/10.1080/13600818.2016.1160043.

Ziyadov, Tural, and Aygun Huseynova. "Azerbaijan's Victory in the Second Karabakh War and Its Impact on Energy Projects in the Region." Energy Strategy Reviews 34 (2021): 100721.
https://doi.org/10.1016/j.esr.2021.100721.

Official Online Sources

The White House.
"President Trump Brokers Another Historic Peace Deal." August 8.2025.
https://www.whitehouse.gov/articles/2025/08/president-trump-brokers-another-historic-peace-deal/

United Nations Security Council.
Resolutions 822, 853, 874, and 884 on the Nagorno-Karabakh conflict.
https://www.un.org/securitycouncil/

European Parliament.
Resolutions and official statements on Armenia–Azerbaijan relations and the South Caucasus.
https://www.europarl.europa.eu/

Organization for Security and Co-operation in Europe (OSCE).
Official statements, Minsk Group documents, and related communiqués.
https://www.osce.org/

U.S. Department of State.
"Nagorno-Karabakh: Basic Facts" (archived).
https://2001-2009.state.gov/p/eur/rls/or/13508.htm

Office of the President of the Republic of Azerbaijan.
Official speeches, decrees, and statements.
https://president.az/en/
State Committee on Work with Diaspora of the Republic of Azerbaijan.
Official releases and policy statements.
https://diaspor.gov.az/en/
Prime Minister of the Republic of Armenia.
Official statements, policy documents, and press releases.
https://www.primeminister.am/en/

Note on Official Online Sources

This book references a limited number of official online sources to document public statements, agreements, and institutional positions related to the Armenia–Azerbaijan conflict and its aftermath. These materials are used as records of publicly available policy positions rather than as interpretive or analytical authorities. Academic scholarship and published sources listed in the bibliography remain the primary foundation of the analysis.

Audiovisual and Media Sources

In addition to published academic literature and policy documents, this book draws on extensive viewing of publicly available audiovisual material, including televised interviews, official press briefings, documentary films, frontline footage, and civil society discussions circulated through broadcast media and digital platforms such as YouTube. These materials were used for contextual understanding, timeline verification, and analysis of public discourse rather than as primary evidentiary sources. No unpublished or private recordings were used.

Photo Credits

Adam Jones. *Dashalti village near Shusha*, June 2015. Via Wikimedia Commons. Licensed under CC BY-SA 2.0.

Armenian Museum of Photo and Video Materials. *Armenian protests in Martuni, Nagorno-Karabakh*, 1988. Via Wikimedia Commons. Licensed under CC BY-SA 2.0.

Asgarov Ruslan. *Road toward Shusha through Dashalti, with the rock formation on which the city stands*, via Wikimedia Commons. Licensed under CC BY-SA 4.0.

Asgarov Ruslan. *Ruins of Aghdam following the First Karabakh War*, via Wikimedia Commons. Licensed under CC BY-SA 4.0.

Aykhan Zayedzadeh. *Memorial complex to those fallen in the Second World War, Shusha*, bearing later war damage, 2022. Photograph taken during the Shusha Human Rights Project organized by the Baku Human Rights Club. Via Wikimedia Commons. Licensed under CC BY-SA 3.0.

Azerbaijan State News Agency. *Civilian car crushed during Soviet military operations in Baku (Black January)*, 1990. Via Wikimedia Commons. Licensed under CC BY-SA 4.0.

Azerbaijan State News Agency. *Soviet armored column in Baku*, 1990. Via Wikimedia Commons. Licensed under CC BY-SA 4.0.

Ilgar Jafarov. *Azerbaijani refugee camp*, 1993. Via Wikimedia Commons. Licensed under CC BY-SA 4.0.

Ilgar Jafarov. *Azerbaijani military conscripts during the First Karabakh War*, early 1990s. Via Wikimedia Commons. Licensed under CC BY-SA 4.0.

Ilgar Jafarov. *Azerbaijani refugees from Karabakh during the war*. Via Wikimedia Commons. Licensed under CC BY-SA 4.0.

Julian Nyca. *Ruins of the Ashagi Govhar Agha Mosque, Shusha*, 2017. Via Wikimedia Commons. Licensed under CC BY-SA 3.0.

Mahammad Turkman. *Azerbaijani environmental protesters facing a Russian peacekeeping post on the Lachin Corridor*, 2023. Via Wikimedia Commons. Licensed under CC BY-SA 4.0.

President.az. *New residential construction in Aghdam as part of postwar rebuilding efforts*, 2025. Via Wikimedia Commons. Licensed under CC BY 4.0.

Stepan Lohr. *Ruins of Aghdam following the First Karabakh War*, via Wikimedia Commons. Licensed under CC BY-SA 4.0.

U.S. Department of State. *Key West peace talks, Florida*, 2001. Presidents Heydar Aliyev and Robert Kocharyan with U.S. Secretary of State Colin Powell and OSCE Minsk Group representatives. Public domain (U.S. government photograph).

White House. *Signing of the Armenia–Azerbaijan declaration*, 8 August 2025. Official White House photograph. Public domain.

Unknown photographer. *Ruins of Shusha*, 1920. Public domain. Via Wikimedia Commons.

Index

About the Author

Rustam Musevi, Ed.D., is a veteran of the US Army and an independent researcher and writer whose work spans the modern history of the South Caucasus, post-Soviet political transitions, conflict resolution, and the dynamics of displacement and diaspora. Born and raised in Baku, he experienced the final years of the Soviet Union and the onset of the First Karabakh War during his formative years. His research draws on archival sources, policy documents, media reporting, and qualitative interviews conducted with members of the Azerbaijani diaspora in the United States as part of a broader research project. This book reflects his long-standing engagement with the region, combining historical analysis with sustained attention to the lived experiences that have shaped its conflicts and narratives.